Political Verse and Song
from Britain and Ireland

SEVEN SEAS BOOKS

A Collection of Works by Writers in the English Language

Political Verse and Song
from Britain and Ireland

Political Verse and Song from Britain and Ireland

Edited by
Mary Ashraf

Seven Seas Publishers
Berlin

SEVEN SEAS BOOKS are published
by SEVEN SEAS PUBLISHERS Berlin
DDR 108 Berlin · Glinkastrasse 13–15

76-471472

Published as a Seven Seas Book 1975
Copyright (c) Mary Ashraf, 1974
Cover Design by Lothar Reher
Printed by Elbe-Druckerei Wittenberg
License Number: 306/136/75
Order Number: 652 103 9
Manufactured in the German Democratic Republic

Contents

PREFACE   21

ANONYMOUS   31
  The Plowman
  The Blacksmiths
  John Ball's Letter ...
  King Richard the Second's Favourites ...
  Lamkin

SIR JOHN HARINGTON   39
  Of Treason

WILLIAM SHAKESPEARE   40
  A London Riot against Foreign Journeymen 1517

ANONYMOUS   41
  A Lanthorne for Landlords

JOHN MILTON   44
  ... Upon His Blindness
  Riches Grow in Hell
  Oppression and Sword-Law
  Conquest

GEORGE WITHER   47
  The Stroke of Death

GERRARD WINSTANLEY   48
  The Diggers' Song

ANONYMOUS   51
  The Sea-Martyrs

JOHN GAY   56
  The Candidate

ANONYMOUS   58
  The New Peers

SIR JOHN BYROM   59
  On Midas's Art

CHRISTOPHER ANSTEY (?)   60
  A Remedy for Unrest

ANONYMOUS   61
  The Port Admiral
  The Genius of Britain

THOMAS SPENCE   66
  A Warning to Usurpers and Oppressors
  The Propagation of Spensonianism
  When the Romans Ruled the Land
  The Dispersion of the British Convention

ANONYMOUS   74
  The Gallic Rush-Light

CHARLES MORRIS   77
  "Captain Morris": A New Irish Song

ANONYMOUS   79
  Burke's Address to the "Swinish Multitude"

DANIEL EATON (?)   82
  Two Ways Pointed Out ...

THOMAS HOLCROFT   83
  Prologue to a Revolution

ANONYMOUS   84
  The Fate of Those Who Go for Soldiers

THOMAS PAINE   86
  Epitaph for a Crow

THOMAS "CLIO" RICKMAN   87
  Sonnet to an Infant at the Breast
  Impromptu Reply to Impertinence
  Sonnet to Thomas Paine

ROBERT BURNS   89
  Second Epistle to J. Lapraik
  Such a Parcel of Rogues in a Nation

WILLIAM BLAKE   92
  Holy Thursday
  The New Order

EDWARD RUSHTON   95
  Be Free!
  The Leviathan
  Toussaint to His Troops

ANONYMOUS   99
  The Wrongs of Man by Feudal Landlords

THOMAS EVANS   101
  Salvation of Empire

GEORGE GORDON, LORD BYRON   103
  An Ode to the Framers of the Frame Bill
  Song for the Luddites
  War-Profiteering Landlords
  One Common Cause

The Poet Laureate and Castlereagh
They Never Fail
Time to Act

PERCY BYSSHE SHELLEY   110
  Mighty Eagle
  This is the Day
  Men of England

EDWARD BLANDFORD   115
  London Railings

ROBERT ANDERSON   117
  Aul Englan

ANONYMOUS   119
  The Keelmen's Stick
  Loyal Festivities

WILLIAM MIDFORD   124
  Picture of Newcastle

ANONYMOUS   127
  Inaugural Address of the Duke of Wellington ...

ROBERT TAYLOR   131
  Swing's Revolution

ANONYMOUS   136
  Union Hymn

JOHN CLARE   137
  Remembrances
  The Fallen Elm

CHARLES COLE   143
   Ode to His Grace The Duke of Wellington
   Dawn of Freedom

EBENEZER ELLIOTT   149
   Song
   Caged Rats
   Song

HUGH WILLIAMS   153
   The Horn of Liberty

CAPEL LOFFT   155
   Public Opinion

ROBERT NICOLL   159
   The Puir Folk
   The Bacchanalian

ANONYMOUS "M"   163
   The Hungry Dogs and the Hides

GEORGE BINNS   165
   To the Magistrates ...

ANONYMOUS   166
   The Poor Man's Wedding

"JOHN BROWN"   168
   A Royal Marriage Ode

THOMAS COOPER   173
   The Lion of Freedom

ANONYMOUS   174
   Hardie's Last Letter to His Sweet Heart

DAVID WRIGHT 176
  Yes, We Are Free

SAMUEL SUMNER JONES 177
  On the Opening of the Present Session of Parliament

J. MCOWEN 185
  Father! Who Are the Chartists?

THOMAS OSBORNE DAVIS 186
  Tone's Grave

JOHN DE JEAN FRASER 188
  The Prisoner at the Bar
  A Word to the People

JOHN ARNOTT 191
  A Song Addressed to the Fraternal Democrats

ERNEST JONES 193
  The New World
  Free Speech
  The Future

EBENEEZER JONES 200
  A Coming Cry
  Song of the Kings of Gold
  Escape
  I Believe

ROBERT JOHNSON 209
  The Sheep Stealer's Defense

JAMES CLARENCE MANGAN 210
  For Soul and Country
  Curtain the Lamp

ALFRED FENNEL   214
  The Red Flag

WILLIAM JONES   216
  The March Wind
  The Peasant's Epitaph

ANONYMOUS   219
  The Southwark Brewers and the Austrian Butcher

R. SHELDON CHADWICK   221
  The Capitalist
  Lady, Spare a Jewel

JAMES MACFARLAN   224
  A Man of Feeling
  The Foundry Boy
  The Lords of Labour

GEORGE GODWYN BARMBY   228
  The Poetry of Spring

ANONYMOUS   231
  The Hulks

BEN PRESTON   233
  Human Progress
  My Gronfathur's Grave

WILLIAM MACCALL   237
  Africa

ANONYMOUS   238
  Three Songs of the National Agricultural
  Labourers' Union

DAVID WINGATE   242
  The Collier's Ragged Wean

"TIMOTHY WACKSTRAW", i. e.
JOHN BEDFORD LENO   244
  Grase the Fat Sow

JOHN BEDFORD LENO   246
  Song
  Labour

WILLIAM MORRIS   254
  A Death Song

SAMUEL LAYCOCK   255
  Beware

W. H. HOBART   258
  A Ballad of Trafalgar Square

JAMES SLIMMON   262
  Robert Burns
  Diogenes the Swineherd

JOHN LESLIE   267
  The Paris Commune 1871

JOHN FRANCIS ADAMS   270
  England in Egypt
  Hong Kong Lyrics
  To Queen Victoria in England
  To Karl Marx

CHARLES ALLEN CLARKE   278
  The Voice of the Manufacturing Slave

JOHN DAVIDSON   279
    Thirty Bob a Week
    War Song
    The Testament of Sir Simon Simplex ...

ERNEST T. COOMBE   292
    Our Common Cause

G. W. S.   294
    Taff Vale

ARTHUR HICKMOTT   296
    Labour Insurgent
    Robert Owen
    Street Propaganda

GEORGE MILLIGAN   300
    A Day's Work at the Docks
    The Tearaway Boss

ETHEL CARNIE   304
    Freedom
    Immortality
    Earth's Song to Her Children

PATRICK MACGILL   308
    Run Down
    The Song of the Drainer

ALBERT YOUNG   311
    Two Poems Dedicated to Karl Marx
    And It Shall Come

JAMES CONNOLLY   314
    A Dying Socialist Speaks to His Son

PADRAIC PEARSE   316
  The Rebel

TOM ANDERSON   319
  Arise Ye Sons of Labour

REV. P. O'NEILL   321
  The Foggy Dew

LIAM MACGABHANN   323
  "A Man Like That –"
  The Levellers

WILFRED OWEN   326
  The Parable of the Old Men and the Young
  Dulce et Decorum Est

H. F. CONSTANTINE   328
  The Glory of War

W. H. DAVIES   330
  The Sleepers

W. N. EWER   331
  Remember Scarborough
  May Day, 1917
  A Ballade of Reconstruction

WILFRED WILSON GIBSON   334
  Comrades
  Out of the Pit
  Fire
  Unity
  The Answer
  Murderers

JOHN S. CLARKE   337
    Karl Marx
    To the Memory of Liebknecht and Luxemburg
    The Proletarian Pedigree
    The Soul of Silas

ELEANOR FARJEON   345
    Oak-Leaves
    Nine Men's Morris
    Promises

ANONYMOUS   348
    Meditations of a Trade Unionist . . .

MATTHEW BIRD   349
    To the Memory of John Maclean

T. E. NICHOLAS   351
    Hail to the Revolution

JOE CORRIE   353
    The Image o' God

ANONYMOUS "SPARTACUS"   354
    The Awakening

SALME DUTT   356
    The Abandoned City

JULIUS LIPTON   358
    Love's Hope
    Wherefore this Change?

HUGH MACDIARMID   361
    For Greater Things
    The Skeleton of the Future

IDRIS DAVIES   363
  In Monmouthshire
  Poems of the General Strike
  Come Down
  William Morris

EDGELL RICKWORD   368
  To the Wife of a Non-Interventionist Statesman
  Luxury

MARY BROOKSBANK   373
  Foondry Lane

VINCENT EDWIN CROSSLAND   374
  The International Brigade
  Thoughts of a Country-Loving Miner

WILLIAM SOUTAR   376
  To Karl Marx
  Advent of Spring of 1939
  Direction

DAVID MARTIN   378
  Soldiers 1939
  South Welsh Prophecy

ALUN LEWIS   381
  Observation Post: Forward Area
  Sacco Writes to His Son
  Destruction

HUW MENAI   385
  Stalingrad
  Back in the Return

MAURICE CARPENTER   387
  George Loveless

DONALD BISHOP   388
  Colour Bar

DAI ALEXANDER   389
  The Miner

JOHN SINGER   391
  Stepney Green

ANONYMOUS   392
  Greek Tragedy

LESLIE DAIKEN   395
  Nostalgie d'Automne

PETER BLACKMAN   396
  Stalingrad
  All Men

ALEXANDER RUSSELL   401
  Unity on the Clyde
  Song of the Moulder

HELEN FULLERTON   405
  The Legend of County Louth
  Cypriot Question
  My Country
  Socialism

NANCY BUSH   414
  Guiana Johnny's Song

WILLIAM DUTSON   415
  The Roberts-Arundel Tuba

LEON ROSSELSON   417
   Battle Hymn for the New Socialist Party

BEVERLEY ROBINSON   419
   Black or White
   Decadegeneration
   Praise to Our Class

MERRYN WILLIAMS   422
   Cuba

RUTH MOSS   423
   The Price of Coal

FELICITY WHITE   424
   The Dragon of Wales

LYNWEN LLOYD JONES   425
   Aberfan

N. O. M.   426
   Long Live Vietnam

LARRY WRIGHT   428
   Treasure Island

ANONYMOUS   430
   The Streets of Derry Town

JAMES CONNELL   432
   The Red Flag

EUGÈNE POTTIER   434
   The Internationale

INDEX OF AUTHORS   439

Preface

The democratic movement of the late eighteenth century can be regarded as the starting point of political anthologies which went beyond the songbooks and collections of topical verse and current political party satire. This was indeed the golden age of popular political ballad both for quantity and quality. It was now that broader lower-class masses were drawn into active agitation in a more organized way, not as mere supporters of this or hat political leader or as a mob incited to riot for this or that immediate demand, but a broad opposition with distinct political principles and a radical programme.

Cheap songbooks and verse collections played an important part in this awakening of political consciousness and helped to keep the movement alive in the years of violent reaction following the French Revolution. While the Government attempted to close down even the workingman's "free and easy" in the taverns because they showed a preference for allegedly seditious songs, Thomas Spence advised his followers "to meet and sing and sing and meet" to keep up their spirits, adding

> "A song that awakens applause
> Is better than speaking or preaching."

In order to reach the wider, less educated public and to deepen understanding of democratic traditions, a few anthologies were published which included a varied assortment of prose and verse, old and new, in support of the rights of man, civil justice, political reforms and so on, or introduced the utopian-socialist and egalitarian ideas which were then penetrating the radical section of the disenfranchised lower classes.

Thus began a political anthology tradition which was extended in Chartist and Owenite publications in the first half of the nineteenth century. With the socialist songbooks and anthologies of the new movements in the late nineteenth and early twentieth century, the political verse anthology became a regular feature of the modern labour movement, serving a broadly educational purpose over and above providing songs for meetings. Several excellent selections of poetry or verse and prose combined appeared in the years between the two world wars, but except for a recent re-issue of Joan Beauchamp's "Poems of Revolt" all these have long been out of print.

No matter how widely the anthologist ranged, each collection was suited to its time and every anthologist had his or her own idea of what was politically useful or aesthetically justified. A new anthology today necessarily makes a different choice. There is however one aim that all political anthologies share or ought to share: the contents must have direct impact and be more or less easily understood. This does not mean of course that the selection is limited to the simplest kinds of verse, or that poetry simple and direct in form is always devoid of subtlety or depths.

Although a number of international socialist songs became incorporated as part of the British socialist singing repertoire, only one of these has been included – "The Internationale". Our own literature and popular poetry offer an abundant source of political verse, ranging from the very simple or the very crude or the very scurrilous to the high eloquence of major poets.

The aim of the present volume is twofold – to show, however incompletely, something of this great range and variation of expression, and along with less well known verse, some of which is here reprinted for the first time, to include old favourites of the traditional socialist anthology and classics of political poetry.

Since today everybody understands that politics spring from the social-economic relations which prevail, this collection differs from many of the older ones in giving more attention to the expression of needs, grievances and protests, the conditions of labour, working-class ethics and so on, which politics in the narrower sense reflect. For the rest the selection is bound to depend to a great measure on the compiler's personal ideas of what seems important, interesting, typical, sincere, witty or poetical as the case may be; and as this bias will be self-evident from the contents of the book, there is no need to explain or excuse it here.

There has been no attempt to represent periods or different movements, nor to illustrate the historical development of political verse. Nevertheless politics are a day-to-day practical affair and words like "liberty", "justice", "patriot" carry different associations and represent very different notions and conditions in the course of history. So that although it is a recognized practice to quote anachronistically taking the face value of words to fit a modern point of view or assuming that there is an analogy of situation and feeling, some historical perspective can enrich the reader's appreciation. The poems have therefore been arranged roughly in chronological order, although as it was also desirable to keep the poems by the same author together, there is considerable overlapping. The author's dates are shown under the name in the right-hand top corner of the page, and the date or more usually an approximate date of composition or first publication is shown on the left following the poem. Arranged in this way something of the development of ideas and the changing problems of successive stages should be visible.

Poems which refer to forgotten events or obscure historical personalities have generally been avoided unless sense and situation can be seen from the poem itself. It does not matter now who the original Vicar of Bray was, nor is it necessary to know the details of church politics; the song is a classic portrait of the time-server or yes-man in any walk of life, in any age.

Many of the poems associated with the working-class movement in the nineteenth and twentieth century were by obscure workingmen and women. Sometimes their trade can be guessed from their poems, but in general it is immaterial for our present purpose what the author was, or to distinguish professional writer from popular poet and casual versifier. The poem can be judged on its merits, and that in the case of political and social poetry obviously includes the aptness and soundness for its time of the political idea which is expressed and the reality of the situation and the people described.

The so-called source books of historical documentation, social history or political thought often distort as much as they illuminate. A selection of political verse would be an equally poor guide not only to social developments but to the relation of this kind of poetry to the problems of literature. A poetry anthology has quite a different function. It is not meant to be a textbook or a specialist's book. It will always have its value in extending the general reader's range and including the odd poem and the minor writer otherwise lost and forgotten. Old anthologies have often been the gateway to that immense heritage of poetry little of which is to be guessed at from the shelves of public libraries and not all of it to be found in "collected works" nor hinted at in standard histories of literature.

A rough classification of political and social poetry according to subject might be made like this:

1. Protest and complaint, direct or indirect, against exploitation and oppression.
2. Aspiration towards a better life, a juster society.
3. Topical satire of governments, politicians, landlords, capitalists.
4. Political-philosophical themes; political and ethical ideals.
5. Campaign songs of particular parties and movements.
6. The commemoration of popular struggles past and present.
7. Tributes to heroes and martyrs in the popular cause.
8. The expression of international working-class solidarity.
9. Comment on industrial conditions and working life and the rôle of the trade unions.
10. The creative power of labour; the image of the worker (including satire and caricature).

Protest and grievance run through all phases of class society, but of course the standard of what people considered their due, whether they appealed to compassion, to abstract justice or to consciousness of certain rights, and the degree of political understanding which accompanies the protest have radically changed in the course of time. The first poems in this volume introduce themes which the transition from feudalism to capitalism did not exhaust.

"The Plowman" hardly needs comment. Here as vividly as any modern documentary the condition of the mediaeval husbandman is laid bare in all its hopelessness, but also in all its humanity — not only because the poet is indignant at the sight of the family reduced to this brute level of existence but because he brings in that other essential feature, the plowman's spontaneous fellow-feeling for another in distress. It is that detail which gives the uncouth figure its substantial, startling reality after six centuries. The poet's contemporaries could have filled in a number of other hard facts about feudal servitude from this description for which the modern reader might need explanatory notes, but the essentials are all there. Actually the poet was using this image of poverty in order to expose the corruption and avarice of the clergy and monastic orders to which he attributed the material as well as the moral ills of his day, and he had no solution to offer other than spiritual regeneration.

For this wretched peasant the good life might very well have seemed a fantastic wonderland of inexhaustible food and drink which is the subject of another mediaeval poem, "The Land of Cokaygne" which is not included in this volume.* The daydream begins with two full meals a day and no worries, no out in all weathers, no stables to muck out, no lice and fleas. Where such things were unattainable luxuries, imagination might as well run wild and add geese flying in ready roast and rivers of wine. Again this author was satirizing the loose living of the monasteries and nunneries, and by no means meant that the good life was only a matter of a full belly and uninhibited wenching, although there is every indication that he was enjoying the fantasy. Such extravagances were simply the flagrant opposite of the poor man's reality, like the old folk-tales of "Table, lay thyself", fairy gold and other wishful thinking. In modern terms, they reflected the contradictions in mediaeval society ripening (at the time of our first poem) towards the Reformation and the Peasants' Revolt.

Such was the mediaeval utopia of the frankly impossible, not yet an ingredient of systematized political thought. For long the Golden Age was imagined only in the past or in the return to a more primitive and patriarchal way of life. An ideal of a hard, simple life of subsistence agriculture

* For a full modernized version see A. L. Morton, "The English Utopia" (Seven Seas Books, Berlin, 1968)

shared by a free community inspired "The Diggers' Song" (page 48). But with the rise of the modern proletariat the vision of social justice progressively became the "Good Time Coming" and took on ever more concrete and more believable forms based on a rational critique of existing society. The utopia was given revolutionary pathos and certain practical political implications in the poems about Spence's Plan and Robert Owen's Co-operative Commonwealth, or in Shelley's "Masque of Anarchy" and "Prometheus Unbound" and Ernest Jones's "The New World".

Many of the old poetic images and allegorical abstractions clung for generations in popular verse, although their meaning changed. The "Union Hymn" (page 36) originally implied the political reform union and club movement which campaigned for Parliamentary Reform. It became attached to the upsurge of the trade union movement and is particularly associated with the Tolpuddle Martyrs. But as ideas in general advanced and modern conditions of class struggle demanded a scientific basis of socialism, the theme of the just society of the future could no longer remain at the level of utopian daydream and painless transition. The best political verse spoke of the actual and future struggle towards the workers' conquest of power, of freedom as man's understanding of necessity and consciously developed ability to control his own destiny in all senses.

The theme of "The Blacksmiths" (page 33) presents Labour itself, the pride, strength and skill of the craftsmen, their indispensability, their claim to honour. No proletarians these. Whether masters or journeymen, they are a special kind of ancient labour aristocracy monopolizing an all-important art, the mediaeval Krupps and Churchills who supplied the armies of feudal kings and barons and made more swords than ploughshares, plunder not productivity being then the watchword of the overlords. No doubt what interested this poet was not any social lesson but the word-picture for its own sake and the rendering of the rhythm and sound of the hammers. There was a song in the forge in those days as there is for the modern class-conscious moulder in Alexander Russell's poem (page 403). The creative rôle of Labour, the self-confident image of the workingman and woman, grew new dimensions in socialist poetry with each stage of political development.

In the poem "Lamkin" (page 36) – there is the mason defrauded of his pay and resorting to terrorist revenge, aided and abetted by the nursemaid who has a long repressed grievance against her haughty mistress. Perhaps this ballad was preserved simply for the sake of its sadistic horror, but in fact it tells the story of a piece of crude class warfare and reflected the long and bitter struggle which united all producers in the town guilds against the feudal nobility when the bourgeoisie was in its very early infancy. Lamkin had no legal remedy to enforce the contract against the baron's arbitrary power, and the ballad is true history in as much as it expressed that phase of class conflict. Anyone would have *felt* murderous in such a case and might have sought consolation in imagining a bloody revenge. Nor should it be overlooked that insult was added to injury, when a tradesman of some repute was not addressed as "Master Lambert" but given a contemptuous nickname by everybody in my lord's household. The story ends on the law-and-order note, in punishment no less barbarous than the crime. But most of the old protests and exposures ended with conventional expressions of loyalty to the powers that were (compare "The Sea-Martyrs", page 51), or pious resignation to the will of heaven. The story is thought to record some real incident, who knows where or when. The ballad might have arisen out of sympathy for Lamkin, or his crime might have been highly coloured in order to warn others of the wickedness of men expecting to be paid for building castles. The feudal baron disappeared from the scene; the wages struggle in its manifold forms continued unending between capitalist and worker. And since it was always a major concern of both, it also developed as a subject of political poetry along with the hundred and one other common issues of industrial life and production relations.

These themes, then, run through the whole history of class society from mediaeval times to the present era of the approaching end of capitalism. Alongside this protest and statement poetry emerged direct political comment and satire, and verse concerned with the theory and practice of government, with class relations as such, and eventually with the question of power in the state. "King Richard the Second's Favourites" (page 35) may serve as a specimen of early political satire attacking unpopular ministers as individuals, not the policies or class interests which public enemies represent.

As wide a selection of these many approaches as there was room for has been given in the present volume; but as poets do not set out to chronicle history or the development of ideas, and as poetry is not a systematic record of anything, there was nothing to be gained by attempting to classify our specimens according to their subjects. These were bound to overlap and it is up to the reader whether he or she thinks about the contents of poems historically or reads them at face value.

This is not intended as a book of reference for academic purposes. There are therefore no textual or historical notes. It is a selection meant to be enjoyed without special knowledge of history. But since it does inevitably illustrate how living issues got into poetry, what inspired poets or how deeper feelings and convictions can be expressed in the brevity of verse forms, perhaps this book may prove of help to younger poets and song writers who are seeking their own modern idiom of communication. With that in mind, the editor has not always been guided by personal taste in such matters but included what has been suggested by a number of other people kind enough to be interested in the idea of an anthology. The ideal way of compiling such an anthology would be to collect suggestions from as wide a circle of working people as possible, for in the editor's personal experience there are a great many more politically conscious people who like poetry than is generally thought to be the case and many who themselves write poetry from time to time most of which never sees publication.

The original title of the poem is given, when it has one. In the case of extracts from long poems the compiler has taken the liberty to supply a heading to indicate what the particular passage is about. The name of the original work from which it is taken is given below. Similarly where a short poem was originally published without a title, a heading has been supplied. Nothing else has been changed or added. Where a poem has been abridged by omitting lines this is shown by dots (...). A few poems had footnotes by the authors. A few more have been added by the present editor. Prose remarks explaining the poem are printed as they appear in the source used for this edition.

Berlin, 1975   MARY ASHRAF

The Plowman

. . .

Then I went forth and talked to myself
Of the falsehood of these folk how faithless they were.
And as I went by the way weeping for sorrow
I saw a simple man near me straining on the plough.
His coat was of coarse cloth that is called carymary,
His hood was full of holes and his hair stuck out through it,
With his clumsy shoes all knotted and cobbled
His toes coming through as he trod on the earth,
His hose hanging over his hams on either side,
All besplattered with sludge as he steered the plough.
Two miserable mittens made up of rags
The fingers frayed out and dripping full of muck,
This man wallowed in mud over his ankles.
Four heffers went before him that had grown so feeble
Their ribs could be reckoned so wretched they were.
His wife walked beside him with a long goad
In a cutty coat curtelled up high,
Shrouded in a winnowing sheet to shield her from the
                                                weather,
Barefoot on the barren ice so that the blood followed.
And by the bottom of the field lay a little crumb-bowl
And thereon lay a little child lapped in rags
And two of two years old on t'other side.
And they all sang the same song that was sorrowful to hear.
They cried with one cry a note of cruel woe.
The poor man sighed and said: Children be still.

This man looked at me and let the plough rest
And said: Poor man, why sighest thou so sadly?
If thou lackest for livelihood I will lend to thee
Whatever good God has given; let us go dear brother.

14th Century

From *The Plowman's Crede*
(Modernized)

The Blacksmiths

Swarte smekyd smethes smatered wyth smoke
Dryve me to death wyth den of here dyntes.
Such noys on nyghts ne herd men never:
What navens cry and clateryng of knockes!
The cammede kongons cryen after "col, col!"
And blowen here bellewes, that al here brayn breasts:
"Huf, puf!" saith that on; "Haf, paf!" that other.
Thei spitten and spraulyn and spellyn many spelles;
Thei graven and gnacchen, thei groanys togedyr,
And holden hem hote wyth here hard hamers.
Of a bole-hyde ben here barm-fellys;
Here shankes ben shakeled for the fere flunders;
Here hamers thei han, that hard ben handled,
Stark strokes thei stryken on a stelyd stokke:
Lus, bus! las, das! rowtyn be rowe.
Such doleful a dreme the devil it todryve!
The mayster longith a litel, and laschet a lesse,
Twineth hem twain, and toucheth a treble:
Tik tak, hic hac, tiket taket, tyk tak!
Lus bus, las das! sych lyfe thei ledyn
Alle clothemerys: Cryst hem give sorwe!
May no man for brenwaterys on nyght han hys rest!

14th Century

John Ball's Letter to the
Peasants in Essex

Johan the Mullere hath ygrounde smal, smal, smal;
The Kynges sone of heuene schal paye for al
Be war or ye be wo;
Knoweth your friend fro your fo;
Haueth ynow, and seith "Hoo";
And do well and bettre, and fleth synne,
And seketh pees, and hold you therinne;
And so biddeth Johan Trewman and alle his felawes.

1381?

King Richard the Second's Favourites –
Busshy, Baggot and Green

There is a bush that's overgrown
Crop it close and keep it down
        Or else it will run wild.
The long grass that is so green
It must be mowed and raked clean;
        It has overrun the field.

That great bag that is so wide
It shall be trimmed and smaller made,
        The bottom's nearly out;
It is so rotten through and through
That never a stitch will hold thereto
        To patch it with a clout.

                (Modernized)

C. 1399

ANONYMOUS

Lamkin

It's Lamkin was a mason good as ever built wi' stane,
He built Lord Wearie's castle, but payment gat he nane.

"O pay me Lord Wearie, come pay me my fee."
"I canna pay you, Lamkin, for I maun gang o'er the sea."

"O pay me now, Lord Wearie, come, pay me out o' hand."
"I canna pay you, Lamkin, unless I sell my land."

"O gine ye winna pay me, I here sall make a vow,
Before that ye come hame again, ye sall ha'e cause to rue."

Lord Wearie's gat a bonny ship to sail the saut sea faem;
Bade his lady weel the castle keep, ay till he should come
hame.

But the nourice was a fause limmer as e'er hung on a tree;
She laid a plot wi' Lamkin, whan her lord was o'er the sea.

She laid a plot wi' Lamkin when the servants were awa'
Loot him in at a little shot-window, and brought him to
the ha'.

"O whare's a' the men o' this house, that ca' me Lamkin?"
"They're at the barn-well thrashing: 'twill be lang or they
come in."

"And whare's the women o' this house, that ca' me Lamkin?"
"They're at the far well washing; 'twill be night or they
come hame."

"An' whare's the bairns o' this house, that ca' me Lamkin?"
"They're at the school reading; 'twill be night or they
come hame."

"O whare's the lady o' this house, that ca's me Lamkin?"
"She's up in her bower sewing, but we soon can bring her
doon."

Then Lamkin's ta'en a sharp knife, that hang doon by his
gaire,
And he has gi'en the bonny babe a deep wound and a sair.

Then Lamkin he rocked, and the fause nourice sang,
Till frae ilka bore o' the cradle the red blood out sprang.

Then out it spak the lady, as she stood on the stair:
"What ails my bairn, nourice, that he's greeting sae sair?"

"O still my bairn, nourice, O still him wi' the pap!"
"He winna still, lady for this nor for that."

"O still my bairn, nourice, O still him wi' the wand."
"He winna still, lady, for a' his faither's land."

"O still my bairn, nourice, O still him wi' the bell."
"He winna still, lady, till ye come doon yoursel."

O the firsten step she steppit, she steppit on a stane:
But the neisten step she steppit, she met him Lamkin.

"O mercy, mercy, Lamkin, ha'e mercy upon me.
Though you've ta'en my young son's life, ye may let
mysel be."

"O sall I kill her, nourice, or sall I let her be?"
"O kill her, kill her, Lamkin, for she ne'er was good to me."

37

"O scour the basin, nourice, and make it fair and clean,
For to keep this lady's heart's blood, for she's come o'
noble kin."

"There's need no basin, Lamkin, lat it run through the
floor;
What better is the heart's blood o' the rich than o' the
poor?"

But ere three months were at an end, Lord Wearie came
again;
But dowie, dowie was his heart when first he came hame.

"O wha's blood is this," he says, "that lies in the chamer?"
"It is your lady's heart's blood; 'tis clear as the lamer."

"And wha's blood is this," he says, "that lies in my ha'?"
"It is your young son's heart's blood; 'tis the clearest ava."

O sweetly sang the blackbird that sat upon the tree;
But sairer grat Lamkin, when he was condemned to dee.

And bonny sang the mavis, out o' the thorny brake;
But sairer grat the nourice when she was tied to the stake.

15th – 16th Century

SIR JOHN HARINGTON
1561–1612

Of Treason

Treason doth never prosper: What's the reason?

For if it prosper, none dare call it treason.

WILLIAM SHAKESPEARE
1564–1616

A London Riot against
Foreign Journeymen 1517

Sir Thomas More: Alas poor things what is it you have got
   Although we grant you get the thing you seek?
Bett: Marry, the removing of the strangers which cannot
chose but much advantage the poor handicrafts of the City.
More: Grant them removed and grant that this your noise
Hath chid down all the majesty of England,
Imagin that you see the wretched strangers
Their babies at their back, with their poor luggage
Plodding to th' ports and coasts for transportation,
And that you sit as kings in your desires,
Authority quite silenced in your brawl,
And you in ruff of your opinions clothed,
What had you got? I'll tell you, you had taught
How insolence and stronghand should prevail,
How ordered should be quelled, and by this pattern
Not one of you should live an aged man;
For other ruffians, as their fancies wrought,
With self-same hand, self-reasons and self-right,
Would shark on you and men like ravenous fishes
Would feed on one another.

> From *Sir Thomas More* (of which this scene
> is ascribed to Shakespeare)

A Lanthorne for Landlords

Tune: *The Duke of Norfolke*

With sobbing grief my heart wil break
      Asunder in my brest,
Before this story of great woe
      I truely have exprest:
Therefore let all kind-hearted men,
      and those that tender be,
Come beare a part of this my griefe,
      and joyntly say with me,

      "Wo worth, wo worth, wo worth them all,
          Wo worth to them I say;
      Wo worth, wo worth, wo worth them all,
          Wo worth to them away."

Not long agoe in Lincolne dwelt,
      As I did understand,
A labouring man, from thence set forth
      to serve in Ireland:
And there in Princes' warres was slaine,
      As doth that Country know,
But left his widdow great with child
      as ever she could goe.

This woman having gone her time,
      Her husband being dead,
Of two fine pretty Boyes at once
      was sweetly brought to bed;

Whereat her wicked Landlord straight
        Did ponder in his minde
How that their wants hee must relieve,
        and succour for them finde:

For, being borne upon his ground,
        This was his vile conceit, –
That he the mother should maintaine,
        and give the other meat;
Which to prevent, he hyed fast
        unto this widdow poore,
And, on the day she went to Church,
        he turn'd her out of doore.

Her houshold goods he 'straynd upon,
        To satisfie the rent,
And left her scarce a ragge to weare, –
        so wilfull was he bent.
Her pretty Babes, that sweetly slept
        Upon her tender brest,
Were forced, by the Miser's rage,
        by nights in streets to rest.

Quoth she, "My husband, in your cause,
        In warres did lose his life;
And will you use thus cruelly
        His harmlesse wedded wife?
O God! revenge a widdowes wrong!
        That all the world may know
How you have forst a Souldier's wife
        a begging for to goe."

From Lincolne thus this widdow went,
        But left her curse behind,
And begged all the Land about,
        her maintenance to find.

At many places where she came,
                    She knew the whipping post,
Constrained still, as beggars be,
                    to taste on such like rost.

And, weary of such punishment,
                    Which she had sufferd long,
She daily thought within her heart
                    shee had exceeding wrong:
And, comming neere to Norwich gates,
                    In griefes shee sate her downe,
Desiring God that never shee
                    might come in that same Towne;

"For I had rather live," quoth shee,
                    "Within these pleasant fields,
And feed my children with such food
                    as woods and meddowes yeeld,
Before I will of rich men beg,
                    Or crave it at their doore,
Whose hearts, I know, are mercilesse
                    unto the needy poore."

16th – 17th Century

JOHN MILTON
1608–1674

To Mr. Cyriac Skinner.
Upon His Blindness

Cyriac this Three years day, these Eyes though clear
    To outward view of blemish or of Spot,
    Bereft of Sight, their Seeing have forgot:
    Nor to their idle Orbs doth day appear,
Or Sun, or Moon, or Star, throughout the Year;
    Or Man, or Woman; yet I argue not
    Against Heaven's Hand, or Will, nor bate one jot
    Of Heart or Hope; but still bear up, and steer
Right onward. What supports me, dost thou ask?
    The Conscience, Friend, to have lost them over ply'd
    In Liberties Defence, my noble task;
Of which all *Europe* rings from side to side.
    This thought might lead me through this World's
                                vain mask
    Content, though blind, had I no other Guide.

c. 1655

Riches Grow in Hell

. . . Mammon led them on,
Mammon, the least erected Spirit that fell
From heav'n, for ev'n in heav'n his looks and thoughts
Were always downward bent, admiring more
The riches of Heav'ns pavement, trod'n Gold,

44

Then aught divine or holy else enjoy'd
In vision beatific: by him first
Men also, and by his suggestion taught,
Ransack'd the Center, and with impious hands
Rifl'd the bowels of thir mother Earth
For Treasures better hid. Soon had his crew
Op'nd into the Hill a spacious wound
And dig'd out ribs of Gold. Let none admire
That riches grow in Hell; that soyle may best
Deserve the precious bane.

1667   From *Paradise Lost* I

Oppression and Sword-Law

Such were these Giants, men of high renown;
For in those dayes Might onely shall be admir'd,
And Valour and Heroic Vertu call'd;
To overcome in Battle, and subdue
Nations, and bring home spoils with infinite
Man-slaughter, shall be held the highest pitch
Of human Glorie, and for Glorie done
Of triumph, to be styl'd great Conquerours,
Patrons of Mankind, Gods, and Sons of Gods,
Destroyers rightlier call'd and Plagues of men,
Thus Fame shall be achiev'd, renown on Earth,
And what most merits fame in silence hid.

1667   From *Paradise Lost* XI

Conquest

They err who count it glorious to subdue
By Conquest far and wide, to over-run
Large Countries, and in field great Battels win,
Great Cities by assault: what do these Worthies,
But rob and spoil, burn, slaughter, and enslave
Peaceable Nations, neighbouring, or remote,
Made Captive, yet deserving freedom more
Then those thir Conquerours, who leave behind
Nothing but ruin wheresoe're they rove,
And all the flourishing works of peace destroy,
Then swell with pride, and must be titl'd Gods,
Great Benefactors of mankind, Deliverers,
Worship't with Temple, Priest and Sacrifice;
One is the Son of *Jove*, of *Mars* the other,
Till Conquerour Death discover them scarce men,
Rowling in brutish vices, and deform'd,
Violent or shameful death thir due reward.
But if there be in glory aught of good,
It may by means far different be attain'd
Without ambition, war, or violence;
By deeds of peace, by wisdom eminent,
By patience, temperance; I mention still
Him whom thy wrongs with Saintly patience born,
Made famous in a Land and times obscure;
Who names not now with honour patient *Job*?
Poor *Socrates* (who next more memorable?)
By what he taught and suffer'd for so doing,
For truths sake suffering death unjust, lives now
Equal in fame to proudest Conquerours.

1671   From *Paradise Regained* III

The Stroke of Death

So long as I have *any* work to do,
I shall have what is needful thereunto.
And when 'tis at an end, no matter whether
The Stroke of Death shall be received, either
By Axe or Halter (so I merit not,
What is by law the Malefactor's Lot)
Or *starving,* or, by one of those diseases
Which ordinarily the body seizes,
For, that shame, which men fear whilst they have breath
By suffering what they count a shameful death,
Is shared among mankind, and every one
Bears part thereof with me, when I am gone.

1661   From *A Triple Paradox*

GERRARD WINSTANLEY
1609–16–?

The Diggers' Song

"You noble Diggers all, stand up now, stand up now,
  You noble Diggers all, stand up now,
The waste land to maintain, seeing Cavaliers by name
Your digging do disdain and persons all defame.
    Stand up now, stand up now.

Your houses they pull down, stand up now, stand up now,
  Your houses they pull down, stand up now;
Your houses they pull down to fright poor men in town,
But the Gentry must come down, and the poor shall wear
                                        the crown.
    Stand up now, Diggers all!

With spades and hoes and plowes, stand up now, stand up
                                        now,
  With spades and hoes and plowes, stand up now;
Your freedom to uphold, seeing Cavaliers are bold
To kill you if they could, and rights from you withhold.
    Stand up now, Diggers all!

Their self-will is their law, stand up now, stand up now,
  Their self-will is their law, stand up now;
Since tyranny came in, they count it now no sin
To make a goal a gin, to starve poor men therein.
    Stand up now, stand up now.

The Gentry are all round, stand up now, stand up now,
  The Gentry are all round, stand up now;
The Gentry are all round, on each side they are found,
Their wisdom's so profound to cheat us of our ground.
    Stand up now, stand up now.

The Lawyers they conjoin, stand up now, stand up now,
  The Lawyers they conjoin, stand up now!
To arrest you they advise, such fury they devise,
The devil in them lies, and hath blinded both their eyes.
    Stand up now, stand up now.

The Clergy they come in, stand up now, stand up now,
  The Clergy they come in, stand up now;
The Clergy they come in, and say it is a sin
That we should now begin our freedom for to win.
    Stand up now, Diggers all!

The tithes they yet will have, stand up now, stand up now,
  The tithes they yet will have, stand up now;
The tithes they yet will have, and Lawyers their fees crave,
And this they say is brave to make the poor their slave.
    Stand up now, Diggers all!

'Gainst Lawyers and 'gainst Priests, stand up now, stand
                                                    up now,
  'Gainst Lawyers and 'gainst Priests, stand up now;
For tyrants they are both, even flat against their oath,
To grant us they are loath, free meat and drink and cloth.
    Stand up now, Diggers all!

The club is all their law, stand up now, stand up now,
  The club is all their law, stand up now;
The club is all their law, to keep poor men in awe;
But they no vision saw to maintain such a law.
    Stand up now, Diggers all!

49

The Cavaliers are foes, stand up now, stand up now,
   The Cavaliers are foes, stand up now;
The Cavaliers are foes, themselves they do disclose
By verses, not in prose, to please the singing boys.
   Stand up now, Diggers all!

To conquer them by love, come in now, come in now,
   To conquer them by love, come in now;
To conquer them by love, as it does you behove,
For He is King above, no Power is like to Love.
   Glory here, Diggers all!"

c. 1650

The Sea-Martyrs; or, The Seamen's Sad Lamentation for their Faithful Service, Bad Pay, and Cruel Usage;

Being a woful relation how some of them were unmercifully put to death for pressing for their pay, when their families were like to starve.

Thus our new Government does subjects serve,
And leaves them this sad choice: to hang or starve.

To the Tune of *Banstead Downs*

Good people, do but lend an ear,
And a sad story you shall hear –
A sadder you never heard –
Of due desert and base reward,
   Which will our English subjects fright
   For our new Government to fight.

Our seamen are the onely men
That o'er the French did vict'ry gain;
They kept the foe from landing here,
Which would have cost the Court full dear;
   And when they for their pay did hope
   They were rewarded with a rope.

The roaring canon they ne'er fear'd,
Their lives and bloud they never spar'd;
Through fire and flame their courage flew,
No bullets could their hearts subdue.

Had they in fight but flincht at all
King James had now been in Whitehall.

Thus England, and our new King too,
Their safety to their valour owe;
Nay, some did 'gainst their conscience fight
To do some great ones too much right;
  And now, oh, barbarous tyranny!
  Like men they fought, like dogs they dye.

Thousands of them their lives did lose
In fighting stoutly with their foes,
And thousands were so maim'd in fight
That 'twas a sad and piteous sight;
  And when they hop'd their pay to gain
  They have their labour for their pain.

Their starving families at home
Expected their slow pay would come;
But our proud Court meant no such thing,
Not one groat must they have till spring;
  To starve all summer would not do,
  They must still starve all winter too.

It might a little ease their grief,
And give their mis'ry some relief,
Might they in trade ships outward go,
But that poor boon's denied them too,
  Which is as much as plain to say,
  You shall earn nothing, nor have pay.

Their poor wives with care languishéd,
Their children cried for want of bread,
Their debts encreast, and none would more
Lend them, or let them run o' th' score.
  In such a case what could they doe
  But ask those who money did owe?

Therefore some, bolder than the rest,
The officers for their own request;
They call'd 'em rogues, and said nothing
Was due to them untill the spring:
   The King had none for them, they said
   Their betters, they must first be paid.

The honest seamen then replied
They could no longer want abide,
And that nine hundred thousand pound
Was giv'n last year to pay them round:
   Their money they had earnt full dear
   And could not stay another half-year.

A council then they streight did call
Of pick-thanks made to please Whitehall,
And there they were adjudg'd to dye;
But no man knows wherefore, nor why.
   What times are these! Was't ever known
   'Twas death for men to ask their own?

Yet some seem'd milder than the rest,
And told them that, their fault confest,
And pardon askt and humbly crav'd,
Their lives perhaps might then be sav'd;
   But they their cause scorn'd to betray
   Or own't a crime to ask their pay.

Thus they the seamen's martyrs dyed,
And would not yield to unjust pride;
Their lives they rather would lay down
Than yield it sin to ask their own.
   Thus they for justice spent their blood
   To do all future seamen good.

Wherefore let seamen all and some
Keep the days of their martyrdom,
And bear in mind these dismal times,
When true men suffer for false crimes;
    England ne'er knew the like till now,
    Nor e'er again the like will know.

But now suppose they had done ill,
In asking pay too roughly, still
When 'twas their due and need so prest,
They might have pardon found at least;
    The King and Queen some mercifull call,
    But seamen find it not at all.

To robbers, thieves, and felons they
Freely grant pardons ev'ry day;
Only poor seamen, who alone
Do keep them on their father's throne,
    Must have at all no mercy shown:
    Nay, tho' there wants fault, they'l find one.

Where is the subjects' liberty?
And eke where is their property?
We're forc'd to fight for nought, like slaves,
And though we do we're hang'd like knaves.
    This is not like Old England's ways:
    'New lords, new laws,' the proverb says.

Besides the seamen's pay, that's spent,
The King for stores, ships, and what's lent,
Does owe seven millions at the least,
And ev'ry year his debt's encrease;
    So that we may despair that we
    One quarter of our pay shall see.

Foreigners and confederates
Get poor men's pay, rich men's estates;
Brave England does to ruine run,
And Englishmen must be undone.
   If this trade last but one half-year
    Our wealth and strength is spent, I fear.

God bless our noble Parliament,
And give them the whole government,
That they may see we're worse than ever,
And us from lawless rule deliver;
   For England's sinking, unless they
    Do take the helm, and better sway.

Early 18th Century

The Candidate

When sly Jemmy Twitcher* had smugg'd up his face
With a lick of court white wash and pious grimace
Awooing he went where three sisters of old
In harmless society guttle and scold.

Lord! Sister, says Physic to Law, I declare
Such a sheep-biting look, such a pick-pocket air,
Not I, for the Indies! You know I'm no prude;
But his nose is a shame, and his eyes are too lewd!
Then he shambles and straddles so oddly I fear –
No; at our time of life, 'twould be silly, my dear.

I don't know, says Law, now methinks for his look,
'Tis just like the picture in Rochester's book.
But his character, Phyzzy, his morals, his life;
When she died, I can't tell, but he once had a wife.

They say he's no Christian, loves drinking and whoring,
And all the town rings of his swearing and roaring;
His lying, and filching, and Newgate-bird tricks: —
Not I, – for a coronet, chariot and six.

Divinity heard, between waking and dozing,
Her sisters denying, and Jemmy proposing.
From dinner she rose with her bumper in hand,
She stroked up her belly, and stroked down her band.

* Earl of Sandwich.

What a pother is here about wenching and roaring!
Why David loved catches, and Solomon whoring.
Did not Israel filch from th' Egyptians of old
Their jewels of silver and jewels of gold?

The prophet of Bethel, we read, told a lie:
He drinks; so did Noah: he swears; so do I.
To refuse him for such peccadillos were odd;
Besides he repents, and talks about God.

Never hang down your head, you poor penitent elf!
Come, buss me, I'll be Mrs Twitcher myself.
D--n ye both for a couple of Puritan bitches!
He's a Christian enough that repents and that --.

The New Peers

In former times (but Heav'n be praised
        We've no such doings now)
Some men to peerages were raised,
        The world knew why and how.

The modern method is to sink
        Contempt in one short word,
For when a name begins to stink,
        We call the thing a – Lord.

176–

SIR JOHN BYROM
1692–1763

On Midas's Art

Midas, they say, possessed the art of old,
Of turning whatsoe'er he touch'd to gold;
This modern statesmen can reverse with ease;
Touch them with gold, they'll turn to what you please.

176–

A Remedy for Unrest

Ah! Well they know that if the Poor
Were cloathed and fed, they'd work no more;
That nothing makes mankind so good,
So tractable as Want of Food;
And like those frugal Politicians,
Who take their maxims from Physicians,
Think Starving is the best foundation
Of popular subordination.

1780   From *Speculation or,*
                       A Defense of Mankind

The Port Admiral

'Twas at the landing place that's just below Mount Wyse,
Poll leaned against the sentry's box, a tear in both her eyes:
Her apron twisted round her arms, all for to keep them
warm,
Being a windy Christmas Day, and also a snow-storm.
   And Bet and Sue
   Both stood there too,
     A-shivering by her side;
   They both were dumb,
   And both look'd glum
     As they watched the ebbing tide.
   Poll put her arms a-kimbo:
     At the admiral's house look'd she;
   To thoughts before in limbo,
     She now a vent gave free.
You have sent the ship in a gale to work,
 On a lee-shore to be jammed;
I'll give you a piece of my mind, old Turk:
 Port Admiral, you be damned.

Chorus
We'll give you a piece of our mind, old Turk:
 Port Admiral, you be damned.

Whoever heard in the sarvice of a frigate made to sail
On Christmas Day, it blowing hard, with sleet, and snow,
and hail?
I wish I had the fishing of your back that is so bent,
I'd use the galley poker hot, unto your heart's content.

Here Bet and Sue
Are with me too,
A-shivering by my side;
They both are dumb,
And both look glum,
And watch the ebbing tide.
Poll put her arms a-kimbo:
At the admiral's house look'd she;
To thoughts that were in limbo,
She now a vent gave free.
You've got a roaring fire, I'll bet:
In it your toes are jammed;
Let's give him a piece of our mind, my Bet:
Port Admiral, you be damned!

Chorus
Let's give him a piece of our mind, my Bet:
Port Admiral, you be damned.

I had the flour, and plumps all picked, and suet all
chopped fine,
To mix into a pudding rich, for all the mess to dine:
I pawn'd my ear-rings for the beef, it weighed at least a
stone:
Now my fancy man is sent to sea, and I am left alone.
Here's Bet and Sue
Who stand here too,
A-shivering by my side;
They both are dumb,
They both look glum,
And watch the ebbing tide.
Poll put her arms a-kimbo:
At the admiral's house look'd she;
To thoughts that were in limbo,
She now a vent gave free:

You've got a turkey, I'll be bound,
  With which you will be crammed;
I'll give you a bit of my mind, old hound:
  Port Admiral, you be damned.

Chorus
We'll give you a bit of our mind, old hound:
Port Admiral, you be damned.

I'm sure that in this weather they cannot cook their meat:
To eat it raw on Christmas Day will be a pleasant treat;
But let us all go home, girls; it's no use waiting here:
We'll hope that Christmas Day to come they'll have a
                                            better cheer.

        So Bet and Sue,
        Don't stand here too,
          A-shivering by my side;
        Don't keep so dumb,
        Don't look so glum,
          Nor watch the ebbing tide.
        Poll put her arms a-kimbo:
          At the admiral's house look'd she;
        To thoughts that were in limbo,
          She now a vent gave free.
So while they cut their raw salt junks,
  With dainties you'll be cramm'd;
Here's once for all my mind, old hunks:
  Port Admiral, you be damned.

Chorus
So once for all our mind, old hunks:
Port Admiral, you be damned.

Early 19th Century

The Genius of Britain

(On the Mutiny at Spithead)

The Genius of Britain went hovering round,
  For she fear'd that fair Freedom was fled;
But she found to her joy that she was not quite gone,
  But remain'd with the fleet at Spithead.
Rejoic'd at the news, to the *Charlotte* she flew,
  Where fair Freedom she heard sat enthron'd:
They all man'd the yards as the goddess came in,
  For Britain and Freedom they own'd.

The fleet hail'd the goddess with three hearty cheers
  As she stood on the *Charlotte's* gangway,
She drop'd a sad tear as she look'd on her sons
  Who so long neglected had lay;
She was led to the cabin. Fair Freedom was there,
  True Loyalty sat by her side;
Britannia sat down in a transport of joy:
  'All hail to my heroes!' she cry'd.

Every ship in the line sent two seamen so brave,
  Whom the goddess receiv'd with a smile:
They assured her that if they were treated like men
  They would still guard her favourite isle.
'Go on, my brave sons, in the steps you now tread,
  Be virtue your guide and your guard,
And God, who rules over the land and the sea,
  Will your honest endeavours reward.'

The Genius of Ireland came in with her harp,
  She saluted fair Freedom with tears,
They man'd the yards to welcome her o'er,
  And every ship gave three cheers.
Success to the seventeen united bright stars,*
  Let their praise echo round every shore,
And the fifteenth of April will ne'er be forgot
  Till Britannia and Freedom's no more.

* Ships' Delegates to the Strike Committee of the Fleet.

1800

THOMAS SPENCE
1750–1814

A Warning to Usurpers and Oppressors,
Alias – Giants and Men of Renown

Ye children of men I pray you attend
Hear what I've to say, a willing ear lend;
I'll show the dire vengeance which on you awaits
In following the sins, which a Just God most hates.
                         Sing Fa-la ye Men of Renown.

The cruelty and violence of seizing the ground,
The cause chiefly was of the old world being drown'd;
The Brutish usurpers then swelling with pride,
Thought it high renown o'er their fellows to ride.

These warriors, these giants, these heroes of old,
Corrupted the manners of all we are told:
Now violence and robbery only have charms,
All honour's confined to the curs'd trade of arms.

Now war being the fashion and Plunder the trade,
The world is as wicked as it can be made;
All now were ambitious of being mighty men,
At butchering their fellows – oh! what a world then!

These monsters although great in each other's eyes,
God blush'd for, and did the proud reptiles despise;
Heart sick of their Baseness, these men of renown,
He like rats and vermine did all of them drown.

No part in this violence and plunder had Noah,
For he was a Just man, the text tells us so;

Nor lost by it. No – See his vast recompence,
The whole world he had for his inheritance.
                    Then here if you please, is a man of renown.

A warning then take now my dear fellow men,
Don't tempt the Almighty with such deeds again;
The field-getting trade abolish it quite,
Dividing your rents and then all will be right.
                    Nor e'er strive more to be men of renown.

The Propagation of Spensonianism

Written in Shrewsbury Jail in the Year 1801

Tune: *The Lillies of France*

One night as a slumb'ring I lay on my bed,
A notable Vision came into my Head;
Methought I saw Numbers forth going to teach,
And Justice and Peace among mankind to preach,
            Saying, "Men mind your interest if your've
                                Common sense,
            And hearken to Reason and Friend Thomas
                                Spence."

Tune: *Derry Down*

"Lo! See but how Eden Spence has set in View,
And who keeps us from it, he has shown us too;
The Cherubim Gentry with their Flaming Sword,
Encamp right before it all with one Accord.

"Thus these Sons of Anak, by Force and by Might,
Keep our promised Land, unto which they've no Right;

Even Towns which we've builded and fields that we've
dress'd,
While we all like Strangers are quite dispossess'd.

"Then hark to this Guide who has spied out the Land,
So plain he instructs you, you must understand;
Take Courage, these Giants we're able to rout,
Their walls must fall down if we give but a shout.

"Then rise, take possession, the whole Human Race,
No wilds we've to traverse we're at home in each Place;
The Cities are ours when we please, where we live,
And Fields without Purchase, we've Nothing to give.

"With sorrow no more then, we'll eat of the ground,
The Curse being removed from all the world round;
The end of Oppression and Lordship being come,
We'll then all rejoice in the bless'd millennium.

"No Shame or Reproach can attach to this cause,
In forming Society, by such Just Laws;
All but some vile Judas must wish us Success,
And ages to come our Names they will bless.

"Now what is there wanting of you careless Men,
But only your Countenance to us to lend;
The Business is done if you only approve,
And every Obstacle straight will remove."

Tune: *The Lillies of France*

I beheld till these Preachers were well understood
When the People in all Places arose like a Flood;
All ancient Oppressions were then swept away,
And Virtue and Freedom for ever did sway.
        Then Men mind your Interest if you've
                             Common sense
        And listen to Reason and Friend Thomas Spence.

An Old British Song

When the Romans Ruled the Land

Long may great Caesar live
To him your treasure give,
         Gen'rous and free!
His feelings are so tough
You ne'er can give enough;
Why keep you back the stuff?
         Rebels ye be.

See, on the gold so fair,
His graceful picture there,
         Which as you view,
Worship – and let it be
Sent to his Treasury;
Send it to him, that he
         May worship too!

You have a house and bed,
And you are cloth'd and fed.
         Temp'rate and bare;
Still let it be your aim,
Pride and excess to tame,
For your kind masters claim
         All you can spare.

Great Caesar let us own
Each on his marrow bone,
         Britons so true;
He shall ride over us!
Happy and glorious,
For ne'er victorious
         Rebels ye knew.

'Cheer up each mournful face,
See what a hopeful race,
           Now all alive!
O how it swells the song!
Princes so young and strong,
Might draw a dray along,
           Ready to drive.

Long live our NOBLE king,
To him your treasure bring,
           Gen'rous and free!
Let it our heart elate,
Still to support the great –
Proud of our low estate
           Still let us be!

The Dispersion
of the British Convention

In the good town of Edinburgh, a woeful thing befel, sir,
And if you will attend to me, the occasion I will tell, sir;
The things which happened there, caused each pensioner
                                            to wonder,
And turn up his eyes, as a duck does in thunder.
                    Bow, wow, wow;
        Down with the swine and rabble, bow, wow, wow.

A set of hair-brain'd fellows met upon a daring plan, sir;
No less than to discuss the rights and liberties of man, sir;
But no man of sense would e're listen to their babble, sir,
For almost all belong'd to the GRUNTERS, or the
                                    RABBLE, sir.
                    Bow, wow, wow &c.

To reform our constitution, these same fellows did intend,
                                                        sir,
When every placeman knows this truth, that 'tis too good
                                               to mend, sir;
And the magistrates have prov'd they had an infamous
                                                  intentiton,
Or else they never would have dar'd to call themselves
                                                convention.
                         Bow, wow, wow &c.

Still further to evince their horrible design, sir,
They call'd each other Citizen, and that increas'd their
                                               crime, sir,
Who if their convention to their nature they would suit, sir,
Instead of *Fellow Citizen,* they'd grunt out *Brother Brute,*
                                                      sir.
                         Bow, wow, wow &c.

Nay, more; in every thing they did, to seem as bad as
                                               France, sir;
THEY framed their committees of instruction and finance,
                                                      sir;
But if instruction were to spread, how horrible were that,
                                                     sir!
Good lord, why the rabble might begin to smell a rat, sir.
                         Bow, wow, wow &c.

Then they said, that a man, sir, in any rank or station,
Had a right by his vote to share in legislation;
And that when from the pockets of the poor the money
                                               went, sir,
They had a right to ask in what manner it was spent, sir.
                         Bow, wow, wow &c.

They talked as if your taxes were become a grievous
weight, sir,
And that sinecure places did no service to the state, sir;
But if it be but *justice* to pay men for doing something,
sir,
'Tis *generous*, I'm sure, to pay men for doing *nothing*, sir.
Bow, wow, wow &c.

Then they wish'd too that all enmity 'twixt nations should
be o'er, sir,
That the sword should be sheath'd, and that blood be no
more, sir;
But what man in oppression could possibly go further, sir,
Than to take away the bread of those who live by murder,
sir.
Bow, wow, wow &c.

So mad at last were they become, that I am almost sure,
sir,
They thought that the rich were no better than the poor, sir;
And at length they had scattered quite a panic through the
city,
By appointing FOUR men on a secret committee.
Bow, wow, wow &c.

The magistrates alarm'd at this, and rousing one and all,
sir,
With all the myrmidons of power, set off to attack the
hall, sir;
And they never would have suffer'd them to come to such
a pass, sir,
But they had not yet receiv'd their orders from Dundas,
sir.
Bow, wow, wow &c.

But as soon as master Harry had sent his orders down, sir,
Uprose at his command, all the rulers of the town, sir;
And some profanely whisper, that on entering the room,
                                                    sir,
These tools of power shed an unsavoury perfume, sir.
                                   Bow, wow, wow &c.

Indictments on each friend of freedom followed close
                                            behind, sir;
The judges very kindly taught the juries what to find, sir;
Though this indeed was useless, for I'll venture to assure
                                                    ye,
They had taken care enough before to pack a proper jury.
                                   Bow, wow, wow &c.

Objections were repell'd, brought in any form or shape,
                                                    sir,
For SEDITION was the crime, and not a simple RAPE,
                                                    sir;
And at length this dire fancy for reform to allay, sir,
They decreed a trip for fourteen years to Botany Bay, sir.
                                   Bow, wow, wow &c.

Thus every method has been tried to quench this daring
                                            spirit, sir,
May both magistrates and judges meet with that reward
                                        they merit, sir;
For each method they've pursued, that all honest placemen
                                            ought, sir,
And if poor freedom be not STABBED – I'm sure 'tis
                                        not their fault, sir.
                                   Bow, wow, wow &c.

1794

The Gallic Rush-Light

In the wide domain of France, where the Graces trip and
lisp, Sir,
A mighty light arose, like will-of-the-whisp, Sir;
This light it shone as bright as Moses' famous Bush-light,
But the Emperor of Germany said, 'twas only a little
Rush-light.
So he puff'd at the Rush-light, the little Gallic Rush-
light,
But all he could do, could not blow out the Rush-
Light.

His mighty Prussian Neighbour he smiled at this resistance,
And offer'd for to lend his aid, but kept aloof his distance;
For though he screw'd the bayonet on, determined for to
push light,
And puny was the push he made at blowing out the Rush-
light;
When he puff'd at the Rush-light, the little Gallic
Rush-light,
And all that they can do, cannot blow out the Rush-
Light.

The Pope he stood aghast, to see this scene of slaughter,
And thought to put it out with a squirt of Holy water;
He said the French were blinded, because they had too
much light,
So with Bell, Book and Candle he curst the Gallic Rush-
light:

So he puff'd at the Rush-light, the little Gallic Rush-
light,
But all he could do, could not blow out the Rush-
Light.

The Tygress of the North,* so famed for spoil and
plunder,
Whose eyes can dart forth lightening, with voice as loud as
thunder;
With her Pettycoat she raised a wind, she surely thought
must crush light,
But it only serv'd to fan the flame that issued from the
Rush-light:
When she puff'd at the Rush-light, the little Gallic
Rush-light,
But all she could do, could not blow out the Rush-
Light.

The Don he curl'd his whiskers, and the little King of
Naples, Sir,
The crazy Queen she promised to do more than she was
able, Sir,
With a host of foes from Piedmont, determined to crush
light,
But tho' all have been blowing since, they've not put out
the Rush-light:
Though they've puff'd at the Rush-light, the little
Gallic Rush-light,
But though all have been blowing since, they've not
put out the Rush-Light.

Then Royal George of England soon join'd the haughty
Gang, Sir,
And sent his dear son, Frederick, these Democrats to
hang, Sir;

* Catherine II of Russia.

75

But on the plains of Germany, the Boy was forc'd to brush
light,
Confounded by the glorious rays that issued from the
Rush-light.
So he ran from the Rush-light, the brave Gallic Rush-
light,
And tho' they've all been blowing, still the brighter
shines the Rush-Light.

1794

CHARLES MORRIS
d. 1838

"Captain Morris"

A New Irish Song

Tune: *Oh dear! What can the matter be?*

Be easy with wars! there's a fine piece of bother on't,
Faith I can't make either one thing or t'other on't,
Devil may burn both the father and mother on't;
      Billy's undone us by war.
        Oh Lord! what will the damage be? &c. &c.

Pat can you tell what the devil's he driving at?
What is't we're fighting for, what is't he's striving at?
A foul bit of work the d -- d Tory's conniving at!

For the poor out of bread what a fine consolation too;
Winter at hand and all trade in stagnation too;
Nothing to swallow but lumps of taxation too;

Then what are our gains, for the millions he squanders now,
Plentiful loss of brave troops and commanders now,
Rotting like sheep in the big bogs of Flanders now!

We've murdered by thousands and pay for the slaughter too,
Nothing to drink, to the a -- e up in water too;
Dutch running off and ourselves marching after too.

Our Floats and our gunboats won't answer their uses too;
Horse of no service for ditches and sluices too;
Cannon too late, and all left as the duce is too.

We're fluxed till our life streams away from our bowels too,
Drench'd so with rain, you might scrape us with shovels too;
Cattle all glander'd and all full of rowels too.

Tents we have few, since we left 'em behind us too,
Dogs wouldn't lie on the *wet straw* they find us too;
All sorts of death by my soul, they've consigned us to!

Then faith with *mistrust* we're a little dejected too,
Prussians withdrawn, and the Dutch disaffected too,
Troops that we've *hir'd* not too much *respected* too.

By my soul it's a sin, that we e're should want harmony,
When we all fight for the Emperor of Germany,
And *John Bull* has promised to pay all the war money.

Then you bitch'd us at *home,* and your word did not keep,
my dears;
Leaving brave lads to be cut up like sheep, my dears;
TOBY sham fighting, and C -- m* asleep, my dears.

By my troth, there's a damnable sin and omission here,
Tho' it's hush'd up, it must rise in revision here;
Murder cries out, for a *state inquisition* here.

Then your Cabinet calls it a war of *existence* now,
That's in plain Irish to die at a distance now,
And help the work forward by *backward assistance* now.

Troth, you've purchased at Toulon a slippery station too,
Laid out our cash in a wild speculation too,
And united all France in a d -- n'd indignation too.

A wise figure we make, to be starv'd to help slavery,
Fighting for others with a profitless bravery;
Oh, get out! you'll undo a good nation with knavery.
Billy's undone us with war. &c. &c.

* Chatham, Second Earl of, Master General of the Ordnance.

1794

78

Burke's Address
to the
"Swinish Multitude"

Tune: *Derry, down, down*

Ye vile SWINISH herd, in the Sty of Taxation,
What would you be after? — disturbing the Nation?
Give over your grunting – Be off – To your Sty!
Nor dare to look out, if a KING passes by:
    Get ye down! down! down! – Keep ye down!

Do you know what a KING is? By *Patrick* I'll tell you;
He has Power in his Pocket, to buy you and sell you:
To make you all Soldiers, or keep you at work;
To hang you, and cure you for Ham or Salt Pork!
      Get ye down! &c.

Do you think that a KING is no more than a Man?
Ye Brutish, Ye Swinish, irrational Clan?
I swear by his Office, his Right is divine,
To flog you, and feed you, and treat you like Swine!
      Get ye down! &c.

To be sure, I have said – but I spoke it abrupt –
That "the State is *defective* and also *corrupt.*"
Yet remember I told you with Caution to peep,
For Swine at a Distance We prudently keep –
      Get ye down! &c.

Now the Church and the State, to keep each other warm,
Are married together. And where is the Harm?
How healthy and wealthy are Husband and Wife!
But Swine are excluded the conjugal life –

> Get ye down! &c.

The State, it is true, has grown fat upon SWINE,
And *Church's* weak stomach on TYTHE-PIG can dine;
But neither you know, as they roast at the Fire,
Have a right to find fault with the Cooks, or enquire.

> Get ye down! &c.

"What use do we make of your Money?" – you say;
Why the first Law of Nature: – We take our own Pay –
And next on our Friends a few *Pensions* bestow —
And to you we apply when our *Treasure* runs low.

> Get ye down! &c.

Consider our *Boroughs*, Ye grumbling SWINE!
At Corruption and Taxes, they never repine:
If we only *Proclaim*, "YE ARE HAPPY!" – They say,
"We ARE *Happy!*" – Believe and be *Happy* as they!

> Get ye down! &c.

What know ye of COMMONS, of KINGS, or of LORDS,
But what this dim Light of TAXATION affords?
Be contented with that – and no more of your Rout:
Or a new *Proclamation* shall muzzle your Snout!

> Get ye down! &c.

And now for the SUN – or the LIGHT OF THE DAY!*
"It doth not belong to a PITT?" – You will say;
I tell you be silent, and hush all your Jars:
Or he'll charge you a *Farthing* a piece for the Stars.

> Get ye down! &c.

* Window Tax.

Here's MYSELF, and *His Darkness*, and *Harry Dundas:*
Scotch, English, and *Irish,* with fronts made of Brass –
A Cord plated Three-fold will stand a good pull,
Against SAWNEY, and PATRICK, and old *Johnny Bull*!!!
                    Get ye down! &c.

To conclude: Then no more about MAN and his RIGHTS,
TOM PAINE, and a Rabble of *Liberty Wights:*
That you are but our "SWINE", if you ever forget,
We'll throw you alive to the HORRIBLE PIT!
                Get ye down! down! down! – Keep ye down!

179–

DANIEL EATON (?)

Two Ways Pointed Out by
Which any Poor Manufacturer Deprived
of Work by this Blessed
War may be Enabled to Obtain
a Morsel of Bread

Being thrown by this ruinous war out of work,
Dick blessed, in his way, Dundas, Pitt and Burke;
Then his wits he employed to find out a way
To prevent being forced to keep fast on chopt hay.

After puzzling a while, he cried out in a rage
That times are so bad that one cannot engage
One's belly to fill without selling one's soul –
To slaughter our Brethren, or wolves-like to prowl.

For no way I see there's to weather the Storm,
But 'list for a soldier, or rogue-like, inform.

1793

THOMAS HOLCROFT
1745–1809

Prologue to a Revolution

. . .
Our author had mounted on the stilts of oratory and
                                        elocution:
Not but he had a smart touch or two, about Poland,
                        France and the – the Revolution,
Telling us that Frenchman and Polishman and everyman is
                                        our brother,
And that all men, aye even poor Negro men, have a right to
                                be free, one as well as another.
Freedom at last, says he, like a torrent is spreading and
                                        swelling
To sweep away pride, and reach the most miserable
                                        dwelling;
To ease, happiness, art, wit, genius to give birth –
Aye, to fertilize a world and renovate old earth.
Thus he went on, not mentioning a word about the play:
For, he says, prologues are blots that ought to be wiped
                                        away.
A Gothic practice, and in spite of precedent, none the
                        better for being old.

1794   From *The Road to Ruin* Prologue

The Fate of Those
Who Go for Soldiers

When into the Village or Town,
    A Recruiting the Soldiers do come;
With lies and with bullying around,
    They rattle away with the Drum;
When large sums of Money they promise,
    That they never intend for to pay,
But of this my brave fellows be certain
    You'll be shot at for Six-pence a day.
                  Shot at for Six-pence a day.

With Thieves of all sorts they'll unite you,
    From the Gallows that's made their escape;
Your friends and relations will slight you,
    Then heart breaking sorrow's your fate;
With such wretches engage not to serve,
    Nor join in the Murderous lay;
If you do you'll justly deserve,
    To be shot at for Six-pence a day.
                  Shot at for Six-pence a day.

Then away to the Wars they will drag you,
    And victuals you'll get when you call;
But war gives the Soldier in battle,
    A Breakfast of Powder and Ball.
Then should you be so foolishly bold,
    And advice you should throw far away;

You ne'er will live to grow old,
    When you'r shot at for Six-pence a day.
                Shot at for Six-pence a day.

Then ne'er mind the sound of the drum,
    Stay at home with your sweethearts and wives;
Free from harms to the Soldier that come,
    That lops off their limbs and their lives;
For the Captains will get all the Gold,
    And the Men lose their lives in the Fray;
Is not he a damned fool young or old,
    That is shot at for Six-pence a day?
                Shot at for Six-pence a day.

Sixty Thousand Englishmen have been killed this last year in Holland. – Ten Thousand more in the West Indies, and Forty Thousand taken Prisoners. – Soldiers, or Sailors, Death or Misery is your Portion.

1797?

Epitaph for a Crow

Here lies the body of John Crow,
Who once was high, but now is low;
Ye brother Crows take warning all,
For as you rise, so must you fall.

c. 1744

THOMAS "CLIO" RICKMAN
1761–1834

Sonnet to an Infant at the Breast

Dear, lovely babe! Equal by birth to all!
While thus thou drainst my breast, my blood runs chill;
I ask, if thou some future day must fall,
And despots send thee to be kill'd or kill?
For thousands daily drop, who each, like thee
Once claimed a mother's ever-anxious love;
Hung on her bosom, sported on her knee,
And valued were, a world of kings above. –

    Tormenting thought! Oh! ere thou grow'st mature
May all wars cease, or tyrants, if there be,
Fight their own battles, and each man secure
By equal rights and equal laws be free. –
    So may no mother's care be thrown away,
    Nor one hurl millions from the face of day.

1795

Impromptu Reply to Impertinence

The sneaking courtier and Corruption's tool,
Thus speak the language of the knave and fool:
"If you dont't like the land you live in – leave it";
My answer is – (in metaphor receive it)
"If BUGS molest me as in BED I lie,
I will not quit my BED for THEM – not I; –
But rout the VERMIN, every BUG destroy,
New make my BED, – and all its sweets enjoy."

Sonnet to Thomas Paine

Hail! genius of truth and life and light!
The purest wisdom marks thy manly page;
'Tis thine to purge from filth the mental sight,
'Tis thine to renovate and bless the age;

To value nought but what is truly great,
To bow to sterling excellence alone,
To treat with scorn the silly face of state,
Nor look with reverence but to Virtue's throne. –
These are the sentiments that fire thy breast,
And when through time, feeling the rights of man,
Shall bless themselves in making others blest,
And model States on Equity's pure plan;
 So men to equal happiness shall rise,
  And truth shall take the place of prejudice and lies.

1803

Second Epistle to J. Lapraik

. . .
Do ye envy the city gent,
Behint a kist to lie an' sklent;
Or purse-proud, big wi' cent. per cent.
      An' muckle wame,
In some bit burgh to represent
      A bailie's name?

Or is't the haughty feudal thane,
Wi' ruffl'd sark an' glancing cane,
Wha thinks himsel nae sheep-shank bane,
      But lordly stalks;
While caps an' bonnets aff are taen,
      As by he walks?

"O Thou wha gies us each guid gift!
Gie me o' wit an' sense a lift,
Then turn me, if Thou please, adrift
      Thro' Scotland wide;
Wi' cits nor lairds I wadna shift,
      In a' their pride!"

Were this the charter of our state,
"On pain o' hell be rich an' great,"
Damnation then would be our fate,
      Beyond remead;
But, thanks to heaven, that's no the gate
      We learn our creed.

For thus the royal mandate ran,
When first the human race began;
"The social, friendly, honest man,
      Whate'er he be –
'Tis *he* fulfils great Nature's plan,
      And none but he."

O mandate glorious and divine!
The followers o' the ragged Nine,
Poor, thoughtless devils! yet may shine
      In glorious light,
While sordid sons o' Mammon's line
      Are dark as night!

Tho' here they scrape, an' squeeze, an' growl,
Their worthless nievefu' of a soul
May in some future carcase howl,
      The forest's fright;
Or in some day-detesting owl
      May shun the light.

Such a Parcel of Rogues in a Nation

Fareweel to a' our Scottish fame,
    Fareweel our ancient glory;
Fareweel ev'n to the Scottish name,
    Sae fam'd in martial story.
Now Sark rins over Solway sands,
    An' Tweed rins to the ocean,
To mark where England's province stands –
    Such a parcel of rogues in a nation!

What force or guile could not subdue,
    Thro' many warlike ages,
Is wrought now by a coward few,
    For hireling traitor's wages.
The English steel we could disdain,
    Secure in valour's station;
But English gold has been our bane –
    Such a parcel of rogues in a nation!

O would, or I had seen the day
    That Treason thus could sell us,
My auld grey head had lien in clay
    Wi' Bruce and loyal Wallace!
But pith and power, till my last hour
    I'll mak this declaration;
We're bought and sold for English gold –
    Such a parcel of rogues in a nation!

Holy Thursday

Is this a holy thing to see
In a rich and fruitful land,
Babes reduc'd to misery,
Fed with cold and usurous hand?

Is that trembling cry a song?
Can it be a song of joy?
And so many children poor?
It is a land of poverty!

And their sun does never shine,
And their fields are bleak and bare,
And their ways are fill'd with thorns:
It is eternal winter there.

For where-e'er the sun does shine,
And where-e'er the rain does fall,
Babe can never hunger there,
Nor poverty the mind appal.

1789–94

The New Order

And Urizen read in his book of brass in sounding tones:
"Listen, O Daughters, to my voice. Listen to the Words of
                                   Wisdom,
So shall you govern over all; let Moral Duty tune your
                                   tongue
But be your hearts harder than the nether millstone."
. . .
"Compel the poor to live upon a Crust of bread, by soft,
                               mild arts.
Smile when they frown, frown when they smile; and when
                           a man looks pale
With labour and abstinence, say he looks healthy and
                                 happy;
And when his children sicken, let them die; there are
                                enough
Born, even too many, and our Earth will be overrun
Without these arts. If you would make the poor live with
                             temperance,
With pomp give every crust of bread you give; with
                            gracious cunning
Magnify small gifts; reduce the man to want a gift, and
                           then give with pomp.
Say he smiles if you hear him sigh. If pale, say he is ruddy.
Preach temperance: say he is overgorg'd and drowns his wit
In strong drink, tho' you know that bread and water are all
He can afford. Flatter his wife, pity his children, till we can
Reduce all to our will, as spaniels are taught with art."
. . .
Then left the sons of Urizen the plow and harrow, the
                               loom,
The hammer and the chisel and the rule and compasses.
They forg'd the sword, the chariot of war, the battle ax,

The trumpet fitted to the battle and the flute of summer,
And all the arts of life they chang'd into the arts of death.
The hour glass contemned because its simple workmanship
Was as the workmanship of the plowman, and the water
wheel
That raises water into Cisterns, broken and burn'd in fire
Because its workmanship was like the workmanship of the
shepherd,
And in their stead intricate wheels invented, Wheel
without Wheel,
To perplex youth in their outgoings and to bind to labours
Of day and night the myriads of Eternity, that they might
file
And polish brass and iron hour after hour, laborious
workmanship,
Kept ignorant of the use that they might spend the days
of wisdom
In sorrowful drudgery to obtain a scanty pittance of bread,
In ignorance to view a small portion and think that All,
And call it demonstration, blind to the simple rules of
life.

1797   From *Vala* or *The Four Zoas*

94

EDWARD RUSHTON
1765–1814

Be Free!

       Power's limpid stream
Must have its source within a people's hearts;
What flows not thence is turbid tyranny.
Rank are the despot weeds that now o'errun
This ample world, and choke each goodly growth.
But that supine, loud vaunting thing called man,
Might soon eradicate so foul a pest
Would he exert those powers that God has given
To be the means of good; and what more good,
More rational – nay, more approaching heaven,
Than the strong joys that flow from Freedom's fount?
You radiant orb, vast emblem of the Power
Who formed him, beams alike on all mankind!
The air, which as a mantle, girts the world,
Is too a common good; and even so
The amplest bounty, Liberty is given.
To man, whate'er his tint – swart, brown or fair,
Whate'er his clime — hot, cold or temperate;
Whate'er his mode of faith, whate'er his state,
Or rich, or poor, great Nature cries – "Be Free!"

178–

The Leviathan

As when the huge Leviathan is seen,
    Torpid and slumbering midst his native ice,
The seamen ply the oar with anxious mien,
    Quick every eye, and noiseless every voice;
And now the keen harpoon its entrance makes,
    At first unfelt, till deeper grows the wound,
When lo! the enormous animal awakes,
    And his broad tail spreads devastation round.
So when a nation, cold, and sluggish lies,
    Silent and slow th' oppressor drives the steel,
At first the wound's unfelt – again he tries,
    Deep sinks the shaft, and now the people feel;
Pierced to the quick the tail soon mounts on high,
And splendour, wealth, and power, in one sad ruin lie.

Toussaint to His Troops

Whether forc'd from burning shores,
Where the tawny lion roars,
Whether doom'd with stripes and chains,
Here to dress your native plains;
Men of noble daring, say,
Shall we crouch to Gallia's sway;
Shall we wield again the hoe,
Taste again the cup of woe,
Or shall we rouse and with the lightenings' force
Blast the relentless foe, and desolate his course?

When the world's eternal sire
Placed on high yon glorious fire,
Were the splendid beams design'd
For a part of human kind?

No! ye sable warriors, no!
All that live partake the glow;
Thus on man th' impartial god
Light, and winds, and rains bestow'd,
And widely thus were pour'd his dearest rights,
And he who slights the gift – th' Almighty donor slights.

Now with canvas white as foam,
See the vaunted legions come,
Nerv'd by freedom once they rose,
And o'erwhelmed a world of foes.
Now of freedom nerv'd no more,
Lo! the miscreants seek our shore;
Yes, the French who waste their breath,
Chaunting liberty or death,
Sweep the blue wave at Usurpation's word,
And bring, oh fiends accurs'd! oppression or the sword.

Men whose famish'd sides have felt,
Strokes by dastard drivers dealt,
Men whose sorrowing souls have borne,
Wrong and outrage, toil and scorn,
Men whose wives the pallid brood,
Have by torturing arts subdu'd,
Friends of Toussaint! Warriors brave!
Call to mind the mangled slave!
And oh! remember, should your foes succeed,
That not yourselves alone, but all you love must bleed.

Fathers, shall the tiny race,
Objects of your fond embrace,
They who 'neath the tamarind tree,
Oft have gaily climb'd your knee;
Fathers, shall those prattlers share,
Pangs that slaves are doomed to bear?

Shall their mirth and lisping tones,
Be exchanged for shrieks and groans?
And shall those arms that round your necks have twin'd,
Be to the twisted thong, and endless toil consign'd!

Towering spirits! ye who broke
Slavery's agonizing yoke;
Ye, who like the whirlwind rush'd,
And your foes to atoms crush'd.
Ye, who from Domingo's strand,
Swept the daring British band;
Ye, oh warriors! ye who know,
Freedom's bliss, and slavery's woe,
Say, shall we bow to Buonaparte's train,
Or with unshaken nerves yon murderous whites disdain?

From those eyes that round me roll,
Wildly flash th' indignant soul;
On those rugged brows I see,
Stern unyielding liberty.
Yes! your daring aspects show,
France shall soon repent the blow;
Soon shall famish'd sharks be fed;
Vultures soon shall tear the dead;
Oh glorious hour! now, now, yon fiends defy,
Assert great Nature's cause, live free, or bravely die.

1806

The Wrongs of Man by Feudal Landlords

Tune: *Lovely Nan*

Let Patriots preach, let Statesmen rave,
There's nought our Freedom now can save,
    From those who rule in state Divan;
From Tyrants grim despotic knaves,
Combined to render mankind slaves,
    In Congress* to devise the plan:
In Pandemonian union bound,
To seize from Freedom all the Ground,
    And so destroy the Rights of Man.

How short the triumph of the Brave,
Who broke the chain of feudal slave,
    And freed from superstition! Man,
That storm'd these holds of Tyranny,
Through seas of blood for Liberty,
    They knew not the Spensonian plan:
How reason's pure unerring course,
Would break down despotism's force,
    And vindicate the Rights of Man.

Draw near if you would understand,
The Rights of Man are in the Land,
    Let feudal Lords say all they can;
A Nation is the People's Farm,
They build, they plant, 'tis their strong arm,
    That till the clod, defend their clan:

* Congress of Vienna.

Who claim the whole, enjoy, enslave,
And doom by millions to the grave,
　　As tho' there were no Rights of Man.

By holy writ in days of yore,
Who move the landmark of the Poor;
　　Are curs'd – so the great fiat ran:
The high command to Moses given,
Thou shalt not covet! what from Heaven,
　　Composed the Great Creator's plan:
Thy neighbour's House, his Wife, or Stock,
His Ox, or Ass, his Goats or Flock,
　　By God decreed the Rights of Man.

Come make with Spence this sacred claim,
And you'll fulfill great nature's aim;
　　Who gave to Woman, Child and Man,
The light and air, the earth and sea,
In Partnership equality,
　　This was the glorious Christian plan:
The Land to let, the Rents divide,
And the oppression would subside,
　　In never ending Rights of Man.

1815

Salvation of Empire

Great Nature may we all adore!
Who yields such never ceasing store
    For all that toil,
Industriously to till the ground,
Or sweep the coast of ocean round
    With netted coil;

Whose bounties flow on ev'ry side,
Are gather'd from the land and tide,
    Whene'er we need;
Shalt thou for ever blessings give,
And myriads on those blessings live,
    And while they feed;

Suppose some visionary god
Bestows those blessings, with a nod,
    To agents few;
And dooms th' unletter'd lab'ring herd
With some grim idol to be scar'd;
    A rabble crew?

And when those sinewy sons of toil
Have heap'd up store from sea and soil
    As rightful heirs;
The few, that never toil'd nor strove,
By seizing, in the name of Jove,
    Shall call it theirs!

Great Nature view, and you will scan,
'Tis she alone that succours man;
   Not sculptur'd god;
Away his name and image fling,
The brass, the stone, or wooden thing;
   And claim the sod.

1815

GEORGE GORDON, LORD BYRON
1788–1824

An Ode to the Framers
of the Frame Bill

I

Oh well done Lord Eldon! and better done Ryder!
 Britannia must prosper with councils like yours;
Hawkesbury, Harrowby, help you to guide her,
 Whose remedy only must *kill* ere it cures:
Those villains, the Weavers, are all grown refractory,
 Asking some succour for Charity's sake –
So hang them in clusters round each Manufactory,
 That will at once put an end to *mistake*.

II

The rascals, perhaps, may betake them to robbing,
 The dogs to be sure have got nothing to eat –
So if we can hang them for breaking a bobbin,
 'Twill save all the Government's money and meat:
Men are more easily made than machinery –
 Stockings fetch better prices than lives –
Gibbets on Sherwood will heighten the scenery,
 Shewing how Commerce, how Liberty thrives!

III

Justice is now in pursuit of the wretches,
 Grenadiers, Volunteers, Bow-street Police,
Twenty-two Regiments, a score of Jack Ketches,
 Three of the Quorum and two of the Peace;

Some Lords, to be sure, would have summoned the Judges,
    To take their opinion, but that they ne'er shall,
For Liverpool such a concession begrudges,
    So now they're condemned by *no Judges* at all.

IV

Some folks for certain have thought it was shocking,
    When Famine appeals and when Poverty groans,
That Life should be valued at less than a stocking,
    And breaking of frames lead to breaking of bones.
If it should prove so, I trust, by this token,
    (And who will refuse to partake in the hope?)
That the frames of the fools may be first to be *broken*,
    Who, when asked for a remedy, sent down *a rope.*

1812

Song for the Luddites

I

    As the Liberty lads o'er the sea
Bought their freedom, and cheaply, with blood,
        So we, boys, we
        Will *die* fighting, or *live* free,
And down with all kings but King Ludd!

II

    When the web that we weave is complete,
And the shuttle exchanged for the sword,
        We will fling the winding sheet
        O'er the despot at our feet,
And dye it deep in the gore he has pour'd.

III

Though black as his heart its hue,
Since his veins are corrupted to mud,
Yet this is the dew
Which the tree shall renew
Of Liberty, planted by Ludd!

1816

War-Profiteering Landlords

See these inglorious Cincinnati swarm,
Farmers of war, dictators of the farm;
Their ploughshare was the sword in hireling hands,
Their fields manured by gore of other lands;
Safe in their barns these Sabine tillers sent
Their brethren out to battle – why? for rent!
Year after year they voted cent. per cent.,
Blood, sweat, and tear-wrung millions – why? for rent!
They roar'd, they dined, they drank, they swore they meant
To die for England – why then live? for rent!
The peace has made one general malcontent
Of these high-market patriots; war was rent!
Their love of country, millions all misspent,
How reconcile? by reconciling rent!
And will they not repay the treasures lent?
No: down with everything, and up with rent!
Their good, ill, health, wealth, joy or discontent,
Being, end, aim, religion – rent, rent, rent!

From *The Age of Bronze* XIV

One Common Cause

But 'twill not be – the spark's awaken'd – lo!
The swarthy Spaniard feels his former glow;
The same high spirit which beat back the Moor
Through eight long ages of alternate gore
Revives – and where? in that avenging clime
Where Spain was once synonymous with crime,
Where Cortes and Pizarro's banner flew
The infant world redeems her name of *"New"*.
'Tis the old aspiration breathed afresh,
To kindle souls within degraded flesh,
Such as repulsed the Persian from the shore
Where Greece *was* – No! she still is Greece once more.
One common cause makes myriads of one breast,
Slaves of the East, or helots of the West:
On Andes' and on Athos' peaks unfurl'd,
The self-same standard streams o'er either world.

From *The Age of Bronze* VI

The Poet Laureate and Castlereagh

If, fallen in evil days on evil tongues,
    Milton appealed to the Avenger, Time,
If Time, the Avenger, execrates his wrongs,
    And makes the word "Miltonic" mean *"sublime"*,
He deigned not to belie his soul in songs,
    Nor turn his very talent to a crime;
He did not loath the sire to laud the son,
But closed the tyrant-hater he begun.

Think'st thou, could he – the blind old man – arise,
    Like Samuel from the grave, to freeze once more
The blood of monarchs with his prophecies,
    Or be alive again – again all hoar
With time and trials, and those helpless eyes,
    And heartless daughters – worn — and pale – and
                                                    poor;
Would *he* adore a sultan? *he* obey
The intellectual eunuch Castlereagh?

Cold-blooded, smooth-faced, placid miscreant!
    Dabbling its sleek young hands in Erin's gore,
And thus for wider carnage taught to pant,
    Transferred to gorge upon a sister shore,
The vulgarest tool that tyranny could want,
    With just enough of talent, and no more,
To lengthen fetters by another fix'd
And offer poison by another mix'd.

An orator of such set trash of phrase
    Ineffably – legitimately vile,
That even the grossest flatterers dare not praise,
    Nor foes – all nations – condescend to smile;
Not even a sprightly blunder's spark can blaze
    From that Ixion's grindstone's ceaseless toil,
That turns and turns to give the world a notion
Of endless torments and perpetual motion.

A bungler even in its digusting trade,
    And botching, patching, leaving still behind
Something of which its masters are afraid,
    States to be curb'd, and thoughts to be confined,
Conspiracy or Congress to be made –
    Cobbling at manacles for all mankind –
A tinkering slave-maker, who mends old chains,
With God and man's abhorrence for its gains.

Where shall I turn me not to *view* its bonds,
    For I will never *feel* them; – Italy!
Thy late reviving Roman soul desponds
    Beneath the lie this State-thing breathed o'er thee –
Thy clanking chain, and Erin's yet green wounds,
    Have voices – tongues to cry aloud for me.
Europe has slaves, allies, kings, armies still,
And Southey lives to sing them very ill.

1818   From *Don Juan* Canto I

They Never Fail

                They never fail who die
In a great cause: the block may soak their gore;
Their heads may sodden in the sun; their limbs
Be strung to city gates and castle walls –
But still their spirit walks abroad. Though years
Elapse, and others share as dark a doom,
They but augment the deep and sweeping thoughts
Which overpower all others, and conduct
The world at last to freedom.

1820   From *Marino Faliero* Act II sc. 2

Time to Act

Had Caesar known but Cleopatra's kiss
Rome had been free. The world had not been his.
And what have Caesar's deeds and Caesar's fame
Done for the earth? We feel them in our shame:

The gory sanction of his glory stains
The rust which tyrants cherish on our chains,
Though Glory, Nature, Reason, Freedom bid
Roused millions do what single Brutus did –
Sweep these mere mock-birds of the despot's song
From the tall bough where they have perched so long, –
Still we are hawk'd at by such mousing owls,
And take for falcons those ignoble fowls,
When but a word of freedom would dispel
These bugbears, as their terrors show too well.

1823   From *The Island* Canto II

Mighty Eagle

(To William Godwin)

Mighty eagle! thou that soarest
O'er the misty mountain forest,
    And amid the light of morning
Like a cloud of glory hiest,
And when night descends defiest
    The embattled tempest's warning!

1817

This is the Day

This is the day, which down the void abysm
At the Earth-born's spell yawns for Heaven's despotism,
    And Conquest is dragged captive through the deep:
Love, from its awful throne of patient power
In the wise heart, from the last giddy hour
    Of dread endurance, from the slippery, steep,
And narrow verge of crag-like agony, springs
And folds over the world its healing wings.

Gentleness, Virtue, Wisdom, and Endurance,
These are the seals of that most firm assurance
    Which bars the pit over Destruction's strength;

And if, with infirm hand, Eternity,
Mother of many acts and hours, should free
    The serpent that would clasp her with his length;
These are the spells by which to reassume
An empire o'er the disentangled doom.

To suffer woes which Hope thinks infinite;
To forgive wrongs darker than death or night;
    To defy Power, which seems omnipotent;
To love, and bear; to hope till Hope creates
From its own wreck the thing it contemplates;
    Neither to change, nor falter, nor repent;
This, like thy glory, Titan, is to be
Good, great and joyous, beautiful and free;
This is alone Life, Joy, Empire, and Victory.

1819   From *Prometheus Unbound* Act IV

Men of England

Men of England, heirs of Glory,
Heroes of unwritten story.
Nurslings of one mighty Mother,
Hopes of her, and one another;

Rise like Lions after slumber
In unvanquishable number,
Shake your chains to earth like dew
Which in sleep had fallen on you –
Ye are many – they are few.

What is Freedom? – Ye can tell
That which slavery is, too well –
For its very name has grown
To an echo of your own.

111

'Tis to work and have such pay
As just keeps life from day to day
In your limbs, as in a cell
For the tyrants' use to dwell.

So that ye for them are made
Loom, and plough, and sword, and spade,
With or without your own will bent
To their defence and nourishment.

'Tis to see your children weak
With their mothers pine and peak,
When the winter winds are bleak, –
They are dying whilst I speak.

'Tis to hunger for such diet
As the rich man in his riot
Casts to the fat dogs that lie
Surfeiting beneath his eye;

'Tis to let the Ghost of Gold
Take from Toil a thousandfold
More than e'er its substance could
In the tyrannies of old.

Paper coin – that forgery
Of the title deeds, which ye
Hold to something of the worth
Of the inheritance of Earth.

'Tis to be a slave in soul
And to hold no strong control
Over your own wills, but be
All that others make of ye.

And at length when ye complain
With a murmur weak and vain,
'Tis to see the Tyrant's crew
Ride over your wives and you –
Blood is on the grass like dew.

Then it is to feel revenge
Fiercely thirsting to exchange
Blood for blood – and wrong for wrong –
Do not thus when ye are strong.

Birds find rest, in narrow nest
When weary of their wingéd quest;
Beasts find fare, in woody lair
When storm and snow are in the air.

Asses, swine, have litter spread
And with fitting food are fed;
All things have a home but one –
Thou, O Englishman, hast none!

This is Slavery — savage men,
Or wild beasts within a den
Would endure not as ye do –
But such ills they never knew.

What art thou Freedom? Oh! could slaves
Answer from their living graves
This demand – tyrants would flee
Like a dream's dim imagery:

Thou art not, as impostors say,
A shadow soon to pass away,
A superstition, and a name
Echoing from the cave of Fame.

For the labourer thou art bread,
And a comely table spread
From his daily labour come
To a neat and happy home.

Thou art clothes, and fire, and food
For the trampled multitude –
No – in countries that are free
Such starvation cannot be
As in England now we see.

1819   From *The Masque of
                    Anarchy* XXXVII-LV

London Railings

. . .
But on we passed and soon the scene reversed,
From those most blest, to those who seem most curs'd;
For here we find an idle few are fed,
To Glutton's excess; – while lacking bread
The slavish million starve, and seem to fear,
Lest wolves and vultures their complaints should hear;
While to the daring, grinding fraud they yield
Of knaves with hearts 'gainst human sufferings steel'd,
Supine in apathy they still are tame,
And have no more of man, than just the name!
Disgraceful to themselves, in mean submission
They wear the galling yoke of imposition;
The pride of insolence they could suppress,
Yet take no measures to enforce redress!

While I beheld this shameful degradation,
My quicken'd pulse beat high with indignation,
That such a grievous system should exist
Of crying wrongs, and men not dare resist
The murderous band of plunderers, who unite
To war 'gainst useful labour's common right; –
"Rouse men," cried I, "and for your freedom fight!"

Scarce had I spoken thus, as so I dream'd,
When Fancy, in my vision, as it seemed,
Turn'd short from these, the sad abodes of woe,
To titled pomp's all-splendid raree-show,

Where had the useless lumber of the state
I mean the mansions of the nick-named *great!*

. . .

    Methought insulted nature seemed amaz'd,
That proud profusion round these miscreants blaz'd,
And on *their* surface shed such brilliant light,
Whose hearts are black, – whose minds are dark as night!
O monstrous guilt of blushless vice, cried I –
Here Fancy cut me short with this reply:

"Could these dumb guards while they these dens
                            surround,
Be *moved* to action, and to sense of sound;
Could these dumb ranks of *iron-railing* speak,
They'd from their stations start, – their yokes they'd break,
And cry aloud, that e'en the deaf might hear,
Quick let the *People* for their *Rights* prepare!
In FREEDOM'S CAUSE we deprecate delay,
When COURAGE shall command us, – we'll obey!!"
The tongueless IRON then in accent steady,
Replied "When wanted you shall find us ready!"

1819   From *A Real Dream or,*
                         Another Hint for Mr. Bull

ROBERT ANDERSON
1770–1833

Aul Englan

Tune: *Oh dear! What can the matter be?*

Oh! dear! – What can the matter be?
Think! think! – What can the matter be?
Say! say! – What can the matter be,
        Fwok munnet whop for Reform!
Our Statesmen hunt pleaces, oppression's their
        pleasure!
They bow man to slav'ry, in whops to gain
        treasure!
Our taxes are numberless; laws beyond
        measure –
        Aul Englan's just lost in a storm!

Oh! dear! – What can the matter be?
Think! think! – What can the matter be?
Say! say! – What can the matter be?
        Fwok munnet whop for Reform!
Wad Rulers, an Judges, an Bishops, forever
Mek gudness their study, an daily endeavour
Aw tyrans to crush – Nay! sec teymes we'll see,
        never –
        Aul Englan's just lost in a storm!

Oh! dear! – What can the matter be?
Think! think! – What can the matter be?
Say! say! – What can the matter be!
        Fwok munnet whop for Reform!

Wer tithes flung asayde, that our country
  disgreaces;
Wer freedom their preyde, that hop into girt
  pleaces;
The Deil meeght sit quiet: now millions he
  cheases –
            Aul Englan's just lost in a storm!

The Keelmen's Stick

Smash! Jamie, aw's glad for t' see that thou's well,
Some rare news aw've getten, mun, now for to tell;
So intiv a yell-house let's set worsels down,
Aw's sae glad for t' see thee, smash aw'll spend a crown.
                                        Fal de ral, &c.

About twelve weeks sine, man, it was a fond trick,
The Keelmen tuick't intiv their heeds for to stick;
They said that their Owners did not use them weel,
So deil a one of them wad enter a keel.
                                        Fal de ral, &c.

Then together the Owners did meet frae a' round,
And laid their brains intiv a steep sae profound,
To consult 'mang theirsels what was best to be duin,
And after they'd met, an' the fray just begun.
                                        Fal de ral, &c.

Then, smash! man, they ca'd out for Branlin's fine corps,
For the Owners were never in sic sets before;
And they ca'd out Hal Liddle's to keep them a' quiet,
For faith, d'ye knaw, they were flaid of a riot.
                                        Fal de ral, &c.

Then one of the Aldermen went iv a bark,
He thowt he cud suin gar them a' gan to wark;
But he suin fand it useless wi' them to use force,
They were just like a whirlwind that wad ha' its course.
                                        Fal de ral, &c.

He teuk some o' Charlie's spruce men wi' him tee,
To bring the keels down frae the spouts, d'ye see;
But they flay'd them se sair wi' a sling and a styen,
That he shiver'd and shak'd, aye, man, every byen.

> Fal de ral, &c.

Then he turn'd his back — let them de what they will,
He thowt o' the Keelmen he'd just had his fill;
And the sowgers a' swore that it vex'd them full sair,
To think that the Keelmen should brag ower them there.

> Fal de ral, &c.

But divent ye think now, for a' they cam back,
That ony o' them, mun, a good pluck dis lack;
For they'll fight till their life's blood run ower their knees,
And they'll spare a' the lives of their warst enemies.

> Fal de ral, &c.

Then efter a while, for to keep a' things well,
They gat a gun ship like a good cockle-shell;
To frighten the Keelmen, it was their design,
But they fand that the Keelmen had pluck on the Tyne.

> Fal de ral, &c.

Next they gat some Mareens and some landsmen an' a',
To bring a' the laden keels down, ye mun knaw:
But they made sic a bummel wi' sail and wi' line,
That they varry near cowpt theirsels intiv the Tyne.

> Fal de ral, &c.

The wives o' Dent's Hole, man, cam out a' full cry,
To see how these fine Dandy Keelmen wad ply;
And as they sail'd past, they set up sic a yell,
Ye wad thowt a' the devils had broke out o' hell.

> Fal de ral, &c.

1821

Loyal Festivities
or, Novel Scenes at Newcastle

A popular Song in the new Farce of the Coronation

The Castle guns were fir'd, and loud
    The bells rang in the morning,
To wake the "Swinish Multitude,"
    And give the public warning:
That, "as in duty bound," the Mayor,
    And loyal Corporation,
Would celebrate, in civic state,
    The day of Coronation!

With matchless liberality,
    They sums of money voted,
That loyalty might be thereby
    Among the herd promoted:
A feast would loyalize the brutes,
    Upon this great occasion,
And make them sing, God save the King!
    At George's Coronation.

Three royal fountains running beer,
    And one to dribble wine O,
Would make them flock from far and near,
    To grunt like loyal swine O.
Two bullocks roasted whole, 'twas thought,
    Would be a grand donation,
To toss among the "rabble rout,"
    At George's Coronation!

'Twas done – the bullocks roasted were,
    The fountains set a flowing;
While Butchers round, upon the ground,
    Huge lumps of beef were throwing:
The loyal swineherds looking on,
    In anxious expectation,
To see each beast enjoy the feast,
    At George's Coronation!

But what was their surprize, to find
    The swinish herd refuse it;
How strange! their tastes were so refined,
    No hog of sense would use it!
Our Gentry now, the loyal few,
    Beheld, with consternation,
The scanty stock of loyalty
    At George's Coronation!

They saw, with grief, the roasted beef
    By saucy swine neglected!
No grateful beast extoll'd the feast,
    Nor loyalty respected!
Their swinish nature sure is changed!
    O! what an alteration!
Time was when pigs would grunt and squeal,
    To grace a Coronation!

But ah! the brutes display, at last,
    The faculty of Reason!
"The age of Chivalry is past!"
    (Reflection most unpleasing!)
And, sad to tell, with that is gone
    "Othello's occupation!"
All servile reverence for a throne,
    And priestly domination!

Then why display this make-believe
    Affection, and profusion!
Ye can no longer swine deceive,
    They see through the delusion.
What then avails this pageantry,
    And useless ostentation?
What signifies your loyalty
    At George's Coronation?

Had Derry-Down* been on the spot,
    And view'd the scene before him,
While beef, and bones, and bricks, like shot,
    Were flying *in terrorem*;
He would have star'd, with wild afright,
    At such a consummation,
And loudly damn'd the useless farce
    Of George's Coronation!

Learn hence, ye Legislators wise,
    Ye guardians of our treasures!
The "swinish multitude" despise
    Your inconsistent measures:
Think not that bayonets will gain
    The people's admiration;
Or fix a Monarch on a throne,
    By a mock Coronation!

* Lord Londonderry i. e. Castlereagh.

1821

Picture of Newcastle
or, George the Fourth's Coronation

Tune: *Arthur McBride*

The firing of guns, and the ringing of bells,
Rous'd me from my dreams about magical spells;
So I'll draw you a sketch, as we're now by oursel's,
      By way of an illustration:
The roads to Newcastle were cover'd almost,
As if Radical thunder had summon'd its host,
Or an enemy's fleet had been seen off the coast,
      On George the Fourth's Coronation.

In the streets what a buz among sweethearts and wives,
And children who ne'er rose so soon in their lives;
All higgledy piggledy through other drives,
      To view what is in preparation.
The oxen are roasting – outsides a mere crust;
They're stuff'd wi' potatoes, and dredg'd well with dust;
While the turnspits were set as if working o' trust,
      On George the Fourth's Coronation.

I next went to view a Boat Race on the Tyne,
For a blue silken flag skill and labour combine;
Gold sovereigns the prizes – to start about nine,
      From Walker, with precipitation.
The Greyhound came first, the old Sandgate-shore gig,
Which went, as if chasing a hare, through the Brig.
No doubt but the wives and the lasses were big,
      On George the Fourth's Coronation.

Then the Gentlemen walk'd in procession to church;
Not even Dissenters did lag in the porch,
But boldly push'd on, amid ruffles and starch,
      To praise and to pray with the nation.
The service being ended, the anthems are sung,
The burnt sacrifice from each furnace is swung,
When the fountains with wine and strong ale 'gan to run,
      On George the Fourth's Coronation.

Then a Female Procession, to heighten the scene,
Paraded the streets, with a bust of the Queen;
When her title was placed where a crown should have been
      Upon the crane top was its station.
Then the Ox was beheaded, and held up to view,
As if he'd done something of Cato-street hue:
A soldier that made his appearance did rue,
      On George the Fourth's Coronation.

Then with squeezing and tearing began the dispute;
Some held by the Pant, and some grappled the spout,
Till as drunk as a lord, and as wise as a brute,
      At this swine-feeding jollification.
They drank out of hats, and old shoes, very keen,
The fights they went round, quite amusing the scene,
While some, in mistake, drank "Success to the Queen!"
      On George the Fourth's Coronation.

The battle grew hot, as they flung round the beef,
Disgusted they sought no Commander in chief;
The fires they demolish'd, while brickbats and beef
      Flew like rockets, in mad desperation.
The Butchers, now thinking their lives very sweet,
Soon threw down their gullies, and beat a retreat,
Not wishing to die, just like dogs, in the street,
      On George the Fourth's Coronation.

Upon the Sandhill, where the fountain ran wine,
The keelmen, quite eager to taste of the vine,
Had the Crown taken down, which was thrown in the Tyne,
            So fix'd was their determination.
There one, tho' stripp'd naked, so great was his drouth
Made a new fashion'd sun-dial, pointing due south,
When the ladies at five of the clock set their mouth,
            On George the Fourth's Coronation.

Among the arrivals at Mansion-house gates,
Were the bones of the oxen, the spits, and the grates,
With a keelman, in petticoats, scratching his pate,
            For a suit from our rich Corporation.
Had the *Den** been but open, the people might say,
For Kill-pudding Joe, and the burdies of prey,
This sunshine would brought a fine "harvest of hay,"
            On George the Fourth's Coronation.

* House of Correction.

1822

Inaugural Address of the Duke of Wellington to the Patrons and Students of King's College

... 'Tis now some five-and-twenty summers since –
   While I was busy teaching Christianity
To the poor Hindoos – that a Quaker man,
    Who doubtless was inflicted with insanity
    Proposed a plan
   By which, at small expense,
The boys and girls of this religious nation,
    With ease and speed,
    Might, every man of them, be taught to read –
    (Almost as well as *we* do) –
    And commence
A general course of useful Education.

The "good old" Genius,* that is dead and gone,
    Look'd on the project with a fav'ring eye –
(At least 'tis *said* so – I think 'tis a libel)
    Its latent treason he did not espy;
But forthwith made his royal wishes known,
That every child should learn to read the Bible.
"And no great harm in *that*," perhaps you'll say;
And so did all the Bishops of the day –
    "But," (said they too)
    "'Twill never do.

* George III.

Does not your gracious Majesty perceive,
That when they once have learned to read their Bibles,
        They'll read the libels
Which the vile Press will scatter in their way?
Let them not read *at all*, illustrious sage –
If we can help it – *for they cannot read
Much good of us* – (the *Standard* and the *Age*,
And the *John Bull* were then, I think, unknown).
            But if, indeed,
            The project must go on,
Let's do our best to counteract the evil,
And send this Joseph Lancaster to the Devil."

Just so they did – they set up Doctor Bell;
And how the plan succeeded, you know well:
When Bishops teach we needn't think the Thames
Will by their pupils e'er be set in flames.
"The snake was scotched," my Lords and Gentlemen,
But treason now another form hath taken;
And we have taken measures once again,
To check its growth, and save the Church's bacon.

      The London University – I see
You shrink with pious horror as 'tis named –
      That steaming hot-bed of iniquity,
Illustrious hearers, was expressly framed
To undermine the Mitre and the Crown,
And turn the Constitution upside down!
What's Phisiology, or Hydrostatics
      Or Larc'ny, or Materia Medica,
Or any other branch o' the Mathematics,
      Or Exact Sciences – what is't, I say,
If Church and State be left without protection,
Or rather given as "subjects for dissection"?
Better, my Lords, "the schoolmaster" were drown'd,
And Harry Brougham ten feet under ground!

But much we strive against this innovation;
We wrote and spoke, and spoke and wrote again;
    We mustered all our ratiocination –
    (And 'twasn't much, God knows) –
        But all in vain:
We said that none but madmen would propose
Such an establishment in Cockneyshire:
        Good Heaven! did they suppose
That learning, virtue, taste, would flourish here;
('Midst tallow, cotton, tea and current prices)
As on the classic banks of Cam and Isis?

This Wisdom cried of old, and no man heeded –
    But suddenly a *new* light on us shone;
We saw at once, *two* colleges were needed;
    And straightway planned a brave one of our own;
So here we are in Bedlam – a fit place
For our proceedings; here are strength and space,
And many circumstances that agree
Surprizingly, with Tory policy.
And here we'll teach the rising generation
    The arts and sciences that we admire;
How to transmute the labour of the nation
    Into such things as Church and State require,
That the Old Couple may be well protected,
Against the malice of the dissaffected.

And if the rogues of Gower Street* should conspire
With other sparks, to – set the Thames on fire,
King's College Mitres will be found, no doubt,
Famous extinguishers, to put it out.

* University College, founded by the Utilitarian-Radical followers
of Jeremy Bentham.

My Lords and Gentlemen,
                    I cannot stay
To say one-half of what I meant to say:
There's Miguel, Nicholas, Lawless and O'Connell
And *many other people,* who go on ill,
        Want looking after. — God be with you, – Oh!
        That one small head should carry all I know.

1828   From *First Book for the Instruction of*
                Students in the King's College

ROBERT TAYLOR
1784–1844

Swing's Revolution

The Archbishop's Palace in a blaze; the Archbishop him-
self flying from Room to Room, in frantic horror.
   Archb. O horrible, most horrible! worse than the
Worst we fear! The lawless mob
Are up in arms in twenty counties at once;
King James hath abdicated his crown, and cast
The great seal of England in the Thames;
The mob pursued Judge Jefferies,
Dodg'd him from street to street, till they found him
Hid in a cellar – and, after most cruel rage,
Have hang'd him on a lamp-post! O Christ,
They've hang'd him. They've hang'd Judge Jefferies,
Hang'd him, hang'd him! O! O! O! O!
The law hath lost its terror; and, worse than all,
The sanctity of the cloth is no protection for the clergy now.
Ah! Ah! Ah! Ah! (*in violent grief.*)
       Enter Dr. Brimstone.
   Brims. My Lord, my Lord, fly! Swing is in your palace,
Swing himself; and a hundred thousand people
Obey him like a God. Swing now is King;
They all throw up their hats, and cry, God save King
Swing.
    (*The crowds without shout,* Swing, Swing for ever!
    Swing, huzza! huzza! God save King Swing!)
       Enter Swing.
As the Archbishop attemps to run away Swing seizes him.
   Swing Stay, old man, stay; that way you rush on

Your destruction – the fire rages in that direction.
Stay here, and you are safe;
Go, and you die!
    Archb. Good God, and am I safe
I' the presence of Swing?
    Swing Swing, Sir, is not *less* than man;
Claim you to be no more and the covenant
Between man and man
Subsists between us, and we are friends;
But no more Grace, no Lordship now, none of your titles:
No Lords, no Bishops, and no Kings now
Shall be endured. We'll have
None of your consecrated idiotcies, to
Madden men's brains out of the remembrance
Of their humanity; to make one part of mankind
Forget their kindred to th' other.
    Archb. (Falls on his knees.) O spare me, spare me!
    Swing I will not spare your craft, Sir;
But your life shall be as dear to me
As my own. Get up, old fool, get up!
Or if thou practisest thus the lesson
Thou and thy wicked craft have taught the people
To cringe and roll thy belly in the dust –
Thou'lt teach me, too, the practice of th' Aristocrats,
And I shall spurn thee. Rise, fellow, rise;
And learn from Swing this lesson –
Nor grace, nor mercy
In any shape, was ever yet obtained
From God or man, – by kneeling.

The assembled Council is the place formerly called the House of Lords; Lords and Bishops on the right hand; Delegates of the People on the left. Archbishop of Canterbury led in between Swing and Richard Jones; the Archbishop places Swing on the Throne.

Archb. My Lords and Gentlemen, but to be Lords
      no more;
The Revolution, that all good men wished
And bad men feared – the People's Revolution –
Has come upon us; the first Revolution
That ever yet, in all the tide of time,
Proposed the People's good. For 'tisn't enough
That we have banished James, and Swing now sits
On England's throne – but we must banish, too,
All tyrannous notions from our own hearts, all scorn
Of those we called the swinish multitude,
And recognise them henceforth by the title of
THE SOVEREIGN PEOPLE. Say, our Citizen-King,
      what is't
That the good People of England, do petition for?
   Swing (descending from the throne.) Nothing.
The good People of England
Will never again be petitioners;
The agricultural labourers, whose voice
Doth speak in mine, have tried petition
Upon petition, prayer on prayer, entreaty on entreaty,
All in vain; denied sufficiency
Of the fruits of the earth, which their own labour tilled,
Till extreme want, and agonizing hunger,
Drave them to madness — madness gave them strength,
Where reason had been weak.
   Archb. What strength mean ye?
   Swing The strength of the first rick-burner, the inspired
      Samson, –
Who, when his Philistine tyrants had put his eyes out,
As you, ye priests, put out the eyes of the people,
And bound him in the temple of their god
Dagon – as your temples are to this day
But forges for welding fetters for the People –
Made him their scoff and jeer, the mighty man

Found that his injuries had given him back
His native strength, and with a giant's grasp
He pulled th' whole edifice upon himself
And them, and crushed god and his priests together:
He died i' th' act himself, but died revenged.

    Jones And now, my Lords, a power
Greater than that of Samson hath passed
Over into the People's hands – a power with which
Your bayonets, your gunpowder, your prisons,
Your legal murders, can compete no longer.
If you would have that power sleep innocent,
Do justice to the People.

    Archb. Do it? As how?

    Jones Visit the poor man's cottage throughout the land,
Not with your vile religious balderdash
And Gospel tracts, to fool him into cowardice,
And tame submission to distresses, which
His wisdom might avert, or his virtue might redress;
Not with deceitful promises of Heaven
Hereafter, to reconcile him to a Hell on earth:
But i' the spirit of honesty and love,
The proper feelings of man's heart to man;
See that he hath the good sufficient meal
His nature craves; nor let your own be sweet to you
Till you are sure your every brother man
Hath a sufficiency. Do this, and ye shall
Possess yourselves of a power greater than
That of fire-balls. Do this, and ye shall
Be fortified in a security – compared to which
Th' array of bayonets and the power of arms
Is but a house of wafers –
Ye shall invest yourselves in triple adamant –
The love of grateful millions.

    (All cry out) We will, we will!

Swing Then Swing resigns his Kingship,
And will return, a British Cincinnatus,
To the plough, from whence he sprang;
Happy to have taught the world, tho' by a fiery lesson –
The noblest moral Heaven itself could give,
"WHO'D LIVE HIMSELF, MUST LET HIS NEIGH-
BOUR LIVE."

1831
From *Swing or, Who are
the Incendiaries?* Act V

Union Hymn

Lo! we answer! see, we come
    Quick at Freedom's holy call.
We come, we come, we come, we come,
    To do the glorious work of all;
And hark! we raise from sea to sea
The sacred watchword, Liberty!

God is our guide! from field, from wave,
    From plough, from anvil, and from loom
We come, our country's rights to save
    And speak a tyrant faction's doom.
And hark! we raise from sea to sea
The sacred watchword, Liberty!

God is our guide! no swords we draw,
    We kindle not war's battle-fires;
By union, justice, reason, law,
    We claim the birthright of our sires,
We raise the watchword, Liberty —
We will, we will, we will be free!

1832

JOHN CLARE
1793–1864

Remembrances

Summer's pleasures they are gone like to visions every one,
And the cloudy days of autumn and of winter cometh on.
I tried to call them back, but unbidden they are gone
Far away from heart and eye and for ever far away.
Dear heart, and can it be that such raptures meet decay?
I thought them all eternal when by Langley Bush I lay,
I thought them joys eternal when I used to shout and play
On its bank at 'clink and bandy,' 'chock' and 'taw' and
                                          'ducking-stone,'
Where silence sitteth now on the wild heath as her own
Like a ruin of the past all alone.

When I used to lie and sing by old Eastwell's boiling
                                          spring,
When I used to tie the willow boughs together for a swing,
And fish with crooked pins and thread and never catch a
                                          thing,
With heart just like a feather, now as heavy as a stone;
When beneath old Lea Close Oak I the bottom branches
                                          broke
To make our harvest cart like so many working folk,
And then to cut a straw at the brook to have a soak.
Oh, I never dreamed of parting or that trouble had a
                                          sting,
Or that pleasures like a flock of birds would ever take to
                                          wing,
Leaving nothing but a little naked spring.

When jumping time away on old Crossberry Way,
And eating haws like sugarplums ere they had lost the may,
And skipping like a leveret before the peep of day
On the roly-poly up and downs of pleasant Swordy Well,
When in Round Oak's narrow lane as the south got black
again
We sought the hollow ash that was shelter from the rain,
With our pockets full of peas we had stolen from the
grain;
How delicious was the dinner-time on such a showery day!
Oh, words are poor receipts for what time hath stole away,
The ancient pulpit trees and the play.

When for school o'er Little Field with its brook and
wooden brig,
Where I swaggered like a man though I was not half so big,
While I held my little plough though 'twas but a willow
twig,
And drove my team along made of nothing but a name,
'Gee hep' and 'hoit' and 'woi' – oh, I never call to mind
These pleasant names of places but I leave a sigh behind,
While I see the little mouldiwarps hang sweeing to the
wind
On the only aged willow that in all the field remains,
And nature hides her face while they're sweeing in their
chains
And in a silent murmuring complains.

Here was commons for their hills, where they seek for
freedom still,
Though every common's gone and though traps are set
to kill
The little homeless miners – oh, it turns my bosom chill
When I think of old Sneap Green, Puddock's Nook and
Hilly Snow,

Where bramble bushes grew and the daisy gemmed in dew
And the hills of silken grass like to cushions to the view,
Where we threw the pismire crumbs when we'd nothing
else to do,
All levelled like a desert by the never-weary plough,
All vanished like the sun where that cloud is passing now
And settled here for ever on its brow.

Oh, I never thought that joys would run away from boys,
Or that boys would change their minds and forsake such
summer joys;
But alack, I never dreamed that the world had other toys
To petrify first feeling like the fable into stone,
Till I found the pleasure past and a winter come at last,
Then the fields were sudden bare and the sky got overcast,
And boyhood's pleasing haunts, like a blossom in the blast,
Was shrivelled to a withered weed and trampled down
and done,
Till vanished was the morning spring and set the summer
sun,
And winter fought her battle strife and won.

By Langley Bush I roam, but the bush hath left its hill,
On Cowper Green I stray, 'tis a desert strange and chill,
And the spreading Lea Close Oak, ere decay had penned
its will,
To the axe of the spoiler and self-interest fell a prey,
And Crossberry Way and old Round Oak's narrow lane
With its hollow trees like pulpits I shall never see again,
Enclosure like a Buonaparte let not a thing remain,
It levelled every bush and tree and levelled every hill
And hung the moles for traitors – though the brook is
running still
It runs a naked stream, cold and chill.

Oh, had I known as then joy had left the paths of men,
I had watched her night and day, be sure, and never slept
                                                    agen,
And when she turned to go, oh, I'd caught her mantle then,
And wooed her like a lover by my lonely side to stay;
Ay, knelt and worshipped on, as love in beauty's bower,
And clung upon her smiles as a bee upon a flower,
And gave her heart my posies, all cropt in a sunny hour,
As keepsakes and pledges all to never fade away;
But love never heeded to treasure up the may,
So it went the common road to decay.

1834–35

The Fallen Elm

Old elm, that murmured in our chimney-top
The sweetest anthem autumn ever made
And into mellow whispering calms would drop
When showers fell on thy many-coloured shade
And when dark tempests mimic thunder made –
While darkness came as it would strangle light
With the black tempest of a winter night
That rocked thee like a cradle in thy root –
How did I love to hear the winds upbraid
Thy strength without – while all within was mute.
It seasoned comfort to our hearts' desire,
We felt thy kind protection like a friend
And edged our chairs up closer to the fire,
Enjoying comfort that was never penned.
Old favourite tree, thou'st seen time's changes lower,
Though change till now did never injure thee;
For time beheld thee as her sacred dower
And nature claimed thee her domestic tree.

Storms came and shook thee many a weary hour,
Yet steadfast to thy home thy roots have been;
Summers of thirst parched round thy homely bower
Till earth grew iron — still thy leaves were green.
The children sought thee in thy summer shade
And made their playhouse rings of stick and stone;
The mavis sang and felt himself alone
While in thy leaves his early nest was made,
And I did feel his happiness mine own,
Naught heeding that our friendship was betrayed,
Friend not inanimate – though stocks and stones
There are, and many formed of flesh and bones.
Thou owned a language by which hearts are stirred
Deeper than by a feeling clothed in word,
And speakest now what's known of every tongue,
Language of pity and the force of wrong.
What cant assumes, what hypocrites will dare,
Speaks home to truth and shows it what they are.
I see a picture which thy fate displays
And learn a lesson from thy destiny;
Self-interest saw thee stand in freedom's ways –
So thy old shadow must a tyrant be.
Thou'st heard the knave, abusing those in power,
Bawl freedom loud and then oppress the free;
Thou'st sheltered hypocrites in many a shower,
That when in power would never shelter thee.
Thou'st heard the knave supply his canting powers
With wrong's illusions when he wanted friends;
That bawled for shelter when he lived in showers
And when clouds vanished made thy shade amends –
With axe at root he felled thee to the ground
And barked of freedom – Oh, I hate the sound.
Time hears its visions speak, and age sublime
Hath made thee a disciple unto time.

It grows the cant term of enslaving tools
To wrong another by the name of right;
It grows the licence of o'erbearing fools
To cheat plain honesty by force of might.
Thus came enclosure – ruin was its guide,
But freedom's clapping hands enjoyed the sight
Though comfort's cottage soon was thrust aside
And workhouse prisons raised upon the site.
E'en nature's dwellings far away from men,
The common heath, became the spoiler's prey;
The rabbit had not where to make his den,
And labour's only cow was drove away.
No matter – wrong was right and right was wrong,
And freedom's bawl was sanction to the song.
– Such was thy ruin, music-making elm;
The right of freedom was to injure thine:
As thou wert served, so would they overwhelm
In freedom's name the little that is mine.
And there are knaves that brawl for better laws
And cant of tyranny in stronger power,
Who glut their vile unsatiated maws
And freedom's birthright from the weak devour.

1832–36

Ode
To His Grace
The Duke of Wellington

Man of titles – won with blood –
Warrior – victor – who hast stood
Smiling o'er the crimson flood.

Known as battle's dreadful lord,
Coldly tempered as thy sword;
Rest thee, peace hath been restor'd:

Rest thee – gallant war-hound – rest,
For thee a long repose were best,
Thy couch should be the Phoenix nest.

For, though battle's rage is o'er,
Still thou'rt he who heretofore,
Led the fight on India's shore.

How the murder'd people fell,
Hunted by the dogs of hell;
Let the stain'd Mulpurbu tell.

God! 'tis like an hideous dream;
Man's deep groan and woman's scream,
Bubbling through their native stream.

No escape – fierce bayonets shine
Along the shore – a dreadful line;
Wellesley, the deed was thine!

And the cruel boast went round,
Meek-eyed Mercy! what a sound:
Lo! five thousand souls were drown'd!

Heed, not souls in arms were they,
Men, who fled the battle's fray;
But people – mark'd the warrior's prey.

Old age – the mother and the child,
The vicious and the undefil'd,
In one cold heap of murder pil'd!

Lives the heart that does not feel,
Through ev'ry pulse a coldness steal,
While such horrors words reveal?

No — and all remember well
By whose sword the people fell.
Shall he govern? – Briton, tell!

Mark – the people there were slain:
Mind – a people here remain,
Shall he whet his scythe again?
. . .
While freedom lingers in the mind,
Nor Autocrat nor Despot join'd,
Shall servile chains upon us bind:

And, thou their staunchest blood-hound, thou,
Of stubborn heart and stirless brow,
Before thy Masters' lords shalt bow,

Shalt sink into thyself again,
And send these tidings o'er the main,
That e'en Napoleon died in vain.

That Freedom in her march sublime,
By Reason lur'd, and led by Time,
Is stealing on our northern clime;

That threat and promise is the same,
From thee – from all who stoop to shame,
And Faction a detested name.

That Tyranny is quite abhorr'd –
That homage to a senseless lord
Hath ceas'd, and cannot be restored.

And, tell the Fiend who crush'd the Pole,
The Briton still hath nurs'd his soul
Too proudly to endure controul;

And, ever jealous of his right,
His Liberty – his whole delight,
Will yet defend with all his might;

Will, with a power unknown to thee,
Assert and keep that Liberty;
Can'st meet us, Arthur, mentally?

No, thou art only havoc's lord,
Thy trust is solely in thy sword;
Rest, and as warrior be ador'd.

As Statesman, all who know thee hate,
Though nerv'd to guide the ranks of fate,
Thou hast not brains to legislate.

Thou hast not, as Napoleon had,
The soul to make a nation glad,
Dost think thou hast? if so, how mad!

And had'st thou, dost suppose that we
Are sunk to that abhorr'd degree
Of national depravity

As to accept at hands like thine
The richest boons? No, by the shrine
Of Truth – by all that is divine!

By our just pride, the British name,
By our forefathers' honest fame,
By Liberty's undying flame –

We loathe the vile apostate, spurn
The mean in soul, and from them turn,
Till nobler lessons they shall learn.

On, and our triumph is achiev'd,
But, mark! and be these words believ'd,
Who trusts a Foe should be deceiv'd.

1832

Dawn of Freedom

Freedom! gorgeous is the dawn
Of thy brightly coming morn –
Radiantly approaching now –
Flushing ev'ry manly brow
    With a hue, from which Decay
    Coldly glancing wings away,
    Like a baffled bird of prey.

Freeman! with the dawn awake,
And betime to toil betake;
Though the task may be severe,
Yet, the harvest will be dear –
    Doubly dear – to thine and thee:
    Leave, oh! leave thy children free: –
    Dower them with Liberty!

Slave, who to the soil art bound,
Child of sorrow! look around!
Hail the radiant light, with joy;
Ev'ry sparkle will destroy
    A link of that detested chain,
    Power to strengthen strives in vain!
    Thou shalt rank with Man again!

Pale Mechanic! up in haste;
Time is precious, scorn to waste
A moment stirring might improve;
From thy heart the chain remove;
    Issue from thy dungeon gloom,
    Quit the anvil, quit the loom;
    Unite, and seal Oppression's doom!

Trading Tyrant! clear thine eyes,
Read salvation in the skies:
Hunger murmurs at thy gate,
Hope, with patience, bids him wait;
    Cruelty is in the mart;
    With the blood of Labour's heart,
    Cease to play the vampire's part.

Ruling Tyrant! mark that light!
Struggling into splendor bright:
Vain it were should myriads bleed,
Striving millions must succeed;
    Pour thy legions on the plain,
    Drench the earth with blood like rain,
    This thou may'st, but, – still in vain!

Hail: O People! hail that light,
Bordering the veil of Night
With growing radiance! ev'ry hour
Gifts it with more potent pow'r:
    Hail it, rising, ev'ry one,
    As the Persian did the Sun,
    When, of old, the day begun!

'Tis the light that Freedom sheds;
As, its glorious influence spreads,
Hearts shall gladden, souls shall know
Wisdom's intellectual glow;
    Mind – immortal mind – shall be
    Bright with Reason – cloudless – free!
    Hail the dawn of Liberty!

1833

Song

This is law all England o'er –
  Palaced pauper's law I guess:
Less they give for more and more –
  More they want for less and less.
This is law all England o'er –
  Palaced pauper's law, I guess:
Wheat to-day and roots to-morrow,
Harder work for deeper sorrow.

Work for idlers, or we sin:
  Day and night, rob board and bed;
Work, and give the Sunday in –
  Nine days' work for three days' bread!
Wrong is right – they make it so;
  This is wrong, full well we know:
Wealth for sloth – for labour sorrow;
Roots to-day and salt to-morrow.

Law for us is law for them;
  If we prove it, we rebel;
Us and our's they soon condemn,
  If we bring less work to sell.
Law for us is law for them;
  If we prove it we rebel –
Nine days' wages! "Hey Saint Monday!"
Work three days – rest three, and Sunday!

"Land's the state, and land's betray'd" –
  We're the State, if fraud's undone –
"Would ye ruin England's trade?"
  We can starve when trade is gone.
"If ye strike, ye ruin trade!"
  You can starve when we're undone –
"Whip that dog! Hark, how the hound yells!"
"See the rascals!" cry the scoundrels.

Caged Rats

Ye coop us up, and tax our bread,
  And wonder why we pine;
But ye are fat, and round, and red,
  And fill'd with tax-bought wine.
Thus twelve rats starve while three rats thrive,
  (Like you on mine and me)
When fifteen rats are caged alive,
  With food for nine and three.

Haste! Havoc's torch begins to glow –
  The ending is begun;
Make haste! Destruction thinks ye slow;
  Make haste to be undone!
Why are ye call'd "my Lord," and "Squire,"
  While fed by mine and me,
And wringing food, and clothes, and fire,
  From bread-tax'd misery?

Make haste, slow rogues! *prohibit* trade,
  Prohibit honest gain;
Turn all the good that God hath made
  To fear, and hate, and pain;

Till beggars all, assassins all,
   All cannibals we be,
And death shall have no funeral
   From shipless sea to sea.

Song

Land of the men who brought before
   All nations, in all times,
A king, soul-gorg'd with crime and gore,
   And slew him for his crimes!

Shall we not name thy name with pride,
   Fam'd mother of the brave?
Who would not die as Hampden died,
   That looks on Sidney's grave?

O'er it thy mountain summits rise,
   Thy dewy roses bloom;
We stand upon it – here he lies!
   Thou, Britain, art his tomb!

Yet scorners say, thy hills and vales
   Are curs'd from sea to sea;
The land of palaces and jails,
   Derision nameth thee.

Where demons tax the air and light,
   And taint with plague the air,
For shameful stripes thy children fight,
   Or labour in despair.

Land of the great, the wise, the good!
  When wilt thou break thy chains?
And startle into honest blood
  The filth in tyrants' veins?

When wilt thou, with the voice of God,
  Alarm thy damn'd of old?
Call Hampden's spirit from the sod?
  And wake the dead and cold?

All power, but our's, as dust is weak,
  When million minds are one:
Great voice, of outraged millions, speak!
  Great will of God be done!

The Horn of Liberty

The Herald of Freedom sounds far in the dale
Its notes full of rapture sweep loud through the gale;
Gay prelude of Liberty's heart-thrilling voice, –
"Now's the hour, my sons, to assert your free choice;
Your efforts I'll aid to destroy the fell foe,
So greet the death-struggle with patriot glow!"

She comes, lo, she comes to our blood-reeking land, –
She sighs at the wails of her long-faithful band;
Her Martyrs she cheers, who indignantly scowl
As Despots add insults to injuries foul;
Fair Truth and Humanity honour her train,
While Justice rejoicing thrice blesses her reign.

Uphold those brave comrades who suffer for you, –
Who nobly stand foremost demanding your due;
Away with the timid – 'tis treason to fear, –
To surrender or falter when danger is near;
For now that our Leaders disdain to betray
'Twere base to desert them, or succour delay!

'Tis time that the Victims of labour and care,
Should reap the reward that is labour's fair share;
'Tis time that their voices in counsel be heard,
The rather than pay for the law of the sword.
All power is ours with a will of our own.
We conquer united, – divided we groan!

Then hail, brothers hail! the shrill sound of the horn; –
For ages deep wrongs have been hopelessly borne;
Despair shall no longer our spirits dismay,
Nor wither the arm when upraised for the fray;
The conflict for Freedom is gathering nigh, –
We live to secure it, or gloriously die!

The horn of liberty sounded for the attendance of the populace on the long bridge across the Severn, by Llanidloes where they were addressed by speakers from the parapet, after which they hurried to the rescue of their comrades, apprehended for training or acquiring the art of self-defence, held as dangerous by partial and jealous legislators to the peace and security of despotic government, and moral duty therefore converted into legal offence; whereupon the authorities and their force (consisting of some two hundred or more armed police and hireling special constables from a neighbouring district, rivals in ancient feuds, and suddenly ushered into the town for the purpose of thereby suppressing their meetings) were completely put to the rout. – April 30th, 1839.

1839

Public Opinion

Oh, mighty Man! lord of this goodly earth!
Thy lordship but shows forth thy littleness;
For thy low life dwarfs down even the huge
And stately globe that doth belong to it,
To the sand-grain, that's all in all to it –
Such as it is, against the Universe,
E'en such thou art, against what thou should'st be.
Oh! if angers could laugh, what merry shouts
Would shake the vault of heaven; to see this ball,
This wondrous ball, rolling in endless room,
With such a pigmy bragging from its perch,
This power and glory is mine – yet 'tis not that –
To be the dwindled body that thou art,
I scorn thee not: for greatness is in good,
Not good in great; but thou'rt a dwarf in soul,
'Fraid of thyself with a most silly fear:
Yes, truly, afraid of thy most silly self –
Nay – but thy shadow – for in very truth,
The world's Opinion, unsifted, is nought else –
A shadow, yet in dark o'erruling awe,
Most strong, although its substance is so weak.
Truly, when God gave Reason for thy gift
He knew thee well – a trimmer – a weathercock,
Unworthy of so high godly a grace;
And so withal He gave thee something else
Beside the Reason that thou could'st not rule,
And would'st not listen when it should rule thee –
Something might suit thee better, a half-thing,

Nay, unthing – nought but a name – Opinion –
Much liker truth to call it apishness;
However called, a grovelling slave in kind –
Slave of the Alazonocracy,* self-styled
Aristocrat: yet crawling from slave bonds
As other eunuchs do, to sovereign sway.
Such is Opinion, also called the public:
Flimsy and fickle; yet by noodledom
Upcried for surety and substance – liar! – avaunt!
The public – what is that – the people! ah, no –
But floating o'er it, like a lazy scum
O'er the wholesome working stream: a flighty cloud
Of many hues, no shape – shifty and slight;
Begotten by light newsreadings on brains
Yet washier; idle and wayward, cowardly
And selfish, for so wealthy leisure is wont;
Sick of its own stagnation, and for lack
Of wholesome working channels to drive will's
Stream onward, craving like a froward child,
Ever some new strange and sense-stirring show;
Slander or ruin, earthquake, gossip-toy,
To draw its soul from its own sink: and hence
Tho' fearful, it loves war for excitement's sake,
And loathes, as mere stagnation, steady peace.
Would'st have a sample of its soul? look there,
On yonder crowd of helpless countrymen,
Untaught, yet teachable, kind-hearted, mild,
Most patient under most oppressive rule,
Summoned as wrongdoers, for their good work
Wrought on waste ground in faith of their full right;
They stand, unarmed, unware, thinking no ill,
Wayworn, in loose talk waiting the award:
But see – that sheet of fire, that storm of shot,

* The ruling class based on self-interest and illusion of its own
greatness.

Those shrieks, those yells, this sudden slaughter strange,
What means it? it means nought but the coward hate
And outrage of bloodthirsty, rancorous hearts,
Madden'd by their own panic. Those who o'erlive
Flee wildly – find and seize weapons hard by.
Turn on the trampler and slay the slaughterers.
Was ever rage more righteous? but no – Rulers
Can ne'er be wrong; resistance never right.
Tho' a drunk soldier strike ye all down – who cares?
Must drown their manly spirit in their blood –
Up then, cries cowardly State-flunkeydom,
Up – play the devil in God's name – shoot, smite,
Burn all the country – homes – crops – havock all –
Spare none – whoe'er flees from ye shoot him down,
Guilty or not – no odds – only make one
Hell of the whole black country – turn not, ere
Ye've done that duty. Well, they did it – clean
And clear – wondrously well – glory to God!
There then Opinion! there thou Public! swill
Thy full – they have set running for thy thirst
Hogsheads of bloody excitement – at the news
Up they throng – noodles, doodles. The whole soft
Handed, hard hearted Alazonocracy,
With its flunkeys, clinging, draggling at its tail,
And proud to be so fouled by it. In they rush
Gloating on cheap thrilling bloodstir – "Ah, good,
Why this is talk indeed – stirs us right thro'.
Worth living for – they got it well, those slaves –
That dared kill back – but the heroes – hip-hurrah.
True Tories – scrunched the workmen – Tories true.
They've given us a week's sensation – a month's.
Crowns and white robes for them – make them knights, peers.
Spout, pray for them – shout, sing, subscribe for them."
Aye, well ye may, so doth the Devil too –
But God, o'erseeing all, overlooks none –

And when the day comes, as come surely it will,
And the black man in manhood shall uprise
Backed by his warrior brethren, conquerors
Of the south, to avenge sternly this hell-blotch;
Then will the noodle public look aghast;
Draw a feint, fearful breath, and each in the slouched
Ears of his brother; "that sensation of ours
So cheap, looks now as tho' it might come dear.
What, war, and soldiers among Christian men,
Bloodshed, and six-pence more of income-tax!
And those our heroes, now so unhero-like!
Ah horror! who'd have thought it?" Nay thy thoughts
Thou noble noodle, to sound deepest truths,
Are something shallow. Thine is no thought-brain:
Its emptiness but echoes noodledom
Needlessly.

               To thy brethren, then, away!
Doodle and Foodle, Poodle, Toodle and all –
We want the stage clear for the working-man –
We'll none of them, nor thee – nor of this same
Most puffy public, that now monkey-like
O'errules the people: and thou, Noodledom,
For thy idols fear not – thou hast set them up –
We too – upset them – weep not; for thy mud
Heroes, mud-daubed with blood, are easy made.
But hence – avaunt – with thy fool trash – for now
'Tis Manhood's time – We must bethink us well –
Henceforth the people's Conscience, how unlike
Public Opinion, that old flaunting jade,
In true self-sure weal-working righteous Faith
Shall lead life onward. So God grant it, and so
Evermore speed it.

1839   From *Ernest; or*
                          The Rule of Right

The Puir Folk

Some grow fu' proud o'er bags o' gowd,
   And some are proud o' learning:
An honest poor man's worthy name
   I take delight in earning.
Slaves needna try to run us down –
   To knaves we're unco dour folk;
We're aften wrang'd, but, deil may care!
   We're honest folk, though puir folk!

Wi' Wallace wight we fought fu' weel,
   When lairds and lords were jinking:
They knelt before the tyrant loun –
   We brak his crown I'm thinking.
The muckle men he bought wi' gowd –
   Syne he began to jeer folk;
But neither swords, nor gowd, nor guile,
   Could turn the sturdy puir folk!

When auld King Charlie tried to bind
   Wi' airn saul and conscience,
In virtue o' his right divine,
   And ither daft-like nonsense –
Wha raised at Marston such a stour,
   And made the tyrants fear folk?
Wha prayed and fought wi' Pym and Noll? –
   The trusty, truthfu' puir folk!

Wha ance upon auld Scotland's hills
  Were hunted like the paitrick,
And hack'd wi' swords, and shot wi' guns,
  Fra' Tummel's bank to Ettrick, –
Because they wouldna' let the priest
  About their conscience steer folk?
The lairds were bloodhounds to the clan –
  The Martyrs were the puir folk!

When Boston boys at Bunker's Hill
  Gart Slavery's minions falter;
While ilka hearth in a' the bay
  Was made fair Freedom's altar;
Wha fought the fight, and gained the day?
  Gae wa', ye knaves! 'twas our folk:
The beaten great men served a king –
  The victors a' were puir folk!

We saw the corn and haud the plough,
  We a' work for our living;
We gather nought but what we've sawn –
  A' else we reckon thieving: –
And for the loun wha fears to say
  He comes o' lowly, sma' folk,
A wizen'd soul the creature has –
  Disown him will the puir folk!

Great sirs, and mighty men o' earth,
  Ye aften sair misca' us;
And hunger, cauld, and poverty
  Come after ye to thraw us:
Yet up our hearts we strive to heeze,
  In spite o' you and your folk;
But mind, enough's as gude's a feast,
  Although we be but puir folk.

We thank the Powers for gude and ill,
  As gratefu' folk should do, man;
But maist o' a' because our sires
  Were tailors, smiths, and ploughmen.
Good men they were, as staunch as steel;
  They didna wrack and screw folk
Wi' empty pouches – honest hearts –
  Thank God, we come o' puir folk!

The Bacchanalian

They make their feasts, and fill their cups –
  They drink the rosy wine –
They seek for pleasure in the bowl: –
  Their search is not like mine.
From misery I freedom seek –
  I crave relief from pain.
From hunger, poverty and cold –
  I'll go get drunk again.

The wind doth through my garments run –
  I'm naked to the blast;
Two days have fluttered o'er my head
  Since last I broke my fast.
But I'll go drink, and straightway clad
  In purple I shall be;
And I shall feast at tables spread
  With rich men's luxury!

My wife is naked, – and she begs
  Her bread from door to door;
She sleeps on clay each night beside
  Her hungry children four!

She drinks – I drink – for why? it drives
 All poverty away;
And starving babies grow again
 Like happy children gay!

In broadcloth clad, with belly full,
 A sermon you can preach;
But hunger, cold, and nakedness,
 Another song would teach.
I'm bad and vile – what matters that
 To outcasts such as we?
Bread is denied – come, wife, we'll drink
 Again, and happy be!

The Hungry Dogs and the Hides

(From the Original Greek of Aesop)

Some hungry dogs, upon a gusty day,
When creeping mists along the forests lay,
By famine stung, rush'd to a river's brink,
Yelling for *food,* they car'd not aught for *drink:*
Across the water, near the farther side,
A glorious chance! some steeping hides they saw,
Though tough – a god-send to a hungry maw.
Loud yelp'd the rout, but how to reach the prize
They knew not, – and their howling pierced the skies:
At last the gravest cur of all the pack,
Showing his tusks – howl'd forth – "Base dogs, stand back!
Why would you madly rush to certain death?
See how the whirling waters boil beneath;
Yet in your fury you would madly dare
To cross the stream, and end your hunger *there;*
Silence your yelpings: – list what I advise –
'Tis even to reach dry-shod, the glorious prize!
Come, let us drink the rushing stream quite up,
Then, on these pageant hides, dear souls, we'll sup."

Yells of delight greeted with loud acclaim
This eloquent cur – this sage without a name.
Down rushed the pack, and of the rabble rout,
Lapping the torrent, every tongue was out.
"Drink, my dear curs. Behold, the shrinking tide!"
Yell'd our bold orator – then gasped and died.

And *still* they drank, 'till the same endless wave
Yielded the hungry pack "a watery grave"!

Moral

See yon tall chimneys, which salute the skies,
Funnels, whence steaming clouds of vapour rise;
Carrying aloft and scattering in thin air
The deep mine's product and the workman's prayer!
And yet they toil in vain, yes! even for those
Who feed them – and who live on labour's woes.
Hark! how they call, and raise the senseless cry; –
"Assist your bounteous masters – or you die!
Rouse, workmen, rouse, nor e'er forget your right,
Tyrants to thwart – and show your virtuous might.
Down with those imposts that would madly rise
To bar the products of more genial skies,
And give you chaff instead – Ye were not born
Britons for this – down with the bonds on corn!"

Thus like the hungry curs they vainly try,
With widening mouths, to drink that river dry,
Which from its old, unfailing fountains pours
An ebbless deluge round its winding shores;
And strive to lull those efforts into peace,
To bridge the gulf, and bid corruption cease;
Let the curs yelp – their howlings still despise,
And in your CHARTER learn *your* safety lies.

1839

GEORGE BINNS
1816–1848

To the Magistrates who Committed me to Prison
Under the Darlington Cattle Act
For Addressing a Chartist Meeting

Oh! bind your fetters fast as hell
    Can forge them for your master,
I smile to think they ring your knell,
    I'LL WEAR THEM FOR THE CHARTER!

And ope' your dismal dungeon's jaws
    To those who will not barter
For tinsel rank, a noble cause,
    I'LL ENTER FOR THE CHARTER!

And herd me with the base and bad,
    Because I'll not surrender
The rights of England to your nod,
    I STILL WILL LOVE THE CHARTER!

Then bind my limbs and lash THE DUST,
    My soul you cannot fetter;
Its chainless wing flies with the just,
    ROUND ENGLAND AND HER CHARTER!

The Switzer's Tell – the Tyrol's pride,
    The noblest blood of Sparta;
The men who've nobly liv'd and died,
    CRY ONWARD WITH THE CHARTER!

1840

The Poor Man's Wedding

I wed thee, girl, as poor men wed,
  To share a lot of toil and care;
No gems will deck our bridal bed,
  But love will strew his roses there.
No cringing slaves, no menial throng
  Will seek our nuptial hovel's thatch;
No steeds will bear us swift along –
  For ours is not a Coburg match!

I did not seek thee for thy gold,
  For wealth thy fancy might bestow;
My love was not a feeling sold,
  For e'en as I am, poor art thou.
I woo'd not with a tongue to which
  The lust of Mammon lent its art;
I do not seek thee to be rich –
  For mine is not a Coburg heart.

Thou dost not take me to thine arms,
  By State necessity impelled,
While condescension yields thy charms,
  To be with humble reverence held.
I choose thee my poor lot to cheer,
  To shed a radiance o'er my life,
And not to frown or domineer –
  For thou art not a Coburg wife!

When time the pleasing hope shall give
　　That soon a pledge will bless our love,
That in *another* we shall live –
　　Another prized ourselves above –
No Court physician will be fee'd,
　　(Puffed in the public prints) to watch,
Lest some mishap should spoil the breed –
　　For our's is not a Coburg match!

And when our infant's cry is heard –
　　Sweet music to a parent's ear –
No flattery foul, no pomp absurd,
　　Will greet the little stranger here.
The public money will not keep
　　Our babe, by princely titles styled;
Peers will not rock that babe to sleep –
　　For ours will be no Coburg child!

Oh, no! our union will not bear
　　The seal of interest – stamp of shame!
But yet our lot will be more fair
　　Than those who boast a higher name.
For to unite us two, at least
　　No groaning people sighs and smarts!
No nation's taxes spread our feast –
　　For ours, love, are not Royal hearts!

1840

A Royal Marriage Ode

Fackeltanz and Fackelzug
In the workhouse of St. Luke,
Stately lords and courtly dames
In the Palace of St. James –
Hurrah for the Prussian bold!
He is come to sack our gold;
Foot it, flunkies, small and grand,
In one huge snob saraband;
He is come to claim his bride –
Share of hard-wrung tax beside;
Rose of England he shall wed,
English rose in German bed.

Fackelzug and Fackeltanz: –
Prick your pauper with a lance;
Crush him, guardsman cas'd in steel;
Shoeless foot with iron heel,
Stout policeman, wield thy staff,
Strike out mid the shrinking raff;
Slaves and lackeys swelter, crawl,
Frantic blessings eager bawl,
Till your foul and noisome breath
Stink, like Royalty in death,
On white-vested bellies creep
To obtain a courtier's peep.

Prostitutes of Regent Street
Be decorous, as 'tis meet,
Laboucherre and Mayne
Else shall bar your wretched gain;
Britain soon must imitate
Morals clean of Belgian State.

Thus a prudent people may
Double their Field Marshal's pay –
Workmen struggling for employ
With wash'd faces yell for joy;
This is what ye sweat for, see,
Children of stark misery.

Fackeltanz and Fackelzug!
Flabby corpse of deaf old Duke
Fresh embalm'd to grace the tomb
Lead the torch-walk down the room,
And with ghost of bloated bawd
Trip it to a verse of "Maud".
Woe and Want and Grief among
Mingle with that nuptial throng:
Sempstress, who the garments made,
Ere in crowded churchyard laid,
With one thin hand on your side
Bear the train up of the bride;
Soldiers, whose unburied bones
Pave the way to Indian thrones;
Widows who those soldiers weep
Wake your little ones from sleep,
Don your faded weeds and crowd,
Through yon wreathed portals proud!

Fackelzug and Fackeltanz; –
Parish grave and Royal dance;

Here, the Court's rich pageantry
Dazzles the offended sky;
There, Starvation's funeral –
With a borrow'd thread-bare pall,
Mouldy mourning-coach and pair,
Death's own horses – takes the air:
Fackeltanz and Fackelzug!
Hurrah! for thy pomp, St. Luke –
Six sham mourners pack'd within
Claiming with the dead man kin,
(Hohenzollern he or Guelph
Bak'd in Adam's vulgar delf)
Chuckling horribly have lied,
To obtain a gratis ride;
They a coffin full of stones,
Or dissection's scraps and bones,
Follow to the grave instead
Of a nameless pauper dead –
Would you view him pickled, call
Great sir, at the hospital –
All that link'd him with his race
A rare tumour on his face.

Fackelzug and Fackeltanz!
People, wake not from your trance;
Though a leader in your "Times"
Point to list of tragic crimes,
That the nation's withers wrung
All from Royal weddings sprung,
Gape, with wide mouths open'd wide,
Stare at bridegroom and at bride:
'Tis not long since, we are told,
English king his daughter sold,
Price he took in Hessian boots
Holding some few thousand brutes;

Hirelings paid to slaughter freedom
As old Israel dealt with Edom;
Take this warning and believe it,
Or, doom'd idiots, spurn and leave it;
Ere long, ye shall know the measure
Of a despot's Royal pleasure.

Fackeltanz and Fackelzug!
In the madhouse of St. Luke,
"Noble" lords and "virtuous" dames
In thy catacomb, St. James!
Nation of glib hypocrites
Eating rottenness, like mites,
"Raise on high a joyous song,
In a torrent full and strong,"
And "your sorrows all forget,"
Not "an eye with grief be wet";
Mix with Hohenzollern's glee
Pauper mirth and jollity,
While the "great Guelph" squat in "Heaven"
Leers down on the rabid leaven.
Gallants, I beseech you all,
Lead fair ladies down the hall,
Bosoms heaving in the dance
Shall not crimson 'neath your glance;
Tread a Polonaise on ashes
Though flame through them leaps and flashes,
Though around ye gathering gloom
Mutters of a day of doom;
Fate's black curtain rent aside
Might reveal a mourning bride,
Show the agony and sorrow
Match like this brings on the morrow.

What are they this stir have made?
Paupers in brief masquerade,
Poorer in the heart and brain,
Than those wedded but to pain;
Dust and ashes are they all
Trick'd out for a festival!
Dance of fools it is they lead,
Million breasts around them bleed;
Canopy there hangs o'er all
Tyranny's dark funeral pall;
Who should sleep beneath it? say,
Freedom, on thy nuptial day.

1840

THOMAS COOPER
1805–1892

The Lion of Freedom

The lion of freedom comes from his den,
We'll rally around him again and again,
We'll crown him with laurels our champion to be,
O'Connor, the patriot of sweet liberty.

The pride of the nation, he's noble and brave,
He's the terror of tyrants, the friend of the slave,
The bright star of freedom, the noblest of men,
We'll rally around him again and again.

Though proud daring tyrants his body confined,
They never could alter his generous mind;
We'll hail our caged lion, now free from his den,
And we'll rally around him again and again.

Who strove for the patriots? was up night and day?
And saved them from falling to tyrants a prey?
It was Feargus O'Connor was diligent then!
We'll rally around him again and again.

1841

Hardie's Last Letter
To His Sweet Heart

O Peggy, dear Peggy! my heart bleeds for you,
While lonely I bid thee my last fond adieu!
But weep not, dear Peggy! O weep not for me!
Cold death brings me joys, love, for thy Hardie is free.

If Stirling's strong castle, this cell, or this chain,
The heart of a free Caledonian could pain,
O then, my dear Peggy, a slave would I be,
But these I all scorn, love, for thy Hardie is free.

Soon, soon, my dear Peggy, I go to that place
Where no partial jury shall sit on my case –
Where kings will be judg'd by a holy decree,
And there, my dear Peggy, shall thy Hardie be free.

And when I am dead, love, as soon I must die,
Should slander's proud minions my mem'ry belie,
O take my part, Peggy, though slaughter'd I be,
And tell them, exulting, that thy Hardie died free.

Ah! think not the axe of the monsters I fear,
Although these last lines are bedewed with a tear!
No! it fell for my ill-fated country and thee;
For nature hath ties, love, tho' thy Hardie is free.

Then farewell, my Peggy, I will say no more;
Hope's bright visions rest on a friendlier shore –
Where life's bloody scenes shall be far, far from me:
Farewell, farewell Peggy, thy Hardie is free.

1841

Yes, We Are Free

Yes, we are free, to plough the sea
    And dig the earth for treasure;
And when we do, the ruling few
    Can take our gains at leisure.

We're free to fight with all our might
    In every Whiggish battle,
And when we do, the ruling few
    Treat us like slaves or cattle.

And free we're born to sow the corn,
    And free when ripe, to cut it;
And when we do, the ruling few,
    Are free to take and eat it.

We are free to weep while tyrants sleep,
    And starve while they are feasting;
And when we do, the ruling few
    Feed us with scorn and jesting.

We pay the tax laid on our backs
    And seldom try to stop it;
And when we do, the ruling few
    Can take by force and pocket.

And thus you see that we are free
    To labour for starvation,
Because they take all that we make
    To pay their d -- d taxation.

1841

On the Opening of the Present Session of Parliament

Parliament assembled at a time when there can be no longer any doubt as to the distress, *which presses with more or less severity,* upon all the industrious classes. – *Public Press of the United Kingdom, the day after the assembling, February 4, 1842.*

I

Blazed banners waving high,
   Marchings of martial men,
Shoutings that rend the sky,
   Loud cannons' roar – and then –
'Mid a right loyal stir,
   Tongues blessing, hats off cast,
All regal gold and fur
   The royal pageant past!
Crowds run before – they fly,
   They turn again to greet,
The Queen! the Queen! they cry,
   To bid her Senate meet!
     Ha! do ye meet? what now –
      See to it, ere ye part,
    What – for the nation's brow?
     What – for the nation's heart?

II

What? lo she enters in,
  Our own, our young, our fair;
With what a festive din
  Her people fill the air,
With homage how august,
  Her stately nobles rise,
'Then all to the All Just,
  The ruler of the skies,
Bend low in humble prayer,
  And help and grace entreat
To have vouchsafed there,
  Where Britain's Senate meet.
    Ha! do ye meet? what now –
      See to it ere ye part.
    What – for the nation's brow?
      What – for the nation's heart?

III

What? hush! soft from the throne
  The Queen's, the *Woman's* voice,
That tremble in the tone,
  Tells how the fond rejoice.
Her people's grace has found
  This answer in her breast.
'Tis o'er, and they around
  Our youthful monarch prest,
Again the eager crowd
  Throng through the swarming street,
Huzzaing long and loud,
  She bade her Senate meet!
    Ha! are ye met? what now –
      See to it ere ye part;
    What – for the nation's brow?
      What – for the nation's heart?

IV

What? ye have answer now;
    Home! mother, young and fair!
Home to the infant brow
    Thou hast all-cradled there:
"God bless her!" thousands shout,
    Shout to her palace-gates.
'Tis well – disperse this rout,
    For them no answer waits;
Fools of the show they came,
    The fools they came, they go;
They dream not of a people's claim
    To shout Ho! Senate, ho!
        Have ye met at last? what now –
          See to it ere ye part;
        What – for the nation's brow?
          What – for the nation's heart?

V

Its brow is black and fierce,
    Yet meagre – twitched with woe;
Its heart hath cries to pierce
    The heavens ye mocked so.
But the still heavens are dumb?
    Believe it not! find men
Whose famine-hour has come;
    Assemble them – and then –
From the top of the midnight-sky
    This answer shall have birth;
Ye ask'd – hear my reply –
    Cowards ! *I* gave you *Earth*!
        Ha! was it so? but now –
          Ye see to it ere ye part;
        What – for the nation's brow?
          What – for the nation's heart?

VI

What? hark as day goes down,
    Howl sinewy rage-hoarse throats;
See want-stamped brows' fierce frown
    O'er what the *Press* denotes; –
"Speech from the throne!" what then?
    Was it spoken to *our* need?
Has the Queen told her noblemen
    They must her people feed?
They must, they shall, they *will*,
    Since their *gift* but forestalls our *choice.*
Ha! thought ye starved men to fill
    With the sounds of a silver voice?
      We have waited long – but now –
        See to it ere ye part;
      What – for the nation's brow?
        What – for the nation's heart?

VII

What? the gaunt artizan
    In his foodless garret cries,
Ye deny my "Rights of Man";
    Ye *shall* answer to its ties!
Woman! *my wife!* come here –
    You *are* she whom I did wed –
Nay, let me wipe that tear,
    Our children *shall* have bread!
And he smileth long to think,
    By the mother that them bore,
How his babes shall eat and drink,
    So they starve but one day more!
      That day has begun! – what now,
        See to it ere ye part,
      Frowneth the nation's brow,
        Muttereth the nation's heart.

VIII

Ye have met – and know ye where
  They meet by twos and threes?
And an oath is all the prayer,
  And each saith it on his knees!
From their empty homes at night;
  In silent hate they wend –
And the crackling flames are bright,
  Ha! who is the farmer's friend?
We helped to store your hold,
  Was there not *one* grain for us?
We take it not – behold –
  We but *bake* it for you thus;
    Knew ye this? then now
      See to it ere ye part,
    What – for the nation's brow?
      What – for the nation's heart?

IX

By our starved across the main,
  Whose cries in dreams we hear,
Ye are *not* met again
  Emigration bills to cheer:
No! harvests ripen round,
  Beneath God's sun at home,
We have thought on it, and found
  There's *no just cause to roam*;
And we LIKE our English land,
  Do ye understand us now?
How think ye a bold hand,
  Seconds burning heart and brow?
    Such things have been – what now,
      See to it ere ye part,
    What – for the nation's brow?
      What – for the nation's heart?

X

While thus throughout the land,
    Dark – threatening murmurs rise,
Know ye're met upon a strand
    Where the waves have met the skies!
Vaunt how ye put to sea
    In the "Vessel of the State",
Senate of England, see
    Ye not it bears *your* fate?
Prose – how the laws ye found
    Must stand by ye – or fall,
Ye have met on their own ground
    The mighty people all!
        Life is *their* law – what now,
            Press *that* law ere ye part,
        Frowneth the nation's brow,
            Muttereth the nation's heart.

XI

Have ye met this time for nought?
    Will ye again postpone?
Behold! matured in thought,
    How the man-child has grown!
The work his right arm wrought,
    Think ye will strength disown?
Our knowledge be untaught,
    Or pain *put off* its groan?
They mutter low and deep,
    Our wants have long been borne,
And swell ye still *your* heap
    From the plenty-pouring horn?
        "Give, or we take!" – what now,
            See to it ere ye part,
        What – for the nation's brow?
            What – for the nation's heart?

XII

Oh! let the answer come
  From the smiling earth around,
From hearts on which the bloom
  Of *love* may still be found.
There are *men* among ye yet,
  Up, up, ye faithful few,
Her cheeks all sorrow – wet,
  Hark! Freedom calls for you!
Save her from thirst of blood,
  Save her from thought of hate;
A conquest great and good,
    In *peace* to consecrate;
      Up! be your watchword now,
        Love-workers ere ye part,
      Read ye well the nation's brow,
        List well to the nation's heart.

XIII

In the people's hopes ye live,
  Or oppression, old and blind,
They had arisen ere this, to give
  Like chaff before the wind!
Proclaim i' the face of day
  Great thoughts of common good,
In your own persons stay
  The coming multitude!
They are up, up ye, or set
  Is the seal to an awful hour,
When shall meet where ye are met,
  Young might and tottering power!
    Which hath Revenge? Oh! now,
      See to it ere ye part,
      Black is the nation's brow,
        Loud is the nation's heart.

XIV

Give freely of God's gift
   To your human nature given;
Benignly brilliant lift
   Your eyes, and learn from Heaven;
Oft sullen clouds that go
   To oppose the Sun's glad march,
Weep to be bright! and lo!
   The all-gracious promise-arch!
Oft, too, where ocean leaves
   Them *free* – great earthquakes prove
Soft as the sigh that heaves
   Through a woman's breast of love!
Show ye then the frowned brows – that ye *see*;
   Show the panting hearts – that ye *feel*;
In a man's mistakeless sympathy,
   With men *as brothers* deal;
And, *though it be late* – even now,
   Ye may leave us, ere ye part,
Smiles on the nation's brow,
   Peace at the nation's heart.

1842

Father! Who Are the Chartists?

MILLIONS who labour with skill, my child,
On the land – at the loom – in the mill, my child.
Whom bigots and knaves
Would keep as their slaves;
Whom tyrants would punish and kill, my child.

MILLIONS whom suffering draws, my child,
To unite in a glorious cause, my child:
Their object, their end,
Is mankind to befriend,
By gaining for all equal laws, my child.

MILLIONS who ever hath sought, my child,
For freedom of speech and of thought, my child,
Though stripp'd of each right
By the strong hand of might,
They ne'er can be vanquish'd or bought, my child.

MILLIONS who *earnestly* call, my child,
For freedom to each and to all, my child;
They have truth for their shield,
And never will yield
Till they triumph in tyranny's fall, my child.

And they've sworn at a Holberry's grave, my child,
(That martyr so noble and brave, my child)
That come weal or come woe,
Still *onward* they'll go
Till Freedom be won for the slave, my child!

1844

THOMAS OSBORNE DAVIS
1814–1845

Tone's Grave

In Bodenstown churchyard there is a green grave
And wildly along it the winter winds rave;
Small shelter, I ween, are the ruined walls there
When the storm sweeps down on the plains of Kildare.

Once I lay on that sod – it lies over Wolfe Tone –
And thought how he perished in prison alone,
His friends unavenged, and his country unfreed –
"Oh! bitter," I said, "is the patriot's meed!

"For in him the heart of a woman combined
With a heroic life and a governing mind:
A martyr for Ireland – his grave has no stone,
His name seldom named, and his virtues unknown."

I was woke from my dream by the voices and tread
Of a band who came into the home of the dead;
They carried no corpse, and they carried no stone,
And they stopped when they came to the grave of Wolfe
Tone.

There were students and peasants, the wise and the brave,
And an old man who knew him from cradle to grave:
And children, who thought me hard-hearted – for they,
On that sanctified sod, were forbidden to play.

But the old man, who saw I was mourning there said:
"We come, sir, to weep where young Wolfe Tone is laid;

And we're going to raise him a monument, too –
A plain one, yet fit for the simple and true."

My heart overflowed, and I clasped his old hand,
And I blessed him, and blessed every one of his band:
"Sweet, sweet 'tis to find that such faith can remain
To the cause, and the man so long vanquished and slain!"

. . .

In Bodenstown churchyard there is a green grave,
And freely around it let winter winds rave:
Far better they suit him – the ruin and gloom –
Till Ireland, a nation, can build him a tomb.

1843

The Prisoner at the Bar

'Tis a jest to ask me why
For my deed I should not die;
I appeal, for my reply,
    To your thongs!
To my corn beneath the hoof!
To the flame-flag from my roof!
Do ye want more maddening proof
    Of my wrongs?

Honest men, before my eyes,
Have been tortured into lies;
And ye bought from perjured spies
    Priceless blood.
Ye corrupted and debased,
Ye inveigled, trapped, and chased,
Ye o'erswept, deformed, defaced –
    Like a flood.

The loftiest, or the least
In the fight, or when it ceased;
The fair virgin, or the priest,
    Did ye spare?
Till now, by force and fraud,
Human feeling is outlawed,
And oppression stalks abroad,
    Bold and bare.

Ye plunderers of our plains!
Ye exhausters of our veins,
Ye firers of our fanes

              If *I* be
(For resistence when ye trod
Flesh and spirit as the clod)
A dark Felon before God,

                    What are *ye?*

If some tyrant's blood I spilt,
On the tyrant is the guilt;
If I met him hilt to hilt

                 For my own:
And – free me from this chain –
I will dare you thus again,
Though you gird with cannon train

                  Me alone.

And this persisting zeal,
Which all trampled men must feel,
Will defy your fire and steel

                  Till ye yield
The plunder ye have gained,
And the captives you have chained,
To a host – perchance untrained,

                  To the field.

Though my fate be in your hands,
With my life's fast-falling sands,
I will lay my stern commands

                  On my son;
By the honour of his wife,
By his fame in death or life,
To be faithful to this strife,

                  Till 'tis won!

A Word to the People

Behold upon the lonely strand
    A limit to the ocean;
And nothing but the simple sand,
    To check its onward motion!
A mass of moving atoms – link'd
    As by a common labour;
Without a single grain distinct
    Above its tiny neighbour!

Oh! could we thus in concord live,
    As brother should with brother;
And, with no sordid feelings, give
    Our efforts to each other:
With hands so strong, and hearts so firm,
    By freedom's cause anointed,
How soon would be a stinted term
    To tyranny appointed!

What is the patriot, but a spark,
    When men are disunited?
It dies – and leaves but little mark,
    That *any* were ignited!
But let the heavenly essence fall
    Where all agree together:
It grows – and spreads – and kindles *all*, –
    Still most in stormy weather.

A world of hopes! – a nipping blast!
    A still-expecting bosom!
And little fruit to come at last
    Of all the glorious blossom!
Unless the recreant slave shall cease,
    To be the tyrant's minion;
Ah! *then,* how short the tyrant's lease,
    Of his usurp'd dominion!

A Song Addressed to the Fraternal Democrats

On the occasion of their First Annual Festival to celebrate the Anniversary of the French Republic, at the White Conduit Tavern, April 21, 1846.

Air: *Auld Lang Syne*

All hail, Fraternal Democrats,
  Ye friends of Freedom hail,
Whose noble object is – that base
  Despotic power shall fail.
    That mitres, thrones, misrule and wrong,
      Shall from this earth be hurled,
    And peace, goodwill, and brotherhood,
      Extend throughout the world.

Associated to proclaim
  The equal rights of man,
Progression's army! firm, resolved,
  On! forward lead the van.
    Till mitres, thrones, misrule and wrong,
      Shall from this earth be hurled.
    And peace, goodwill, and brotherhood,
      Extend throughout the world.

To aid this cause we here behold,
  British and French agree,
Spaniard and German, Swiss and Pole,
  With joy the day would see.

When mitres, thrones, misrule and wrong,
  Will from this earth be hurled,
And peace, goodwill, and brotherhood,
  Extend throughout the world.

We now are met to celebrate
  The deeds of spirits brave,
Who struggled, fought, and bled, and died,
  Their misrul'd land to save.
    For mitres, thrones, misrule and wrong,
      From France they nobly hurled,
    And would have spread Democracy
      Throughout this sea-girt world.

Though kings and priests might then combine
  To crush sweet liberty,
We tell them *now* that they must bow,
  That man shall yet be free.
    That mitres, thrones, misrule and wrong,
      Shall from this earth be hurled,
    And peace, goodwill, and brotherhood,
      Extend throughout the world.

Oh! may that period soon arrive,
  When kings will cease to be,
And freedom and equality
  Extend from sea to sea.
    Then mitres, thrones, misrule and wrong,
      Will from this earth be hurled,
    And peace, goodwill, and brotherhood,
      Shall reign throughout the world.

1846

ERNEST JONES
1819–1869

The New World

I saw a new heaven and a new earth. – Rev. XXI.1

From freedom born to Time, transcendent birth!
Colossus destined to bestride the earth,
While heaved old empires with unwonted throes,
Man's sanctuary, America, arose.

Dull Europe, startled by thy first wild tones,
Held up thy cradle with her crumbling thrones,
And France, sad nurse of thy rude infant days,
Lulled thy first slumber to her "Marseillaise".

Nations have passed, and kingdoms flown away,
But history bids thee hope a longer day,
Wise witness of an ancient world's decay;
No common guards before thy barriers stand –
The elements themselves defend thy land;
Eternal frost thy northern frontiers meet;
Around thy south is rolled eternal heat;
O'er East and West twin oceans watch afar;
To thee a pathway – to thy foes a bar.
The noblest rivers through thy valley flow;
The balmiest skies above thy myriads grow;
The richest field of earth is spread below:
And thee surround – Oh, blessing past increase!
A race of heroes in a land of peace.
Not thine the trials that the past has known:
Blasphemed altar, crime cemented throne;

Not thine to wash, when wincing at the strain,
With thine own blood, the rust from off thy chain;
Nor thine to struggle painful stages through,
Of old oppressions, and ambitions new;
Of priestly bigotry and feudal pride,
That – even in ruin, still corruption hide,
Young Nation-Hercules! Whose infant grasp
Kingcraft and Churchcraft slew, the twin-born asp!
What glorious visions for thy manhood rise,
When thy full stature swells upon our eyes!
A crown of northern light shall bind thy head,
The South Pole at thy feat its billows spread,
With island-gems thy flowing robe be graced,
And Tyrian-Cameoes glitter at thy waist.
Warm as its skies and spotless as its snow,
Thy mighty heart shall beat at Mexico;
And on that mystic sight of unknown Eld,
A city rise, as mortal ne'er beheld,
Till Europe sees thy sovereign flag unfurled,
Where'er the waters wash the Western World.
Swords carve out titles; but, their seal to set,
The last fine touch of empire's wanting yet;
One speech, one law, one God, alone efface,
From conquered lands the frontier's lingering trace;
Thus Hellas bound the East, mid war's alarms,
More with her army's language than her arms;
And thus, though rent Rome's military rule,
Her colonies are Senate, bar and school.
Thus, when the Saxon tongue shall sound confessed
By all the bold young utterance of the West,
One kindred thought enkindling through the whole,
The proud, imperial form shall feel a soul.

A! That the wisdom here so dearly bought,
Would sanctify thy wild, luxuriant thought,
And righteously efface the stripes of slaves,
From that proud flag where heaven's high splendour waves!
But not the black alone the wrong shall feel,
The white man sinks the prey of gold and steel;
For victory carries glory in her train,
Who dark behind her trails a lengthening chain.
The hordes, ambition taught afar to roam,
Soon rivet links on misery's limbs at home;
The taste of conquest brings the thirst for more,
And death-fraught navies leave the saddened shore.
But when, thy natural limits once possessed,
Thou, too, shalt seek to colonize a West;
Round coral-girt Japan thy ships shall ply,
And China's plains behold thine armies die! —
Unequal burdens press the exhausted land,
Till richer States petition, rise, withstand.
(The poor are still most liberal for their means,
But wealth the greedier grows, the more it gains.)
In Mexico, the spurring courier's bell
Proud senate's distant provinces rebel: —
Then call your legions home, new levies raise;
The more you arm, the more the evil preys;
The *long spared classes* feel the drain at last;
They join the mass and Mammon's hour is past.
Then, where the South sits throned in flame above,
Their hearts as fervid as the land they love,
Swift sinks the white and towering o'er the rest,
The hot mulatto rears his fiery crest: —
Awhile the jarring elements contend,
Till mingling hues with softening passions blend;

Thus wrongs avenged and Afric's burning stain,
Darkens her torturer's brow and floods his vein,
And, in the children, brands the father – Cain.
The Titan fragments slowly break away,
Ripe fruit of ages men misnamed decay;
But from the change no rival powers shall war,
And freedom's friendly union fight no more.

1849   From *The Revolt of Hindostan or,*
           The New World

Free Speech

The Judge decides from high judicial seat,
The right to speak, petition and to meet;
"To meet – in every public space, no doubt,
If the police don't choose to keep you out.
If, at such meeting you may chance to be,
And some one something says to somebody,
Though not one syllable you may have heard,
You're guilty, all the same, of every word!
You may petition, if you like, the Throne –
But then the Ministers decide alone;
Or parliament – and, if they won't attend,
What would you more? – the matter's at an end!
Processions can in no case be allowed –
Except for civil feast, or courtly crowd;
Hunts, too, may sweep the fields with battering feet,
But men not bear petitions through the street.

"If you associate in your common cause, –
That is conspiracy, by Statute-laws!
If Cabinet or Commons you decry, –
That is sedition, rout and felony!

If you suppose the Crown can do amiss,
That's treason! – see our last new Act for this! –
And if against the holy church you rail, –
That's blasphemy! – *to jail, you knaves! to jail!*
You have a right to meet petitioning still, –
Just when we choose, – and say – just what we will."

Yet came their blows so hard, so home their hits,
On cushioned seat the Judge uneasy sits;
With ignorant glibness, reputation tries;
Like Sin, that reasons with its guilt – he lies!
From shallow premise inference false would wrench,
And spouts Economy from solemn bench:
"I drink champagne – that gives the poor man bread –
The grower takes our calico instead –
I keep my hunter – why that brow of gloom?
Does not my hunter also keep his groom?
I roll my carriage – well! that's good for trade!
Look at the fortunes coachmakers have made."
Then, his last argument when others fail –
"TO JAIL! TO JAIL! *You wicked men, to jail!*"

From *The Revolt of Hindostan or.
The New World*

The Future

In sunny clime behold an Empire rise,
Fair as its ocean, glorious as its skies.
Mid seas serene of mild Pacific smiles
Republic vast of federated isles.
Sleepy tradition, lingering, loves to rest,
Confiding child! on calm Tahiti's breast;
But science gathers, with gigantic arms,
In one embrace, the South's diffusive charms;

Nor these alone, she rears the bright domain,
Throughout the world expands her hallowing reign –
Then, bold aspiring as immortal thought
Launched in the boundless, mounts the aeronaut;
While o'er the earth they drive the cloudy team,
Electric messenger, and car of steam;
And guide and govern on innocuous course,
The explosive mineral's propelling force;
Or, mocking distance, send, on rays of light,
Love's homeborn smiles to cheer the wanderer's sight.

Mechanic power then ministers to health,
And lengthening leisure gladdens greatening wealth:
Brave alchemy, the baffled hope of old,
Then forms the diamond and concretes the gold;
No fevered lands with burning plagues expire,
But draw the rain as Franklin drew the fire;
Or far to mountains guide the floating hail,
And whirl on barren rocks its harmless flail.
Then the wierd magnate, bowed by mightier spell,
Robbed of its secret, yields its power as well;
With steely fingers on thin dials placed,
The thoughts of furthest friends are instant traced;
And those fine sympathies that, like a flame,
Fibre to fibre draw, and frame to frame,
That superstition, in its glamour – pride,
At once misunderstood and misapplied,
As virtue ripens shall be all revealed,
When man deserves the trust such arms to wield.

. . .

Those halcyon days shall witness discord cease,
And one great family abide in peace;
While ball and bayonet but remain to tell
That lofty race how low their fathers fell.
One language then endearingly extends

Shall tongues still deviate when hearts are friends?
With Babel's curse war, wrong and slavery came –
Their end was shadowed in the cloven flame.
No parchment deed shall qualify the soil:
God gave to man his title in his toil:
No wild distinction mark his great design
And designate a theft as "mine and thine";
No perjured code shall make his bounty vain,
And say: "For thee the stubble – me, the grain" –
But, 'twixt this dust and heaven's o'erarching span
Man own no nobler name than that of MAN –
No holier law than Christ's great law of Love,
His guide within him, and his Judge above: –
Freed ever more from soldiers, nobles, kings,
Priests, lawyers, hangmen and all worthless things;
For, matchless harmony prevailing earth,
With evil passions, dies each evil birth;
And, all her stubborn elements subdued,
Nature and man forget their ancient feud.

From *The Revolt of Hindostan or,
The New World*

A Coming Cry

The few to whom the law hath given the earth God gives
to all
Do tell us that for them alone its fruits increase and fall;
They tell us that by labour we may earn our daily bread,
But they take the labour for their engines that work on
unfed.
And so we starve; and now the few have publish'd a decree –
Starve on, or eat in workhouses the crumbs of charity;
Perhaps it's better than starvation, – once we'll pray and then
We'll all go building workhouses, million, million men!

We'll all go building workhouses, – million, million hands,
So jointed wondrously by God, to work love's wise
commands;
We'll all go building workhouses, – million, million minds,
By great God charter'd to condemn whatever harms or
binds;
The God-given mind shall image, the God-given hand
shall build
The prisons for God's children, by the earth-lords will'd;
Perhaps it's better than starvation, once we'll pray, and
then
We'll all go building workhouses, – million, million men.

What'll we do with the workhouses? million, million men!
Shall we all lie down and madden, each in his lonely den?
What! we whose sires made Cressy! we, men of Nelson's
mould!

We, of the Russells' country, – God's Englishmen the bold!
Will we, at earth's lords' bidding, build ourselves
                                    dishonour'd graves?
Will we who've made this England, endure to be its slaves?
Thrones totter before the answer! – once we'll pray, and then
We'll all go building workhouses, million, million men.

c. 1843

Song of the Kings of Gold

Ours all are marble halls,
Amid untrodden groves,
Where music ever calls,
Where faintest perfume roves;
And thousand toiling moan,
That gorgeous robes may fold
The haughty forms alone
Of us – the Kings of Gold.

        Chorus We cannot count our slaves,
                  Nothing bounds our sway,
                  Our will destroys and saves,
                  We let, we create, we slay.
                  Ha! ha! who are Gods?

Purple, and crimson, and blue,
Jewels, and silk, and pearl,
All splendours of form and hue,
Our charm'd existence furl;
When dared shadow dim
The glow in our wine-cups roll'd?
When droop'd the banquet-hymn
Raised for the Kings of Gold?

The earth, the earth is ours!
Its corn, its fruits, its wine,
Its sun, its rain, its flowers,
Ours, all, all! – cannot shine
One sunlight ray but where
Our mighty titles hold;
Wherever life is, there
Possess the Kings of Gold.

And all on earth that lives,
Woman, and man, and child,
Us trembling homage gives;
Aye trampled, sport-defiled,
None dareth raise one frown,
Or slightest questioning hold;
Our scorn but strikes them down
To adore the Kings of Gold.

On beds of azure down,
In halls of torturing light,
Our poison'd harlots moan,
And burning toss in sight;
They are ours – for us they burn;
They are ours, to reject, to hold;
We taste – we exalt – we spurn –
For we are the Kings of Gold.

The father writhes a smile,
As we seize his red-lipp'd girl,
His white-loin'd wife; ay, while
Fierce millions burn, to hurl
Rocks on our regal brows,
Knives in our hearts to hold –
They pale, prepare them bows
At the step of the Kings of Gold.

In a glorious sea of hate,
Eternal rocks we stand;
Our joy is our lonely state,
And our trust our own right hand;
We frown, and nations shrink;
They curse, but our swords are old;
And the wine of their rage deep drink
The dauntless Kings of Gold.

> *Chorus*   We cannot count our slaves,
> Nothing bounds our sway,
> Our will destroys and saves,
> We let, we create, we slay.
> Ha! ha! who are Gods?

Escape

Shark's jaws are glittering through the eternal ocean
Now, even as ever; through its topmost seas
That mightily billow, through the secrecy
Of its abysms, where the waters bide
Omnipotently shuddering – scattering fear
Onward they go; their illuminating teeth
Perpetually parting, and ever through
Some dolphin's body nervously they clench.
Hidden within the tropic forest's maze
Now, even as ever, glares the tiger's eye
Over its victim, yellow-circling light:
And there the serpent, with his gaze, still charms
To approach, and into his distended jaws
Shiveringly hie the gaudy chattering parrot.

Or gambolling coney; and shaggy spiders there
Catch in their webs the flitting humming-birds:
And through the golden air, the humming-birds flitting
Slay countless happy insects.

                                Slaughter sways
Supremely, everywhere, where man comes not,
Beasts kill each other; where his empire holds,
There, oh ye gods! on richer aliment
Feeds slaughter, and extends. There armies clash
And at the shock ten thousand human forms
Each with exquisite joints and countless nerves,
Fall bloodily broken. There the priest-piled faggots
Flame round the martyr, and send up to heaven
The smoke of torment. There the blood-stained hands
Of gold-holders sell sustenance to the goldless,
At price of body, at price of mind and heart.
There the goldless pay this price, and breed successors;
A generation of things that never live
But toil, and suffer, and shriek, – undead abortions
That yet are human children! And self-slain
Often humanity. Man's towns and cities
Seem builded on rivers, that the rushing waters
May roll for him the ever-ready tomb
He oft assumes; and self-slain, ever go down
Fond women, who the cup of life spill
Offering it tremblingly to some gallant's lips.
Dire is the woe, when first the vision of slaughter,
Thus everywhere regnant, breaks into the mind
Youthful and loving, and emerging from the home
Where all it knew was that all round it smiled;

And whence ever went its fancies, towards some fate
That should one day lead it through the maze of life,
To seek and share love everywhere. At first,
Stunn'd like a wader out into the sea,
Who thinking he steps upon the sand, finds only
Water yield under him, – the appalled youth,
Reaches out aimlessly and in vain for aid.

Then the howl of the world arouses him; he rises, –
Through heavens and hells, eternities and times,
Wildly he stares; – seeking the power that bids
This terrible reign. Baffled, his gaze retreats;
He strips his being of all control and veil,
With which men gird themselves; and he thinks his teeth
Could grasp Earth's wretched breast, and that he could leap
With her to oblivion. And while thus he dreams,
Steals sensual pleasure to him. The nakedness
To which in his noble rage he smote his being
But exposes him to her dalliance; and he turns
From thought that bids him hurl against the unknown
His life, that itself dishonours in enduring
Sight of the blood-stained universe, – to the arms
Of sensual pleasure, and exhausted there,
Finds ignominious sleep; –
If sleep that be, whereunto ever descend
The visions of possible and gentle glory,
That circled brightly round his youth, and that now
Invite him, from his impotent degradation,
To soar into their joy; – if sleep that be,
From which the sleeper must ever arise, and slay,
With murder worse than parricide, these entreaters; –

Or awake, to find his moral powers gone idiot,
And his intellect sane to watch them.

From *Ways of Regard*

I Believe

Every ship except the one we embark in
                    Gives us dreams
Of bright voyaging, beautious lands afar, and
                    Glorious streams;
Every maiden, until she has consented,
                    Angel seems.

Beautiful is nought, unless some foreground
                    Grasp debar;
All things flying attract us, and all charm till
                    Gain'd they are –
The hills are beautiful but because their summits
                    Soar afar.

What is the argument of thy discontent,
                    Human soul?
Wilt thou, oh haggardest of coursers! ever
                    Find fit goal?
Art thou a wild exception, or knoweth Nature
                    Nothing whole?

Sometimes I dream the law of thy well-being
                    Ceaseless change,
And while thy senses and affections bid thee
                    Narrow range,
Thou, like a bird encaged, and fetter'd, pinest
                    Lost and strange.

But most I pondering deem that it may be,
        That thy sight
To grasp the perfect 'neath Time's imperfections
        Hath no might,
Whilst only before the perfect canst thou expand to
        Fit delight.

And seems it then, whilst each fruit thou pursuest
        Turns to dust,
That, spite of all thy pride in thy pursuing
        'Twere more just
That thou had'st never been unto dead-sea apples
        Thus out-thrust.

Wait, blind-whirl'd Ixion of the flashing wheel
        Life and Death!
This thing is certain, that like ore good grows all
        Ill beneath;
Other than worshippers of dreams and scriptures
        Live by faith.

Tombs yet may rise for us, of lifetimes
        Dark and brief;
We may not see Time's victory, but it comes, and,
        For our grief,
Endurance knows celestial consolations
        Past belief.

Dissatisfaction accident is of Earth,
        Not Earth's plan;
Years come when even its name shall be a riddle
        None may scan;
Perchance even now his plumes outspreads the hour that
        Ends the ban.

Roll on then, Eearth, with all thy soaring mountains
                    Pale as Ghosts!
Enchant, oh maids, and glory in enchanting
                    Man's young hosts;
Toward a new future will we make your victims
                    Road sign-posts.

Mix pigments, study lines, exalt us Nature,
                    Painters all,
Burn fire on all her altars; and, though wearied,
                    Never fall;
What if 'twere come that she a Cleopatra
                    Could not pall.

Hills, shake not off one torrent, nor grow pale thou,
                    Golden Sun!
The music of the world thou light'st up hath not
                    Yet begun.
Get ready women! fitly have ye not yet
                    Once been won.

Nor shake thou mockingly thy darts, oh Death!
                    Know, oh King!
We have made friends with Melancholy and she
                    Thee will bring
Gently among us, yea to teach new music
                    Them that sing.

There is a heaven, though we to hope to pass there
                    May not dare;
Where adoration shall for ever adore some
                    Perfect fair;
And we can wait thee, Death, our eyes enfixed
                    Firmly there.

1859

The Sheep Stealer's Defense

*At the Kildare Quarter Sessions, Robert Johnson and
Martin Murphy, were found guilty of sheep stealing, and
sentenced to seven years transportation. Asked before sen-
tence, what they had to say for themselves, Johnson who
had been discharged during the late reduction of the army,
read a poem of which the following are the first and last
verses. – Northern Star, July 29, 1849.*

I served my Queen and country well
   For seventeen years and over;
I fought where comrades round me fell
    Like leaves in brown October;
I fought, where in his ghastliest guise,
   Grim death around did hover;
Yet I was turned adrift to die,
    A poor disbanded soldier.

For thraldom in some penal clime
   I'll freedom gladly barter;
I'd sooner bear the brand of crime
    Than die starvation's martyr!
Proceed – for seventeen long, long years
   My theme was British glory;
Proceed – this heart's unblanched by fear,
    A soldier stands before ye.

1849

JAMES CLARENCE MANGAN
1803–1849

For Soul and Country

I

Arise! my slumbering soul, arise!
    And learn what yet remains for thee
        To dree or do!
The signs are flaming in the skies;
    A struggling world would yet be free,
        And live anew.
The earthquake hath not yet been born
    That soon shall rock the lands around
        Beneath their base,
Immortal Freedom's thunder-horn
    As yet yields but a doleful sound
        To Europe's race.

II

Look round, my soul, and see and say
    If those about thee understand
        Their mission here, –
The will to smite – the power to slay –
    Abound in every heart, – and hand
        Afar, anear.
But God! must yet the conqueror's sword
    Pierce *Mind,* as heart, in this proud year?
        O, dream it not!
It sounds a false blaspheming word
    Begot and born of moral fear –
        And ill-begot!

III

We still have power with naked hands
The Vergniauds and the Dantons died,
But not in vain.
Their lot was cast 'mid burning sands –
Our own is thrown in pasture wide,
And gardened plain.
They looked for waters where none ran;
They sought for palaced piles and towers
In barren air.
We, taught by them of Soul and Man,
Know well that all save Truth's own powers
Lead to despair!

IV

To leave the world a Name is nought –
To leave a name for glorious deeds
And works of love,
A name to waken lightening thought,
And fire the soul of him who reads,
This tells above!
Napoleon sinks to-day before
The ungilded shrine, the single soul
Of Washington:
Truth's name alone shall man adore!
Long as the waves of Time shall roll
Henceforward on!

1848

Curtain the Lamp

Curtain the lamp, and bury the bowl,
    The ban is on drinking;
Reason shall reign the queen of the soul
    When the spirits are sinking.
Chained lies the demon that smote with blight
    Men's morals and laurels,
Then hail to health, and a long good night
    To old wine, and new quarrels!

Nights shall descend, and no taverns ring
    To the roar of our revels;
Mornings shall dawn but none of them bring
    White lips and blue devils.
Riot and frenzy sleep with remorse
    In the obsolete potion,
And mind grows calm as a ship on her course
    O'er the level of ocean.

So should it be! for man's world of romance
    Is fast disappearing,
And shadows of CHANGES are seen in advance,
    Whose epochs are nearing.
And the days are at hand, when the best shall require
    All means of salvation.
And the souls of men shall be tried in the fire
    Of the final probation!

And the witling no longer or sneers or smiles,
    And the worldling dissembles,
And the black-hearted sceptic feels anxious at whiles,
    And marvels and trembles;
And fear and defiance are blent with the jest
    Of the blind self-deceiver;
But hope bounds high in the joyous breast
    Of the childlike believer!

Darken the lamp, and shatter the bowl,
    Ye faithfullest-hearted!
And as your swift years travel on to the goal
    Whither worlds have departed,
Spend labour, life, soul, in your zeal to atone
    For the past and its errors:
So best shall you bear to encounter alone
    The Event! and its terrors.

184–

The Red Flag

Air: *Dark loch na gar*

'Tis in the Red Flag true Republicans glory;
　　Red is the emblem of Justice and Right –
By martyrs' blood dyed, whose names live in story;
　　The victors, though fallen, in Liberty's fight.
Fast flow our tears for the fetter'd and slaughter'd;
　　And exiles who wander o'er valley and crag.
Too long has the earth by tyrants been tortured;
　　They shall crouch yet, and cower, before our Red Flag!

Away to the winds with the cant "moderation!"
　　Mercy is not with king, tiger, or snake.
Crush to the dust as they've crush'd each nation
　　In the day of our triumph, kings tremble and quake.
"Mercy!" yes, *Mercy* such as *they* gave us
　　Such we'll return, and throneless we'll drag
From their high places those who enslave us,
　　To bow – mean and abject – before our Red Flag!

"Mercy!" whilst Haynau riots in murder,
　　And tiger-like, gloats o'er the blood of mankind;
While the serfs of the Czar poor Poland engirder –
　　The betrayers of France Rome's chains again bind –
Sicily crush'd 'neath the Bourbon lies bleeding –
　　And Hungary curses the Austrian rag,
The nations oppress'd pray the time may be speeding
　　When in triumph and glory shall fly our Red Flag!

That glad time shall come, kings; though patriots you
                                       slaughter,
   Fresh legions shall rise for the martyrs who fall.
Through tempests and sunshine the nations have fought for
   Fair Freedom, benignant, who yet shall bless all;
Then we'll remember wrongs despots have wrought us.
   Of their "Right divine" power no more shall they
                                      brag.
"Moderation" is madness, (experience hath taught us,)
   When at Freedom's next summons we hoist the
                               Red Flag!

1850

WILLIAM JONES
c. 1820–

The March Wind

Hark! hark! 'tis abroad, and no fetters can bind,
Nor tyrant controul it – the mighty March Wind –
It calls the pale worker from factory and frame –
I even imagine it calleth his name!
In a voice deep as thunder, it seems thus to speak –
"Come forth to old Charnwood! come forth to the Peak!
See the tall Clifton Grove, how it bends to the blast!
How around and above the huge shadows sweep past!"
Away! there is vigour and joy for the mind –
There is freshness and health in the mighty March Wind!

How many drear months, since the flow'rs ceas'd to bloom,
Have ye breathed latent death in th' o'ercrowded
workroom.
How oft, when without the thick fogs have hung low,
Have ye sighed for sweet spring and the wild winds to
blow.

Well, the wild winds are blowing and spring now is nigh;
And spots of gold sunshine in low valleys lie;
Haste forth, then, and see; the fresh gale and warm sun –
Call the poor winders, too, and let them have a run,
For there's death in the *wheel,* – but there's life to the
mind –
Nay, there's rapture and bliss in the mighty March Wind!

If it loosen the roots of the sturdy old tree, –
Why, the sap to the top branch will rise the more free.
If the bough that is rotten be dashed to the ground,
'Twill afford the growth-room to those that are sound.
If it thin the old forests, and trouble the seas,
'Twill awake stalwart courage and scatter disease.
Like a true Briton's friendship, though rough, 'tis sincere,
Shouting, "Yonder goes winter, boys, be of good cheer!"
Oh! boundless as genius, as thought unconfined, –
It is grand to enjoy it – the mighty March Wind!

Ye linger. Is tryanny's hest in the way?
Or your limbs are they nerveless the will to obey?
Fear nothing; – when dangers our pathway bespread
Then the sap of true energy tends to the head!
With a crust in your scrip, and a staff in your hand,
And resolve in your hearts, ye the hills rainbow-spanned
May ascend – nay, methinks, I now hear your blithe cheer, –
"Hurrah for blest Freedom! 'tis good to be here!"
"Hurrah!" replies echo, and startles the hind, –
And your voice mounts to heav'n on the mighty March
                                        Wind!

Away, then, nor quail at the sharp-driving sleet;
Away to the wild scenes with firm-planted feet;
There mark how the mountain groves bow the tall head –
For the gale is still rude, though the shadows are fled.
And the shadows of mind too, like clouds disappear;
And the broad disc of knowledge begins to shine clear;
And the Voice of the People loud shakes every shore,
Like the crash of the elements, – hark to its roar!
And their pow'r shall increase till they go forth combined,
Resistless and free as the mighty March Wind!

1850

217

The Peasant's Epitaph

Hard by lieth Timothy Clow;
    Confirmed was his fontal vow!
Always to his "pastors", and eke to his "masters",
    Through life he made, "duly", his bow.

At ten, with plough and with wain,
    He worked on the shelterless plain,
'Mid rain and sleet, till his hands and feet
    Were covered with boil and blain!

At twenty, Love's pleasing smart
    Throbbed keen through his simple heart;
So he married – and, then, went whistling again
    O'er the hill, with his humdrum cart.

At thirty, when sorely rack'd
    With rheum, and his children lack'd
Both raiment and food, his "pastor" so good,
    For charity, gave him – a tract.

At forty, – lo! dull decay
    Came on, and his looks grew grey;
So his "master", at length, in whose service his strength
    He had wasted – turned him away!

At fifty, when sorrow gave
    To Death the poor worn-out slave,
For his worth they allowed him – a Bastile shroud!
    For his bones – a parish grave!

1850

The Southwark Brewers
and the Austrian Butcher

Jolly boys who brew porter for Barclay and Perkins,
The prime London stout of our cans and our firkins
Here's a health, English hearts, whate'er may betide,
For the dose you gave Haynau along the Bankside.

> Derry down, derry down, &c.

The deeds of this butcher we all have heard tell,
How died Bathyani, how Leiningen fell;
Gallant Aulich he hanged like a felon and slave,
Tho' he prayed like a soldier to go to his grave.

> Derry down, derry down, &c.

O the cord for the neck and the lash for the back
When Haynau commanded, they never were slack;
The women he scourged till the red blood ran down,
This chief of the Armies of Austria's Crown.

> Derry down, derry down, &c.

Ye lasses of Southwark a health unto you,
Who aided to give Marshall Haynau his due,
The wretch who flogged women deserves well to meet
Rough welcome like yours in each fair London street.

> Derry down, derry down, &c.

Turn him out, turn him out from our side of the Thames,
Let him go to great Tories and high-titled dames;
He may walk the west-end, and parade in his pride,
But he'll not come again near the "George" in Bankside.

                   Derry down, derry down, &c.

1850

The Capitalist

On the glittering piles of wealth he gazed
      (His heavy coffers hold;)
Till his giddy brain with gold was daz'd,
      His heart was changed to gold.
Soon all human feelings sickening died
      Crush'd by that passion's power;
As the life-parch'd flow'rs of the morning fade
      Scorch'd by noon's blazing hour.
And the blood that coursed through his portly frame
      Forgot its crimson dye –
To the glowing gold pour'd through every vein
      It owed vitality.

He dwells in a mansion whose splendour mocks
      Noble or regal state;
Like a bloated spider their life he sucks
      Whose toils his wealth create.
He throws round his victims the iron net,
      Which want has wove for him,
And he joys to see on their pale cheeks set
      The seal of hunger grim.
He has search'd out what never was known
      To Alchemysts of old –
He taketh his brothers' sinew and bone
      And melts to yellow gold!

The dawn looks forth where his plundered serfs
      Their weary labours ply;

While the latest star which the midnight gives,
    Quits, ere they cease, the sky.
See the bloodshot eye and the haggard form
    The idotic stare,
And consumption's slow insidious worm,
    Are brands his servants bear.
Stern manhood, o'erpowered his sturdy strength,
    Bows to the deadly strife;
And the throbbing brow of opening youth
    With cares of eld is rife.

A hale old age, save in ancient song
    To workers is unknown –
(But a sleepless angel each blighting wrong
    In God's day-book writes down!)
Bravely, O bravely, the golden flood,
    The rich man quaffs the while;
And little he recks if his brother's blood
    Its lustre somewhat soil;
Honours and titles await his call
    With aught earth's confines hold,
For the nations (like they of Dathan) all
    Adore the calf of gold.

O fell is the noble's insane misrule,
    When trampled nations obey;
And blackest of all the plagues of hell
    Is the priest's unbounded sway;
But this goodly earth is more deeply curs'd
    By mammon's blacker slaves,
Who answer the anguished cry for bread
    By digging pauper graves.
O quail ye not lest that skeleton host
    May turn and their tyrants slay?
For the hunter feareth that hour the most
    When the hunted stand at bay.

Say paled not your cheek when that dying howl
    Of hunger past your doors,
Lest your children's clutch of your hoarded spoil
    Should prove less firm than yours?
For the time draws nigh when the reck'ning due
    With brigands shall be made
And the long arrears and interest too,
    In full shall be repaid!
And O when that day of maddening strife, –
    Of long-pent justice comes,
When the people's watchword is – "life for life"
    God help the guilty ones.

1850

Lady, Spare a Jewel

Lady, spare a jewel! Want is knocking at thy door!
The chilly Frost creeps crisping down the hoary
                        blowing-space;
Little babes are shivering through this aching winter-time.
Oh Lady! spare a jewel, but one jewel for the poor,
To hush the whining hounds of Famine, Death and Crime,
And light with heavenly ray Humanity's sad face.

What! not one jewel, Lady, this aching winter-time,
While chilling Frost creeps crisping down the hoary
                        blowing-space,
To blast the three estates of Famine, Death and Crime,
And light with heavenly ray the faces of the poor?
Spare thy jewels, haughty Lady! Death is knocking at
                        thy door;
And thou canst not close it now on his grim and
                        ghastly face.

1856

A Man of Feeling

O much he talked and much he wrote
    Fine words of feeling, nicely blent,
With tender touches, sweet to quote,
    And little thrills of sentiment.

O fine and sympathetic toes
    That turned aside to spare the worm,
Kind heart that disregarded woes
    Which merely took a human form.

Except when far Tahiti's sons
    Could draw his bounty o'er the main,
And leave those hungry wretched ones
    To perish in a neighbouring lane –

O noble soul! surpassing all
    In depths of pity, breadth of sense,
How often has the crowded hall
    Re-echoed to thine eloquence.

And men bepraised the liberal hand,
    And men extolled the mighty views,
And spread the name throughout the land
    That figured in the morning news.

Then reverence the good man's grave,
    And let your grief be like his own,
And give him all *he* ever gave
    That soft and tender thing – a stone!

185–

The Foundry Boy

Mighty furnaces are flaring like a demon's breath of fire,
Forges like great burning cities break in many a crimson
spire;
Tongues of eager flame are lapping all the glory of the
heaven,
While a blush of burning hectic o'er the midnight's face is
driven.
Peals the thunder throat of Labour, hark! the deaf'ning
anvils clash,
Like a thousand angry sabres in the battle's headlong dash.
Hear the thoroughfares of tumult like the midnight Ocean's
roar
As in agony he clutches at the black heart of the shore;
Toiling there the poor Boy-Poet grimes within a dismal
den,
Piles the fire and wields the hammer, jostled on by savage
men.
Burns his life to mournful ashes, on a thankless hearth of
gloom,
For a paltry pittance digging life from out an early tomb:
And the soul is dwarfed within him that was cast in Titan
mould,
And the wealth of Heaven he loses for the lack of human
gold,
And he cannot see the stars arise in splendid sheen of
light —
Like angel watchfires gleaming in the cloudy cliffs of
night!

From *The Wanderer of the West*

The Lords of Labour

They come! They come in a glorious march!
    You can hear their steam steeds neigh,
As they dash through Skill's triumphal arch,
    Or plunge 'mid the dancing spray.
Their bale-fires blaze in the mighty forge,
    Their life-pulse throbs in the mill,
Their lightnings shiver the gaping gorge,
    And their thunders shake the hill.
Ho! these are the Titans of toil and trade,
    The heroes who wield no sabre;
But mightier conquests reapeth the blade
    That is borne by the Lords of Labour.

Brave hearts, like jewels, light the sod,
    Through the mist of commerce shine,
And souls flash out, like stars of God,
    From the midnight of the mine.
No palace is theirs, no castle great,
    No princely, pillared hall;
But they well can laugh at the roofs of state,
    'Neath the heaven which is over all.
Ho! these are the Titans of toil and trade,
    The heroes who wield no sabre;
But mightier conquests reapeth the blade
    That is borne by the Lords of Labour.

Each bares his arm for the ringing strife
    That marshals the sons of the soil;
And the sweat-drops shed in their battle of life
    Are gems in the crown of toil.
And prouder their well-won wreaths, I trow,
    Than laurels with life-blood wet;

And nobler the arch of a bare, bold brow
  Than the clasp of a coronet.
Then hurrah for each hero, although his deed
    Be unblown by the trump or tabor!
For holier, happier far is the meed
  That crowneth the Lords of Labour.

GEORGE GODWYN BARMBY
1820–1881

The Poetry of Spring

XII

Moult with the birds, ye red-cloaked warriors! Change
Your blood-stained raiment, and o'er ploughed fields range,
And man no more from brother man estrange.

Ye souls, so covetous of corn and herds,
Whose jaundiced eyes would turn life's cream to curds
Doff miser robes, and moult ye with the birds.

Moult with the birds, ye lawyers with long curls!
Leave to the moth your chancery twists and twirls;
Off gown and wig! No swine require your pearls.

Ye minds all ignorant and dark and drear,
As owlets' eyes at sunrise, blank and blear;
Moult with day's birds, and let the light appear.

Moult with the birds, ye black-robed priests! and wear
Saints' robes of radiance, and the truth declare
That bids us hope in god and not despair.

Ye tongues, so blistered with deceiving words!
Ye slaves, whip-goaded with dumb, driven herds!
There's spring for all; then moult ye with the birds.

Off feathers frayed and faded, coarse and blurred;
On glossy plumes, and let sweet songs be heard!
Through pain comes pleasure, and so moults the bird.

Ploughman, afield! the dewy morn is fair,
Yet still thy breath is wreathed upon the air;
Harness the team, and fix the shining share.

Now guide the coulter, and with even sight
Force deep the share, and cut the furrow straight,
And turn each black ridge side-ways to the right!

So he who drives the white Parnassian teams
Pages of rag with glorious work redeems, –
Each placed aside, till filled the radiant reams.

Alike as labourers do the Fates regard,
Peasant and ploughman, patriot and bard –
The painter's small palm and the hind's hand hard.

Ye men of tillage, and ye men who write;
For each one common cause – one duty bright;
Two close-clasped hands, whose union is might.

Producers both, your different spheres ye find,
So till the soil, to cultivate the mind,
Direct the heart and train the strong and kind.

Patient the rook pursues the upturning share –
The red worm gaining for his thrifty care;
So speed the plough, that all may have and spare.

Hands to the plough! whoever turneth back
Is not fit workman! By that cloudy rack
Let man work on – Heavens are not slack!

Plough down the hill that's stained with human blood,
Plough the wide plains of human brotherhood;
Plough freedom's fields – the rich glebes of the good.

Plough o'er the palaces of tyrant pride,
And o'er false temples let the bright share glide;
As o'er doomed cities old, spread ruin wide.

To fit the field to take the wondrous seed,
To move the brain its thronging thoughts to breed;
Such ploughman's labor and such patriot's deed.

How wide the uncultured acres spread and lo!
How vast the ignorance, the want, the woe;
So speed the plough – there's mighty work to do.

1860

The Hulks

The Hulks are old vessels kept for the convenience of
imprisoning disobedient sailors, who presume to have
a conscience opposed to the destruction of foreigners who
have no wish on their part to interfere with the private
affairs of other countries. But a warrior should never think,
and if he keeps a conscience he must soon learn to surrender
it to the call of duty (which means the doing acts contrary
to his inclinations, and which may therefore be defined as
unnatural morality), or he will soon feel the reason why.

Great Britain, proud as mistress of the seas,
And proud of her extensive colonies,
Has, like the hen, to scratch that she may keep
Possession of her spoil and profits reap,
From trade that must eventually flow
To England's mart: then why not let them go
That give much trouble – with so little gain?
Because we're proud, and prestige must maintain;

The youth now leaves his home, his work, his friends;
All social happiness on earth he ends,
And learns assassination as a trade,
Which does his Christian feeling deep degrade.
Conscience at last will claim the power to speak,
And now for conscience brave, for duty weak,
In calm refusal to engender strife,
He earns with conscience clear the hulks for life.

Awake – free trade! and teach us better things;
Show earth is for the people, not for kings;
Show man should send his produce to exchange,
Not armies over other lands to range,
And claim possession through success in war.
Free trade! we ask that you at once restore
The Nation's sense of justice, and disperse
Kings, Priests, and Warriors, every nation's curse.

c. 1870   From *Poetry of the Pavement*

Human Progress

To man, the naked, impotent, were given
Courage and skill – the two best gifts of heaven;
With bolder front he then began to roam,
Dislodged the wild beast, and possessed his home.
Struck by his club, the gnashing panther died,
And clothed the victor with his princely hide;
The lion, growling o'er his fleecy prey,
Awed by his burning eye-ball, slunk away;
Caught in his flying noose, the affrighted horse
Resigned to him his swiftness and his force.
At length the furnace roared and raged and glowed,
Till from its fires the spade and ploughshare flowed.
Then melancholy wastes, by labour tilled,
Put forth the rose and, robed in beauty, smiled.

On the sea shore his straining eyes surveyed
Far distant lands in brighter hues arrayed,
He dares the dangerous and the doubtful path,
Launches the bark, and mocks the ocean's wrath.
Nursed for the battle – born to be supreme
He wars with all things – all things war with him.

At last the sage, with holy triumph fraught,
Grasps in his hand imperishable thought;
Eternal voices whispered from the grave,
And age to age its treasured wisdom gave.
Victorious man, with unabated breath,
Lives thro' all time to scoff at baffled Death.

233

Fraught with the wisdom of unnumbered years,
See what a halo round his brow appears;
On proud dominions' airy heigth he stands,
Holding the reins of Nature in his hands.
He bids the breezes toil, the ocean waves
His burdens bear like meek and conquered slaves;
Sublime inventions teach his soul to slight
The eagle's swiftness and the lion's might.

Woes, wants, and ills, since earth's primeval hour,
Have but matured intelligence and power;
Man from each bitter wrings some priceless sweet –
From suffering patience, wisdom from defeat,
From wants ingenious thought, from effort force,
Greatness from sorrow, glory from the curse.

Each flower of joy, that time and being cheers,
Was won from thorns, and nursed with sweat and tears;
Laws, arts, religion – all things great and good
Were born in anguish and baptised in blood.
Strengthened with strife, and dignified with woes,
Man to the stature of the angel grows.

My Gronfathur's Grave

Nut a puff stirred a leaf o' them grand owd trees,
     'At owershaddad the grahnd ov ahr village church,
As I gloared wi' full een on a gerse-grown heap,
     Under t'shade of a knotted an' time-worn birch.

T'owd tree, like a priest in his hoaly robes,
     Stude solemn an' grey anent t'western dlow,
An' liftin' its arms into t'silent air,
     Seemed to pray for t'poar fellah 'at slept below.

Tlois at hand a fine marble wor placed aboon t'squire,
  Thau he stale fro' his tenants ther hard-won breead,
For it's tyrants, 'at grunds us wi' pahr an' brass,
  'At we honour an' worship alive ur deead.

Bud ye'll fynd nauther tablet, nur name, nur date,
  Ovver t'spot wheer my gronfathur sleeps i' t'dark,
For this world tak's na gaum ov a sweatin' slave
  'At can nobbud due useful an' honist wark.

Nut a letter he knew ov his a b c's,
  Nut a pothuke his fingurs could frame to mak'
So they made ov a brother a harnessed beast,
  An' a beast's heavy burden oppressed his back.

Fro' five ov a mornin' to nine at neet
  He slaved for a livin' for forty year,
An' all t'plessure 'at sweetened that bitter life
  Wor a Sunday stretch an' a pint o' beer.

Then they tuke him away fro' his flail an' plew,
  An' they streytened him intuv a sowjer lad,
For his reulers, althau they could read an' write,
  Hed been lakin' a lifetime at "Hell run mad".

An' if ivver, when trodden reyt dahn i' t'muck,
  His heart in a whisper hed said, "Rebel",
His tyrants hed cheyns for body an' sowl –
  I' this life a dungeon, i' t'next a hell.

Hay, dear! hah we suffered thru pride an' greed,
  When t'country wor governed by nowblemen;
Them lords 'at says t'poar isn't fit to reul,
  Sud lewk ovver t'webs they've wovven thersen.

Poor grondad, I wish tha wor here to see
        Hah bravely we've battled wi' pahr an' brass,
Fur t'day draws near when a king munnot craw
        Ovver t'ignarant, impidant workin' class.

When I think o' t'long ahrs an' o' t'slavish wark
        'At browt tha so sooin tuv a naamless tomb,
My courage revives, an' my arm an' neiv
        Gets strung up an' doubled for t'feyt to come.

Africa

Throned on an elephant a woman towers.
Dark as the night is she; her flaming eyes
Rebuke the slow pace of the languid hours,
And give new ardours to the blazing skies.
Bare to the waist is she; her glowing breast
Is passion's hunger, passion's wild unrest.
One hand a scorpion holds, the cruel sign,
The symbol fierce of every power malign;
A horn of plenty fills her other hand,
And pours its treasures on the mighty land.
The scorpion crush, O Africa, and then
Fruits from a second horn shall gladden men.
The scorpion is thy children's slavery,
The second bounteous horn is liberty.

1870–80

Three Songs of the National Agricultural Labourers' Union (founded 1872)

THE WELLESBOURNE TREE

Tune: *Auld Lang Syne*

When Arch beneath the Wellesbourne tree
His glorious work began,
A thrill of hope and energy
Through all the country ran;
But farmer, parson, lord and squire
Looked on with evil eyes,
Some looked with scorn and some with ire
And some in dumb surprise.

> *Chorus*
> The rich and great our cause may hate,
> We care not for their frown;
> The strongest are not strong enough
> To keep the labourer down.

They thought they'd kept us down so low,
Our manhood was crushed out,
So ignorant we should not know
The task we were about;
But now no longer they despise
The men who strive with wrong,
Whom they thought fools they find are wise,
Whom they thought weak are strong.

The squire and parson, for our sin,
Give no more soup or coals,
And poor old folks with Union* kin
Are stopped their parish doles.
Their Poor Law traps they slyly lay,
When threats and lock-outs fail,
And on the wife force parish pay
To thrust the men in jail.

Whene'er it can, the rich man's press
Ignores the wrongs we bear,
To us the law gives no redress,
The parliament no ear;
Sir Michael** hold your railing tongue,
Our lives give you the lie,
But from you all shall yet be wrung
The justice you deny.

  * Workhouse.
** Sir Michael Hicks Beach, afterwards Lord St. Aldwyn.

WE DEMAND THE VOTE

Tune: *Stand Like the Brave*

Hark, hark to the call boys,
Sounding loud, long and shrill,
And voices re-echo
O'er ocean and hill;
    We have now a great army, both loyal and brave,
    We ask for the vote and the vote we will have.

We lift up our banner
In the cause that is right,
Determined to be valiant
In council or fight;
> We have now a great army, both loyal and brave,
> We ask for the vote and the vote we will have.

With Arch our commander
The strife is begun,
We have fought sharp engagements
And victories have won;
> We have now a great army, both loyal and brave,
> We ask for the vote and the vote we will have.

From the mines and the mills,
From the forest and field,
We march in bold order,
Resolved not to yield;
> We have now a great army, both loyal and brave,
> We ask for the vote and the vote we will have.

With strong bone and sinew
And true British heart,
Stand firm by your flag boys,
And play the man's part.
> We have now a great army, both loyal and brave,
> We ask for the vote and the vote we will have.

March on thus brave comrades,
In the cause that is right,
Show wisdom in council,
Show valour in fight.
> We have won many battles, be valiant and brave,
> Stand firm for the vote and the vote we will have.

WE'LL ALL BE UNION MEN

Tune: *A Day's March Nearer Home*

Ye tillers of the soil,
Assert your manhood then,
You get your living by hard toil,
Then all be Union men.

> *Chorus*
> Joe Arch he raised his voice,
> 'Twas for the working men,
> Then let us all rejoice and say,
> We'll all be Union men.

We've been oppressed we know,
By money-making elves,
But Arch and Co. have taught us how
To rise and help ourselves.

Now since we've learnt the plan,
That Arch and Co. have taught,
The Union for the working men,
We'll never give it up.

No never give it up,
Not when the victory's won,
For what we get by Union,
Protect it just the same.

There is a simple rule,
A very short one too,
It's do to others as you would
Have others do to you.

DAVID WINGATE
1828–1892

The Collier's Ragged Wean

He's up at early morning, howe'er the win' may blaw,
Lang before the sun comes roun' to chase the stars awa'
And 'mang a thoosan' dangers, unkent in sweet daylight,
He'll toil until the stars again keek through the chilly night.
See the puir wee callan' 'neath the cauld clear moon!
His knees oot through his troosers, and his taes oot through
his shoon;
Wading through the freezing snaw, and thinking ower
again
How happy every wean maun be that's no a collier's wean.

His cheeks are blae wi' cauld, and the chittering winna cease,
To gi'e the hungry callan' time to eat his morning piece;
His lamp is burning on his heid wi' feeble, flickering ray,
And in his heart the lamp of Hope is burning feebly tae.
Nae wonner that the callan's sweert to face his daily toil,
Nae wonner he sae seldom greets the morning wi' a smile,
For weel he kens he's growing up to face the cauld disdain
That lang the world has measured oot to every collier's
wean.

The puir wee hirpling laddie! how mournfully he's gaun,
Aye dichting aff the ither tear wi's wee, hard, hackit
haun'!
Sair, sair he's temptit 'mang the snaw to toom his flask
o' oil,
But, ah! ae flash o' faither's ire were waur than weeks o'
toil.

242

In vain the stars look on the youth wi' merry twinkling
                                                                    een,
Through clouds o' care sae dense as his their glory is nae
                                                                    seen;
He thinks 'twad be a better plan if coal had 'boonmost
                                                                    lain,
And wonners why his faither made a collier o' his wean.

Oh! ye that row in Fortune's lap, his waefu' story hear,
Aft sorrows no sae deep as his ha'e won a pitying tear,
And lichter wrangs than he endures your sympathy ha'e
                                                                    won —
Although he is a collier's, mind he is a Briton's son.
And ye wha mak' and mend oor laws, tak' pity on the
                                                                    bairn;
Oh! bring him sooner frae the pit; and gi'e him time to
                                                                    learn;
Sae shall ye lift him frae the mire 'mang which he lang
                                                                    has lain,
And win a blessing frae the heart o' every collier wean.

186–

243

Grase the Fat Sow

I'se a poor hignorammus an' knaws leetle or nuffin'
Thanks to squire an' parson, ther church an' ther skule;
No wonder, me thinks, that sum calls I a ruf'un,
An' the folk up in Lunnon a pig an' a fule.
Still, I roikes about wen I goes out a-cartin'
An' I turns up a thort as I follows ma plow,
An' I says to myself wi' a look that means "sartin",
Tha rich be determind ta grase the fat sow.
Grase the fat sow, Grase the fat sow,
    Tha rich be determind to Grase the fat Sow.

I'm danged if I dwon't tak' ta pothooks an' hangers,
An' rite ta tha peepers tha leetle I knaws,
I'll tell bit o' truth 'bout oursels an' our gangers,
An' games as be played by tha hawks an' tha crows.
They gie I ten shillin's a week ta keep six wi'
For seventy-two hours at steeables an' plow;
An' not a bit more ta tha peeple I mix wi',
An' keeps all tha rest ta grase the fat sow.
Grase the fat sow, Grase the fat sow,
    An' keeps all tha rest ta Grase the fat Sow.

Thay telled I 'twere wicked ta sing an' ta whistle,
An' danged if I chirruped for meny a year,
Fur I felt loike a jackass content wi' a thistle,
An' trembled all over wen measter wor near.

Thay tell'd I ta pray, an' I prayed loike a good 'un,
I prayed for a fortin, some sheep an' a cow,
But while I were prayin' they stole all our common,
Bekase it were wanted to grase the fat sow,
Grase the fat sow, Grase the fat sow,
    Bekase it were wanted ta Grase the fat Sow.

Tha squire has jest bin an' taken ma gardin,
An' sent a por chap off ta jail fur a hare;
So I tell ee the loife as we lade is a hard 'un,
An' danged if I think we shall change 'un by prayer.
I'se fund out tha humbug o' parson's religun,
Fur I turns it all over wile driving ma plow;
It prepares a por fule ta be plucked loike a pigeon,
An' helps tha rich squire ta grase the fat sow.
Grase the fat sow, Grase the fat sow,
    An' helps the rich parson ta Grase the fat Sow.

Thare be good texts in Scripture, but parson dwon't heed
                                                    'em,
Thare be sum that por people cud well understand,
An' tha' time's cumin fast wen we por folk'll rade 'um
An' prach 'um a sarmint on labour an' land.
An' thay're prayin' an' prachin's dun leetle or nuffin'
Ta raise such as I from this terribul slough;
I'se fund out thay're sarmints be only goose stuffin',
Or else it be summat ta grase the fat sow,
Grase the fat sow, Grase the fat sow,
    Or else it be summat ta Grase the fat Sow.

1872

JOHN BEDFORD LENO
1820–1895

Song

Judge not a man by the cost of his clothing,
    Unheeding the life-path that he may pursue;
Or oft you'll admire a heart that needs loathing,
    And fail to give honour where honour is due.
The palm may be hard and the fingers stiff-jointed,
    The coat may be tattered, the cheek worn with tears,
But greater than kings are Labour's anointed,
    And you can't judge a man by the coat that he wears.

Give me the man as a friend and a neighbour
    Who toils at the loom – with the spade or the plough,
Who wins his diploma of manhood by labour,
    And purchases wealth by the sweat of his brow.
Why should the broadcloth alone be respected,
    And the man be despised who in fustian appears?
While the angels in heaven have their limbs unprotected,
    You can't judge a man by the coat that he wears.

Judge of a man by the work he is doing,
    Speak of a man as his actions demand;
Watch well the path that each is pursuing,
    And let the most worthy be chief of the land!
And the man shall be found 'mid the close ranks of labour,
    Be known by the work that his industry rears,
And the chiefdom when won shall be dear to his neigh-
                                                    bour,
    And we'll honour the man whatever he wears.

Labour

My theme is Labour, Famine's deadliest foe,
The proud man's scoff, the honest man's delight;
My aim to strike a fierce and deadly blow
At men whose gaze has stricken like a blight,
And left the land as though a locust flight
Had covered all the earth. The time has come
When men who toil must rouse up in their might,
(Scorning to sink like beggars to their tomb,)
And take what they have earned, a comfortable home.

A cupboard lined with plenty of good cheer,
A larder filled with food from stall and sty,
A cellar stocked with honest home-brewed beer –
Meat for the hungry, liquor for the dry;
Good wholesome beds where honest men may lie
And rest their weary bones at close of day,
Till the bright sunbeams fill the morning sky.
Such homes await ye, poor men in dismay,
When ye have strength to drive your ancient foes away.

Show me the weak are treated like the strong,
That scales of Justice are for ever true,
That her administrators, 'voiding wrong,
From her just lines will never turn askew,
Nor sway her beams in favour of the few,
Then I'll recant, and joyfully proclaim
That 'tis a mirage I've been passing through;
Then will I go and wrap myself in shame
And tremble, as though cursed, when men pronounce
                                            my name.

I would that I could think as some have thought,
That Justice, only Justice, ruled the land;

That, like a flower never known to sport,
It held all vagaries in strict command;
That my conclusions have been built on sand,
To vanish like the fabric of a dream:
But, come what may, on this I take my stand –
That wealth in England has a power supreme,
And scales withouten gold will ever kick the beam.

What mockery to prate of Mother Earth
To men who daily walk abroad in fear:
The greatness of the land that gave them birth,
To those who plainly are not wanted here;
Of Nature's kindness to her children dear,
To those who never lose the sense of wrong,
And burthens bear from suffering year to year.
What mockery to feed men with a song,
When nought of joy or mirth to such poor souls belong.

Go! learn what laws they've passed in England's name,
To justify the dark deeds they have done;
How bishops trading in Religion's name,
Have called to witness, God, and Christ, his Son,
To doings prompted by the Evil One.
Go! tell the truth, unmindful of their rage,
Of men whose lust has turned their hearts to stone,
How banded thieves in every clime and age,
Have stripped the sons of toil of God's great heritage.

Go! seek in vain for acres that were free,
That no man living dared to call his own,
Free as the air we breathe, the bounding sea,
The gladd'ning rain, that bursting storms let down;
Go! search to find how prickly hedges, grown,
Shut in the rich, and barricade the poor;

Then to the world their cruel deeds make known,
How parks have grown from common, marsh, and moor,
And honest men are forced to seek the workhouse door.

I write to warn, and not to kindle wrath,
To further Justice in this land of ours,
To check the brambles growing in man's path,
And comfort it with incense-bearing flowers.
I've seen a storm descend in fruitful showers,
That looked as low'ring as the one now near,
I've seen it lose its devastating powers,
And pass away without a trait of fear,
Leaving the sky above from threat'ning dangers clear.

I've often stood and watched the shifting glass,
And tried to read the portents of the sky;
I've longed and longed to see the dark clouds pass
That dim the future, and, with tear and sigh,
I've conjured men to hesitate, and try
To deal with fairness to all human kind.
Alas! alas! they one by one passed by,
As though, like Justice' self, they all were blind,
And every word I spoke was but a breath of wind.

Why talk of conscience leading men aright,
As though the world was, like the gospel, pure;
As though 'twere free from enmity and spite,
And not gone rotten to its inmost core.
Give me the proof that rich men love the poor,
Or, conscience-stricken, turn aside from sin;
That men are better than in days of yore,
And feel the tie of universal kin;
That wrong, in peace or war, is never known to win.

Go! list to all the lecherous, treacherous cant,
From pulpits built on earthly heresies;
How heaven is credited with waste and want,
How God made drones to rob the working bees,
And laws to give them competence and ease.
Mark how religion, of its virtues shorn,
Becomes the pimp to man's iniquities;
How countless toilers, wearing crowns of thorn,
Are taught the truthless lesson "Man was made to mourn".

Who curses those with every want supplied,
The God-denounced, who trample on his laws,
The men who batten on their lust of pride,
Whose carnal promptings know nor break nor pause?
Why should they revel in the world's applause,
And dance to death that beggars reach in pain?
Tell me, ye canting hypocrites, the cause –
Why God has split the human race in twain
The one to sow, the other reap the hurricane!

Out of the way, ye tinselled sons of pride,
Whose every thought has been to swell your store;
To float, like rainbow-bubbles, on the tide,
Unmindful of the cries of England's poor.
The wrongs that fed your revelries of yore,
The robberies that made your merriment,
Are doomed to pass away, in peace or gore.
Those gathering tones of wakening discontent
Proclaim a people's wrath in anger may be spent.

Why preach of bounteous riches unto those
Whom misery follows wheresoe'r they go?
Of mines of wealth that splintered rocks disclose
To those who share not in their overflow?
Whose lives are one consistent round of woe!

These cannot feel the sense of gratitude,
Whatever riches Nature may bestow.
'Twixt life and death, the poor and needy brood
Know no surcease of pain – no cheering interlude.

All labour tends to truth. The shuttle flies,
The millwheel turns, the plow, the pick and spade,
With startling force lay open to the skies
The mysteries of earth and sea. By trade
The nations of the world are wiser made,
And commerce, with her flying pennant, brings
Forth new revealments, to the constant aid
Of truth and knowledge. Honest wealth that springs
From toil, stands first in heaven of all love's offerings.

To do a deed, is both to think and act.
A flash of thought that leads not to a blow
Must die, and, like a vessel wracked,
Lie hidden with its kindred down below.
Though on the surface other thoughts may plough,
That thought is dead, and will not rise again.
The storm may beat, the waves tempestuous flow,
And shake the world by one vast hurricane;
But thoughts that prompt no deed, are numbered with the
slain.

The man who toils not, robs the sick and maimed,
The lonesome widow, and the mental blind,
And he, who, doing this, is not ashamed,
Forfeits the love of all of human kind –
The love of him who tempers the rude wind
To the shorn lamb, within whose gospel's found
The spur to labour, "Seek, and ye shall find";
The parable that Sloth may well confound,
"The tree that bears no fruit encumbereth the ground."

The measure of the world lies in its growth –
Productive growth – not stretch of sea or land;
Within the riches that are held by both.
The fool alone will measure barren sand,
And seas that stubbornly resist the wand
That Labour wields to serve the common good.
The space is lost that lists to no command,
And will not bend to serve the multitude,
Who, starving, cry aloud, "Give us our daily food."

The world has grown, the world must ever grow,
Where Labour treads, it conquers soon or late;
There's many spots where golden harvests show,
And reapers armed with sharpened sickles wait,
That human kind were wont to execrate.
'Twas Toil that built the tanks and turned the stream,
And added acres to the world's estate:
The strength of Intellect and Toil supreme,
Combined, possess the pow'r to fashion, like a dream.

Brave workers of the world, God speed your race!
Your lives alone are truly worth their cost;
Our mother, Earth, reveres the faintest trace
Of all your footsteps; until these are lost,
Her memory will cling to ye as most
Exalted of her sons. Often in pain,
She prayed for ye, and cursed the greedy host,
Whose presence is an everlasting stain,
Born of the guilty hand that wrought the crime of Cain.

The flowers bloom wherever ye have trod,
The birds sing sweeter by the cultured groves,
The rain falls softer, and the living God
Counts ye among the children whom he loves.
His spirit's with ye; day and night, it moves
Over the footpath of your wandering;

Coincident to thine, as thine to his, it roves.
While hovering angels, ever on the wing,
Come laden with heaven's gifts, and earthly comforting.

If Heaven, in wrath, should sacrifice the world,
And leave one toiler but to mark his race,
The banneret of Toil would float, unfurled,
And in earth's ruins, he would quickly trace
How he might live and labour to efface
The marks of punished sin and God's displeasure,
And, from the debris, weave and interlace
Another world, of fully equal measure,
A fitter, better globe, to hold King Labour's treasure.

He would be fruitful as the fruitful seed
From which he sprang, and fail not to prove true
The gospel of his race, in word and deed;
The gospel that was writ for me and you.
What though its worth has failed to reach the few
Who laugh at Toil, and dare its deeds asperse?
Go! mark how wasted cities rose and grew,
How Toil, alone, can gather and disburse;
How dissipate the lie that Labour is a curse.

Ye who have fought fell Famine with success,
And driven back man's most invet'rate foe,
Shall win your guerdon, earthly happiness,
And conquer all ye fain would overthrow.
"The slave that would be free, must strike the blow,"
Is lisped no longer by the tongue of Fear,
The new-born boldness of the crowd shall grow,
Still gath'ring strength from rolling year to year,
Till, in the dark'ning distance, crime shall disappear.

1898   From *The Last Idler*

A Death Song

What cometh here from west to east awending?
And who are these, the marchers stern and slow?
We bear the message that the rich are sending
Aback to those who bade them wake and know.
Not one, not one, nor thousands must they slay,
But one and all if they would dusk the day.

We asked them for a life of toilsome earning,
They bade us bide their leisure for our bread;
We craved to speak to tell our woful learning:
We come back speechless, bearing back our dead.

They will not learn; they have no ears to harken.
They turn their faces from the eyes of fate;
Their gay-lit halls shut out the skies that darken.
But, lo! this dead man* knocking at the gate.

Here lies the sign that we shall break our prison;
Amidst the storm he won a prisoner's rest;
But in the cloudy dawn the sun arisen
Brings us our day of work to win the best.
Not one, not one, nor thousands must they slay,
But one and all if they would dusk the day.

* Alfred Linnel, killed at the Trafalgar Square demonstration
Nov. 26, 1887.

1887

Beware

Beware! for the clouds are gathering,
    And the rumbling noise that we hear
Is the murmur of suffering people,
    That tells us a storm is near.
Shall we dare to despise this warning,
    Pressed upon us again and again?
Beware of the sullen storm-clouds,
    On the brows of desperate men!

We may boast of our vast dominions;
    Of our national wealth and might;
But be sure that God and the People
    Will be found on the side of Right,
When the storm-clouds burst in the heavens,
    And the fiery bolts descend,
The proudest hearts will be shaken,
    And the reign of oppression end.

Why all this magnificent splendour
    Adorning the halls of the rich,
While the toilers who made them their fortunes
    Are pining away in the ditch?
Must the masses be beggared, in order
    To bolster up kingdom and thrones?
Are the bees to be forced into silence,
    While the honey is eaten by drones?

Who amongst us are found most deserving?
    The labourers delving the soil?

Or the inhuman, land-grabbing tyrants,
    Who fatten and feast on the spoil?
Are these to have British protection,
    Their halls and their lands made secure,
While bludgeons, and cowardly insults,
    Break the heads and the hearts of the poor!

Who gave these proud lordlings their mansions,
    The riches with which they are blest?
Who bribed them to use their great influence
    In crushing the weak and opprest?
Were these business transactions done fairly?
    Do they add to our honour and fame?
Ah, no; – but quite the contrary,
    To our lasting dishonour and shame!

Shall England still swagger and bluster?
    Is the world given up to our care?
If so, why not bottle the sunshine,
    And peddle it out with the air!
Look out, for the clouds are gathering!
    Yes, gathering on poor men's brows;
Beware of the pent-up feelings
    Which your heartless acts may arouse!

Feast on, ye proud Belshazzars!
    Let joy fill the banqueting hall;
But be sure of this – that God's finger
    Is writing upon the wall!
So on with the feast, but remember
    That while you are feeding your pride,
The storm-clouds are ready for bursting,
    And Lazarus is starving outside.

What is it we hear from Old Ireland?
    The children's innocent songs?

Oh, no! 'tis the down-trodden, groaning;
    Yes, groaning beneath their wrongs.
Her patriots and priests are in prison;
    Her sons and her daughters in tears;
And yet we have men so degraded
    As to mock them with jibes and jeers!

How long shall the conflict continue;
    This war between Wrong and Right!
And when shall the weak be successful
    In their struggle 'gainst Wealth and Might!
Take heed to the gathering storm-clouds,
    And the writing upon the wall;
For pride goes before destruction,
    And the haughty in spirit must fall!

A Ballad of Trafalgar Square

(With apologies to Macaulay)

Now gather round, my children,
   And I'll relate to you
A story of a wonderous fight,
With unarmed men, in broad daylight,
   And p'licemen dressed in blue.

In Eighteen Eighty-Seven
   To old Trafalgar Square,
A mighty host, with measured tread,
And flag advanced and banners spread,
Marched slowly, with a kind of dread,
   To hold a meeting there.

The P'lice stood calm and silent,
   But frowned upon their foes,
Till a great shout of "Graham"
   From all the vanguard rose.
And forth two men went rushing,
   From out that mighty crowd,
On, on they went, their heads were bent
(To dodge the blows they were intent)
   'Mid cheering long and loud.

But all O'Brien's champions
   Were frightened at the view
Of policemen reinforcing
   Around the hatless two.

And from that hapless scrimmage
>Where those two men had fought
All, turned, like men so faint of heart,
>Burning at first to take a part,
But when their heads with bruises smart,
Felt sorry that they'd made a start
>"Because they didn't ought."

Was none who would be foremost
>To lead such dire attack?
But those behind cried "Forward!"
>And those before cried "Back!"
So Warren and his minions,
>And Matthews and his gang,
Rejoiced to know they'd closed the Square
(And that the soldiers too were there)
Against all meetings, foul or fair,
>Where voices loudly rang.

But meanwhile law and logic
>Had vainly been applied
To show the right and custom
>Were on the people's side.
"Keep back, keep back the specials,"
>Loud cried the Liberals all,
"Back, Warren! Back, O Matthews!
>Back! or your party fall."
But onward marched the specials
>And on went Matthews too.
The Tories laughed, and joked, and chaffed,
>The Liberals looked blue.

At length the Tory party
>From Government resigned,
And Liberals took the places
>Of those they'd so maligned.

Then came the old, old question
            About Trafalgar Square.
The Socialists directly said
(And speedily the news was spread)
Our banners bright, all flaming red,
            Shall wave triumphant there.

But the M. R. Federation
            Had stealthily applied
For "leave" to hold a meeting,
            For five long years denied.
They formed a deputation
            Of well-known coming men
And mostly waiters, I should say
(They're nick-named Fabians to-day),
On Asquith, therefore, *waited* they,
            And "prayed" him there and then.

"Oh, Secretary Asquith,
            To whom we Liberals pray,
Our humble hearts our docile tongues,
            Take thou in charge this day."
So they spake, and speaking bowed
            Their heads in reverence low,
And with true humbleness of heart,
            Forthwith prepared to go.

No answer, good or evil,
            Was heard for many a day,
For Asquith stood, in dumb surprise,
With parted lips and straining eyes,
            And scarce knew what to say.

He knew that he'd defended
        Some men who had been tried,
But little thought that he, one day,
Would have to turn around and say
        What he had then denied.

"I give you leave to go there"
        (Lefevre winked assent)
And then with shouts of triumph
        The Home Office was rent.
"But mostly on a Sunday,
        And sometimes in the week,
We'll say on Saturday afternoon
(Bank Holiday a special boon),
And then you mustn't go too soon,
Nor stay to see the rising moon,
You mustn't laugh, or shout, or spoon,
        In fact — you mustn't speak."

1892

Robert Burns

Syne he sings the charms of Nature
    And the power that awes and thrills,
In the grandeur of the forest
    In the vastness of the hills;
And he sings of sterling friendship
    And its staunch assisting hand;
And he sings the patriot's passion
    For the welfare of his land.
Then his herp like a great river
    Deep in flood and vexed in strife,
Sadly wise with full experience
    Of our varied human life
Sings the weary facht and habble
    That we workin' bodies ha'e –
A' the strive and constant battle
    To get thro' and pey oor way;
For, ah! Rabbie sympathised wi'e
    Frae his muckle, manly heart –
Ca's wha like he wadna hear o't
    But took, aye the puir man's pairt,
Kent himsel' the tragic life o't
    That the feck o' puir folk dree,
Slavin' lang an' sair, and may be
    Dyin' destitute like me.
Syne his voice like organ-music
    Rises solemn, slow, sublime,

And 'Eternity' intoning
    Like a far-off funeral chime
Sings the deathless Hope exalted
    That illuminates our span,
That inborn, rock-fast assurance,
    Man is more than mortal man:
And his great eye glows with vision
    And foresees the certain day
When the Right shall wake to triumph
    And the Evil die away, –
When the implements of warfare
    To the scrap-heap shall be hurled
And the Bloody Beast of Battle
    Execrated oot the world, –
When the long dream of the faithful
    Rich reality shall be,
And the Commonwealth of Mankind
    Rules a planet of the free.

1898   From *Burns Centenary*
                in the Poorhouse

Diogenes the Swineherd

I

Eureka! my fellow-drudges
    Who grub this crabbed Earth,
I have wrung from reticent Nature
    The secret of my Birth:
This lout you fancy a swineherd –
    This louse on the rind of the ball,
Once dwelt a god where none else trod
    Save the Lord God of All.

263

II

I spoke an astral language,
    I sung a supernal song,
In a region beyond ether,
    With a beatific throng;
I willed that world's existence,
    I called to end that sphere,
Ere I fell from the height of my native might
    And was damned into being here.

III

As a semi-conscious sleeper
    Is powerless yet to break
The cumbering chain of slumber
    Which clings to him nigh awake,
I grope this swamp of existence,
    Whose vapours distort and screen,
And may not rise where my inmost eyes
    Might see what they erst have seen!

IV

But the starry vast of midnight,
    A glen dark, lonely, still,
The cry of Ocean's anguish,
    A far off azure hill,
A transient vista of sunset,
    Daybreak o'er a desert shore, . . .
These better betoken than language spoken
    That I lived heretofore.

V

In the silence after the snowfall,
    In the sigh of a parting leaf,
There's an antenatal rapture,
    There's an immemorial grief;

All Poetry – Art – Music
    Is memory's poor assay
To retrieve a glow from the Long Ago –
    A flash from the Far Away.

VI

There's a Star of the Empyrean –
    It wanes for lack of me;
Its people soulless – darkling –
    Its I their Christ shall be;
There's a constellation whirling
    To destinies undivine,
While I its god of salvation plod
    This plash here ... herding swine!

VII

In the Archives of the Ages
    Is the record of my crime
Which hurled me from those altitudes
    And banished me to Time –
The passion – the pride transcendent
    Of the arch-angelic race ...
Did I measure it all by the depths of my fall
    I was first and worst of the base.

VIII

Now I squat in a lousy mudhut,
    I doss at the cattle's feet;
I am slumped with the vile and the riff-raff,
    Have draff and brock for meat;
It's wonder this slaving muckworm
    Should doubt and bedamn his Birth,
And boose in the mire on the swipes of the byre ...
    A virtual spawn of the Earth?

IX

Men whine and tremble hearing
    The Pale White Horse's hoofs, –
With trashy drugs and nostrums
    Would charm his rider aloof;
My Liberator – I know you!
    My cell's but thinly barred –
Come, call me out with a cleaving shout
    When you visit this convict yard.

X

God! let me slough this nature –
    This howf – this hell of sin;
Let the royal Heir in exile
    His rightful kingdom win –
Let the bells of my restoration
    Clash out to the cosmic dome
That my footstep falls in my Father's halls
    And the Son of God's come home.

c. 1898

The Paris Commune 1871

How memory through the lapse of years recalls the
                                        cannon's rattle
    Brings back again the time so grandly dread;
When Paris rose in Labour's name and gave the foeman
                                        battle,
    And sealed her fate with hecatombs of dead.

Yes, memory loves to dwell upon the great defeat
                                        victorious
    Made holy by the life-blood of the brave,
The sacrifice triumphant, for the peerless cause, the glorious,
    The radiant resurrection from the grave.

The blood goes surging through the heart, we hear the
                                        loud defiance
    The cry "To arms!" ringing over France,
And Paris calls the working men of Europe to alliance
    And breaks the spell of twenty years of trance.

The chivalry are charging from the lowly homes of Labour,
    Hear the shock, the shout of conquest from the hill,
When the trained assassins meet their match and fly with
                                        shivered sabre
    From the heroes of the workroom and the mill.

The two proud months! How many times the enemy's
                                            lines were routed!
    'Midst thunder from the cannon came the May,
Yet Paris held the Red Flag high, and still defiance
                                            shouted,
    With the life-blood ebbing from her in the fray.

Fate's fearful shade grows blacker still, contracts the ring
                                            of fire,
    Though fearlessly is given blow for blow;
And Paris, Labour's Mecca shrine, becomes a blazing pyre,
    And nearer, ever nearer, comes the foe.

The line of battle broke at last; in every street and alley
    Unflinchingly are crossed the bayonet blades,
And every inch of ground is fought where Freedom still
                                            can rally
    A single man behind the barricades.

Not yet the time! The curtain falls, and, 'midst the lurid
                                            darkness,
    Death looks on Freedom's soldiers face to face;
And now, the time to try men's souls in all his ghastly
                                            starkness,
    They meet him with the daring of their race.

But who can tell the story of the strife so great, Titanic?
    Or who depict the glory of the fall?
That shook the globe and scattered wide the dragon's
                                            teeth volcanic
    To grow the armed crop to break the thrall?

We treasure in remembrance, too, the awful week of
                                            slaughter
    When the butchers in their fury killed amain;

The murder of the thousands of the people's sons and
                                                daughters,
    And the mitraillades upon Satory's plain.

The glorious dead! They left their Flag and willed us to
                                                preserve it
    As red as when from their dead hands it fell,
To keep it free from spot and stain, and loyally to serve it,
    As they did 'gainst the powers of earth and hell.

The Blood-Red Flag of Liberty! We'll guard it from
                                                pretenders,
    From those who its red meaning would impugn,
And when it floats in battle breeze prove we as true
                                                defenders
    As those who fought and died in the Commune.

1898   (Abridged)

JOHN FRANCIS ADAMS
1862–1893

England in Egypt

From the dusty jaded sunlight of the careless Cairo
        streets,
    Through the open bedroom window where the pale
        blue held the palms,
There came a sound of music, thrilling cries and
        rattling beats,
    That startled me from slumber with a shock of
        sweet alarms.
For beneath this rainless heaven with this music in
        my ears
    I was born, and all my boyhood with its joy was
        glorified,
And for me the ranging Red-coats hold a passion of
        bright tears,
    And the glancing of the bayonets lights a hell of
        savage pride.

        So I leaped and ran, and looked,
            And I stood, and listened there,
        Till I heard the fifes and drums,
        Till I heard the fifes and drums,
        The fifes and drums of England
            Thrilling all the alien air!
        And "England, England, England,"
            I heard the wild fifes cry,
        "We are here to rob for England,
            And to throttle liberty!"

And "England, England, England,"
       I heard the fierce drums roar,
"We are tools for pious swindlers
       And brute bullies evermore!"

And the silent Arabs crowded, half-defiant, half-
       dismayed.
   And the jaunty fifers fifing flung their challenge to
       the breeze,
And the drummers kneed their drums up as the
       reckless drumsticks played,
   And the Tommies all came trooping, tripping,
       slouching at their ease.
Ah Christ, the love I bore them for their brave hearts
       and strong hands, –
   Ah! Christ, the hate that smote me for their
       stupid, dull conceits –
I know not which was greater, as I watched their
       conquering bands
   In the dusty jaded sunlight of the sullen Cairo
       streets.

              And my dream of love and hate
                     Surged, and broke, and gathered there,
              As I heard the fifes and drums,
              As I heard the fifes and drums,
              The fifes and drums of England
                     Thrilling all the alien air! –
              And "Tommy, Tommy, Tommy,"
                     I heard the wild fifes cry,
              "Will you never know the England
                     For which men, not fools, should die?"
              And "Tommy, Tommy, Tommy,"
                     I heard the fierce drums roar,
              "Will you always be a cut-throat
                     And a slave for evermore?"

No, I shall never see it with these weary death-dim
    eyes,
  The hour of Retribution, the hour of Fate's desire,
When before the outraged millions, as at last – at last
    they rise,
  The rogues and thieves of England are as stubble
    to the fire!
When the gentlemen of England, eaten out with lust
    and sin,
  When the shop-keepers of England, sick with
    godly greed as well,
Face the Red-coats and the Red-shirts, as the steel-
    ring closes in
  And hurls them, howling madly, down the precipice
    of hell!

But O, I *knew* that hour,
    Standing sick and dying there,
As I heard the fifes and drums
As I heard the fifes and drums,
The fifes and drums of England
    Thrilling all the alien air!
And "Tommy, Tommy, Tommy,"
    I heard the wild fifes cry,
"It is time to cease your fooling;
    It is time to do or die!"
And "Johnnie, Johnnie, Johnnie,"
    I heard the fierce drums roar,
"It is time to break your fetters
    And be free for evermore!"

1887

Hong Kong Lyrics

III

I stand and watch the soldiers
 Marching up and down,
Above the fresh green Cricket-ground
 Just outside the town.

I stand and watch and wonder
 When in the English land
This poor fool Tommy Atkins
 Will learn and understand?

Zulus, and Boers, and Arabs,
 All fighting to be free,
Men and women and children
 Maimed and murdered has he.

In India and in Ireland
 He's held the People down,
While the robber English Gentleman
 Took pound and penny and crown.

To make him false to his Order,
 What was it that they gave –
To make him his brother's oppressor?
 The clothes and soul of a slave!

O thou poor fool, Tommy Atkins.
 Thou wilt be wise that day
When, with eager eyes and clenched teeth,
 Thou risest up to say:

"This is our well-loved England,
 And I'll free it, if I can,
From every rotten Shop-keeper,
 And played-out Gentleman!"

To Queen Victoria in England

An Address on Her Jubilee Year

Madam, you have done well! Let others with praise unholy,
 Speech addressed to a woman who never breathed
           upon earth,
Daub you over with lies or deafen your ears with folly,
 I will praise you alone for your actual imminent worth.
Madam, you have done well! Fifty years unforgotten
 Pass since we saw you first, a maiden simple and pure.
Now when every robber Landlord, Capitalist rotten,
 Hated oppressors, praise you – Madam, we are quite
           sure!

Never once as a foe, open foe, to the popular power,
 As nobler kings and queens, have you faced us,
          fearless and bold:
No, but in backstairs fashion, in the stealthy twilight hour,
 You have struggled and struck and stabbed, you have
        bartered and bought and sold!
Melbourne, the listless liar, the gentlemen blood-
          beslavered,
 Disraeli, the faithless priest of a cynical faith out-
          worn –
These were dear to your heart, these were the men you
          favoured,
 Those whom the People loved were fooled and flouted
         and torn!

Never in one true cause, for your people's sake and the
          light's sake,
 Did you strike one honest blow, did you speak one
          noble word:

No, but you took your place, for the sake of wrong and
the night's sake,
Ever with blear-eyed wealth, with the greasy respect-
able herd.
Not as some robber king. with a resolute minister slave
to you,*
Did you swagger with force against us to satisfy your
greed:
No, but you hoarded and hid what your loyal people gave
to you,
Golden sweat of their toil, to keep you a queen
indeed!

Pure at least was your bed? pure was your Court? – We
know not.
Were the white sepulchres pure? Gather men thorns
of grapes?
Your sons and your blameless Spouse's, certes, as Galahads
show not.
Round you gather a crowd of horrible hypocrite
shapes!
Never, sure, did one woman produce in such sixes and
dozens
Such intellectual *canaille* as this that springs from you;
Sons, daughters, grandchildren, with uncles, aunts and
cousins,
Not a man or a woman among them – a wretched
crew!

Madam, you have done well! You have fed all these to
repletion –
You have put up a gilded calf beside a gilded cow,
And bidden men and women behold the forms of human
completion –

* e. g. Charles I and Strafford.

Albert the Good, Victoria the Virtuous, for ever –
and now!
But what to you were our bravest and best, man of science
and poet,
Struggling for Light and Truth, or the Women who
would be free?
Carlyle, Darwin, Huxley, Spencer, Arnold? We know it –
Tennyson slavers your hand; Burdett-Coutts fawns at
your knee!

Good, you were good, we say. You had no wit to be evil.
Your purity shines serene over virgins mangled and
dead.
You wasted not our substance in splendour, in riot or revel –
You quietly sat in the shade and grew fat on our
wealth instead.
Madam, you have done well! To you, we say, has been given
A wit past the wit of women, a supercomputable
worth.
Of you we can say, if not "of such are the Kingdom of
Heaven,"
Of such (alas for us!), of such are the Kingdom of *Earth*!

To Karl Marx

Not for the thought that burns on keen and clear,
   Heart that the heat has turned from red to white,
   The passion of the lone remembering night
One with the patience day must see and hear —
Not for the shafts the lying foemen fear,
   Shot from the soul's intense self-centring light —

   But for the heart of love divine and bright,
We praise you, worker, thinker, poet, seer!
Man of the People — faithful in all parts,
   The veins' last drop, the brain's last flickering dole,
   You on whose forehead beams the aureole
That hope and "certain hope" alone impart —
   Us have you given your perfect heart and soul;

Wherefore receive as yours our souls and hearts.

The Voice of the Manufacturing Slave

Fast in a cage of circumstance,
    Whose bars are worse than iron bars,
A woodland instinct stirs my throat,
    And so I sing to sun and stars.

And so, although I feel the pain
    Of fleshly fret and stiffling strife,
I feel some universal joy
    Shine round the sorrow of my life.

And deeper still I feel this truth –
    Would men but harken wisdom's call,
The joy we now but get in crumbs
    Would be the daily food of all.

1895

JOHN DAVIDSON
1857–1909

Thirty Bob a Week

I couldn't touch a stop or turn a screw,
    And set the blooming world a-work for me,
Like such as cut their teeth – I hope, like you –
    On the handle of a skeleton gold key;
I cut mine on a leek, which I eat it every week:
    I'm a clerk at thirty bob as you can see.

But I don't allow it's luck and all a toss;
    There's no such thing as being starred and crossed;
It's just the power of some to be a boss,
    And the bally power of others to be bossed:
I face the music, sir; you bet I ain't a cur;
    Strike me lucky if I don't believe I'm lost!

For like a mole I journey in the dark,
    A-travelling along the underground
From my Pillar'd Halls and broad Surburbean Park,
    To come the daily dull official round;
And home again at night with my pipe all alight,
    A-scheming how to count ten bob a pound.

And it's often very cold and very wet,
    And my missis stitches towels for a hunks;
And the Pillar'd Halls is half of it to let –
    Three rooms about the size of travelling trunks.
And we cough, my wife and I, to dislocate a sigh,
    When the noisy little kids are in their bunks.

But you never hear her do a growl or whine,
　　For she's made of flint and roses, very odd;
And I've got to cut my meaning rather fine,
　　Or I'd blubber, for I'm made of greens and sod:
So p'r'aps we are in Hell, for all that I can tell,
　　And lost and damn'd and served up hot to God.

I ain't blaspheming, Mr. Silver-tongue;
　　I'm saying things a bit beyond your art:
Of all the rummy starts you ever sprung,
　　Thirty bob a week's the rummiest start!
With your science and your books and your theories about
　　　　　　　　　　　　　　　　　　spooks,
　　Did you ever hear of looking in your heart?

I didn't mean your pocket, Mr., no:
　　I mean the having children and a wife,
With thirty bob on which to come and go,
　　Isn't dancing to the tabor and the fife:
When it doesn't make you drink, by Heaven! it makes
　　　　　　　　　　　　　　　　　you think,
　　And notice curious items about life.

I step into my heart and there I meet
　　A god-almighty devil singing small,
Who would like to shout and whistle in the street,
　　And squelch the passers flat against the wall;
If the whole world were a cake he had the power to take,
　　He would take it, ask for more, and eat it all.

And I meet a sort of simpleton beside,
　　The kind that life is always giving beans;
With thirty bob a week to keep a bride
　　He fell in love and married in his teens:
At thirty bob he stuck; but he knows it isn't luck:
　　He knows the seas are deeper than tureens.

And the god-almighty devil and the fool
    That meet me in the High Street on the strike,
When I walk about my heart a-gathering wool,
    Are my good and evil angels if you like.
And both of them together in every kind of weather
    Ride me like a double-seated bike.

That's rough a bit and needs its meaning curled,
    But I have a high old hot 'un in my mind –
A most engrugious notion of the world,
    That leaves your lightning 'rithmetic behind.
I give it at a glance when I say "There ain't no chance,
    Nor nothing of the lucky-lottery kind."

And it's this way that I make it out to be:
    No fathers, mothers, countries, climates – none;
Not Adam was responsible for me,
    Nor society, nor systems, nary one:
A little sleeping seed, I woke – I did, indeed –
    A million years before the blooming sun.

I woke because I thought the time had come;
    Beyond my will there was no other cause;
And everywhere I found myself at home,
    Because I chose to be the thing I was;
And whatever shape of mollusc or of ape
    I always went according to the laws.

I was the love that chose my mother out;
    I joined two lives and from the union burst;
My weakness and my strength without a doubt
    Are mine alone for ever from the first:
It's just the very same with a difference in the name
    As "Thy will be done". You say it if you durst!

They say it daily up and down the land
     As easy as you take a drink, it's true;
But the difficultest go to understand,
     And the difficultest job a man can do,
Is to come it brave and meek with thirty bob a week,
     And feel that that's the proper thing for you.

It's a naked child against a hungry wolf;
     It's playing bowls upon a splitting wreck;
It's walking on a string across a gulf
     With millstones fore-and-aft about your neck;
And the thing is daily done by many and many a one;
     And we fall, face forward, fighting, on the deck.

1894

War Song

In anguish we uplift
     A new unhallowed song:
The race is to the swift;
     The battle to the strong.

Of old it was ordained
     That we, in packs like curs,
Some thirty million trained
     And licensed murderers,

In crime should live and act,
     If cunning folk say sooth
Who flay the naked fact
     And carve the heart of truth.

The rulers cry aloud,
    "We cannot cancel war,
The end and bloody shroud
    Of wrongs the worst abhor,
And order's swaddling band:
    Know that relentless strife
Remains by sea and land
    The holiest law of life.
From fear in every guise,
    From sloth, from lust of pelf,
By war's great sacrifice
    The world redeems itself.
War is the source, the theme
    Of art; the goal, the bent
And brilliant academe
    Of noble sentiment;
The augury, the dawn
    Of golden times of grace;
The true catholicon,
    The blood-bath of the race."

We thirty million trained
    And licensed murderers,
Like zanies rigged, and chained
    By drill and scourge and curse
In shackles of despair
    We know not how to break –
What do we victims care
    For art, what interest take
In things unseen, unheard?
    Some diplomat no doubt
Will launch a heedless word,
    And lurking war leap out!

We spell-bound armies then,
    Huge brutes in dumb distress,
Machines compact of men
    Who once had consciences,
Must trample harvests down –
    Vineyeard, and corn and oil;
Dismantle town by town,
    Hamlet and homestead spoil
Of each appointed path,
    Till lust of havoc light
A blood-red blaze of wrath
    In every frenzied sight.

In many a mountain-pass,
    Or meadow green and fresh,
Mass shall encounter mass
    Of shuddering human flesh;
Opposing ordnance roar
    Across the swaths of slain,
And blood in torrents pour
    In vain – always in vain,
    For war breeds war again!

The shameful dream is past,
    The subtle maze untrod:
We recognize at last
    That war is not of God.
Wherefore we now uplift
    Our new unhallowed song:
The race is to the swift,
    The battle to the strong.

1899

The Testament of Sir Simon Simplex Concerning Automobilism

That railways are inadequate appears
Indubitable now. For sixty years
Their comfort grew until the *train de luxe*
Arrived, arousing in conducted Cook's,
And other wholesale tourists, an envious smart,
For here they recognized the perfect art
And science of land-travel. Now we sing
A greater era, hail a happier Spring.
The motor-car reveals ineptitude
In railway-trains; and travellers conclude
The railway is archaic: strictly true,
Although the reason sounds as false as new: –
Railways are democratic, vulgar, laic;
And who can doubt Democracy's archaic?
The railway was the herald and the sign,
And powerful agent in the swift decline
Of Europe and the West. The future sage
Will blame sententiously the railway age,
Preachers upon its obvious vices pounce,
And poets, wits and journalists pronounce
The nineteenth century in prose and rhyme
The most unhappy period of time.
That nations towering once in pomp and pride
Of monarchs, rank and breeding, should subside
To one dead undistinguishable horde
Sans sceptre, mitre, coronet and sword,
Reverting to a pithecoidal state
May be the purpose of recurrent fate;

But that such folks should to themselves appear
Progressing toward a great millennial year
Is just the bitter-sweet, the chilly-hot,
The subtle metaphysic of the plot.
The last age saw the last stage of the fit
That pestered, when the Roman Empire split,
The catalytic centuries: the strange
Insanity that fed on secular change;
The general paralysis of men
That ended in the railway and the wen
Called London: from the Tiber to the Thames,
From dreaming empire to delirious aims
That move the laughter of the careless fates,
And effervesce in socialistic pates.

But convalescence with the car begins
And petrol expiates our railway sins.
Before we know we shall with joy behold
A world as sane as any world of old;
From labour and electoral problems free,
A world the fibre of whose health shall be,
No Will to be the Mob, but mastering all,
A Will to be the Individual;
For every Mob exhales a poisonous breath,
And Socialism is decadence, is death:
The Mob expropriates, degrades, destroys;
The Individual conquers, makes, enjoys.
Not till the motor was the contrast plain,
Because the separate classes of the train
Deceived us with a choice of company;
And, when he liked, the tame celebrity,
The genius, man of wealth, aristocrat,
By means of tips through any journey sat
In cornered state; or with sufficient pelf
Could purchase a compartment for himself.

He rather would have deemed himself a snob
Than that the train could turn him into Mob,
Till automotion's privacy and pride
Exposed the grossness of the railway ride;
For 'twas the freedom of the motor-car
That showed how tyrannous the railways are.
To go by train from one place to another
You have to brave the station's smoke and smother:
The train derides you there; 'twill never come
To pick you up, nor turn, to see you home,
A single wheel; the getting under way,
The true vexation of a holiday,
The stolid train permits you to deplore;
But with your automobile at the door –
Why, there you are, nor need you stir a foot,
Man and portmanteau instantly *en route!*
You buy a ticket if you go by train
At some offensive loophole, which you gain
After prolonged attendance in a queue –
Whatever class you take, a motley crew:
And to await one's turn, like patient Job,
Unites one with a vengeance to the Mob.
Then you may miss the train; but *you* must wait
Its advent and departure prompt or late.
The motor soothes, the railway racks your nerves;
The train commands, the automobile serves.
The automobile nurses all caprice,
And gives the longest life a second lease;
Indulges indolence, and even in me
Increases individuality.

I thought and many my opinion shared
That the deceased politic who declared
That all were Socialists, had told, perhaps,
A fib, exploited in a studied lapse
Of platform declamation as a sop
To catch erratic voters on the hop,
The strained politeness of a caustic mind,
A dead-lift effort to say something kind.
'Twas more than that: not only had we learned
To suffer Socialism; our souls discerned
A something fine about it; egoists even
Perceived therein at last a mundane heaven.

'Life is a railway journey,' genius thought –
(The erring genius very cheaply bought
With gilded apples of Asphaltites) –
'Thieves bearing swag, and poets sprouting bays,
The ring, the cabinet, scortatory dames,
Bishops, sectarians of a myriad names,
Bankers and brokers, merchants, mendicants,
Booked in the same train like a swarm of ants;
First, second, third, class, mass and mob expressed
Together to the Islands of the Blest –
Each passenger provided with a groat
To pass the Stygian stile for Charon's boat.
Or broad or narrow as the gauge may run,
None leaves the track without disaster; none
Escapes a single stoppage on the way;
And none arrives before his neighbour may.
In the guard's van my sacred luggage knocks
Against the tourist's traps, the bagman's box;
And people with inferior aims to mine
Partake the rapid transit of the line.

But this is culture of the social school,
And teaches me to lead my life by rule
Empirical, of positive descent
And altruistic self-embezzlement.
Life *is* a railway journey: I rejoice
That folk whose purpose, visage, clothes and voice
Offend me will continue to offend
In the same train until the journey's end.'

So spoke the genius in pathetic rage. –
The socialistic and the railway age
Were certainly coeval; machinery too
Equated communism; and every new
Development of electricity
Was welcomed by the Mob with three times three,
Convinced the world at last was through the wood –
Right through to Universal Brotherhood!
Conceive it: – Universal Brotherhood,
With everybody feeble, kind and good!
I, even I, Sir Simon Simplex, know
The world would end to-day if that were so.
What spur does man require, what stinging zest
To do still better than his level best?
Why, enemies; and if he has them not
He must unearth and beat them till they're hot;
For only enmity can train and trounce
The cortex and the muscle to an ounce.
Let Socialists deny, mistaking peace,
That only with the world will warfare cease;
When *we* behold the battle-flags unfurled
We know the fates phlebotomize the world,
And alternative with peace's patent pill,
The old heroic cure for every ill.

Life was a railway journey; foe and friend,
Infected with nostalgy of the end,

Awaited patiently the crack of doom;
But thank the powers that be, the motor boom,
Predestined to postpone the judgment-day,
Arrived in time to show a better way.
And when the automobile came we found
Our incorrupt opinion safe and sound,
Inoculated only by the schism,
For ever proof against all Socialism.
The motor stops the decadence: not all
Are in the same train with the prodigal,
The Christian scientist, the *souteneur,*
The Gothamite, the man from anywhere,
Domestic Gill and idiomatic Jack,
The wheedling knave, the sneak, the hectoring quack;
The man of broader mind and farther goal
Is not entrained with Lubin Littlesoul;
Your gentleman by birth with quickened sense,
Refined requirements and abundant pence,
And men of faculty and swelling aim
Who conquer riches, power, position, fame,
Are not entrained with loafers, quibblers, cranks,
Nor with the Mob who never leave the ranks,
With plodding dullness, unambitious ease,
And discontented incapacities.

Goodwill is in the blood, in you and me,
And most in men of wealth and pedigree;
So rich and poor, men, women, age and youth
Imagined some ingredient of truth
In Socialistic faith that there could be
A common basis of equality.
But now we know and by the motor swear
The prepossession was as false as fair;
Men are not equal; no two intellects
Are of a calibre; desires, defects,

Powers, aptitudes, are never on a par
No more than finger-prints and noses are.
And on my soul and conscience I maintain
Political equality's as vain
As personal: For instance, I would place
The franchise on a principle of race,
And give the Saxon's forward reach a felt
Prepotence o'er the backward-glancing Celt;
And if his chauffeur counts as one, why then
Sir Simon Simplex should be reckoned ten.
I call Democracy archaic, just
As manhood suffrage is atavic lust
For folkmotes of the prime, whose analogue
In travel was the train, a passing vogue:
Th automobile put an end to that,
And left Democracy as fallen and flat
As railway-stock. Wealth and the crafty hand
That gathers wealth had always at command
Horse-carriages for private travel, but
The pace had got beyond that leisured rut;
Class, mass and mob for fifty years and more
Had all to travel in the jangling roar
Of railways, the nomadic caravan
That stifled individual mind in man,
Till automobilism arose at last!
Now with the splendid periods of the past
Our youthful century is proudly linked;
And things that Socialism supposed extinct,
Degree, nobility and noble strife,
A form, a style, a privacy in life
Will reappear; and, crowning nature's plan,
The individual and the gentleman
In England reassume his lawful place
And vindicate the greatness of the race.

Our Common Cause

Tune: *The White Cockade*

As toilers of the earth we stand.
And hail our kin in every land;
No man our country's foe we call,
Save he who is the foe of all.

> *Chorus*
> And as we clasp our comrade's hand,
> We swear to fight in every land,
> Till justice sits upon the throne,
> And all the earth is Labour's own.

One time we thought our foe was he
Who dwelt in lands beyond the sea;
To-day we know across the foam
No foe so great as he at home.

Who owns the factory and the soil
Is enemy of all who toil;
From shore to shore the cry is hurled,
He is the foe of all the world.

How often have we drawn the sword
And fought to swell our master's hoard?
We'll now avenge our martyred dead,
And face our coward-lords instead!

And haply those who told us then
We fought as French or Englishmen,
Will find when battling for the Right,
We still remember how to fight!

And as we march, each new born day
Shall find us farther on our way:
No foeman fierce may bid us pause
If we but trust our common cause.

1901

G. W. S.

Taff Vale

The Trade Unionist

No gouty lord concurring
　　With judges' stern decree,
No rotten-ripe red herring
　　Stale argument or plea
　　　　Cast up in Labour's face
　　　　Brings Labour to disgrace.

When statesmen are for flaunting
　　Cock-feathers in their hats,
Soft flatteries are not wanting
　　To *"Labour's aristocrats"* –
　　　　Then treacherously we're dealt
　　　　This blow beneath the belt.

The fool ran down the mountain
　　Sweet water to obtain,
Ignored each crystal fountain,
　　And found the briny main! –
　　　　For all that's come to pass
　　　　Write *Labour* down an ass.

But better fed the asses
　　The lustier are their kicks,
And Freedom's War on Class is
　　In trade *and* politics:
　　　　No longer let there be
　　　　An aristocracy.

Strong Labour many-sided,
    Gleams like some precious stone,
Divided, sub-divided,
    In facets, anyone
        Of which, if scratched or soiled
        Then is the whole gem spoiled.

March on! We're bound together
    By common interest
Through clear and cloudy weather
    To battle for the best,
        Till man's proud diadem
        Boasts no purer gem.

Through night, between the sinking
    And rising of the sun,
One past old commune linking
    To another not begun,
        From Labour's pangs and cries
        The New World shall uprise.

1902

Labour Insurgent

I

It is only power Wealth heeds;
    Power; with a big sounding name,
Exploiting the people's needs
    For a tinselled fame.
Song, and devotion, and praise,
    For Mammon, enthroned on high,
Grasping the gifts of the days
    While the workers die.

2

Always the substance for Wealth;
    Ever the shadow for Toil;
Riches exalted o'er health;
    And idleness sleek with spoil.

3

It is only power Wealth heeds;
    Not bloodless lips that cry
    When he treads the mart – chin high,
To-day in his servile press,
"Rebellion of Toil," he reads,
And he curses – pretending to bless!

4

It is only power Wealth heeds;
Compulsion by forceful deeds;
    Constraint of swords, or banks,
    Of men in marshalled ranks.

5

Now Toil at last awakes,
The heart of the tyrant quakes,
And he speaks in dulcet tones
　　Soft as a murm'ring rill,
　　"Be gentle, Toil, bear me still
On your back without moan;
Have we not, brother, one aim,
　　One hope, one life interest?
Be guided by me, I claim
　　To know what for you is best.
Unlock your chains, if you must,
　　But dwell in them still the same.
See, they are perished with rust,
　　And only exist in name."

6

But Toil has grown wise and bold,
And cringes not as of old:
　　"I shall take what is mine, what is just,"
He calmly and bravely replies;
"I have listened too long to your lies."
　　And he treads the old serpent to dust.

1910

Robert Owen

　　He stands serene, alone;
　　　　The years have come and gone,
And silent changes worn new channels deep,
Still, still enthroned, his grand old name I keep,
In youth's brief day, he was my sun uprist,
My fount of light, my greatest Socialist.

Greater than Christ to me
His warm constructive soul,
His life was prophecy
Of that exalted goal
To which man treads with sure, if tardy, pace,
Where equity makes beautiful the Race.

He stands serene, alone;
Too often too-forgot;
Yet heard he toilers moan
And passed them not;
Life, fortune, power, fine-natured sympathy,
All these he gave ungrudgingly and free.

He stands serene, alone;
The years have come and gone,
And though behind may drift much gold of youth,
He still upholds for me the lamp of Truth,
'Long ways that wind and twist,
My greatest Socialist.

1910

Street Propaganda

1

At the corner of the street, once again
Voicing the good wise gospel as of old,
While twilight's tender glories slowly wane,
And western clouds grow bright with magic gold.

2

'Tis hard to talk when beauty woos one so,
  When eve's soft splendour lures the willing heart.
Why stand I here? Ah! Why? I scarcely know,
  Some stern deep impulse bids me do my part.

3

Some sympathy bequeathed from sire to son –
  Some deep emotion born of rebel blood –
Wells in my soul, and bids me rise and go
  And stand, perchance as my forefathers stood.

4

The star of eve burns brightly as I talk,
  Toil's scarred worn face is eagerly upturned,
'Tis fine to teach, and yet 'tis sweet to walk
  In glades of green that never poet spurned.

5

Peace! Peace! This is no time for selfish ease,
  For opiate ways of garlanded repose;
The clear heights call, the wise humanities,
  The knowledge that is greater than man's woes.

6

'Tis done. Fold up the flag, the night has come;
  Return with thanks the chair or chance-loaned stool;
Above, the starlit silences are dumb –
  Below, hearts – well at peace with conscience – full.

1910

A Day's Work at the Docks

Before the great world's noises break
    The stillness overhead,
For toiling life begins the strife –
    The day's grim fight for bread.
Where Mersey's mighty greyhounds speak
    The wealth of England's stocks,
Stand, mute and meek, the men that seek
    A day's work at the docks.

Behold them now – a motley throng,
    Men drawn from every grade:
Pale, florid, puny – weak and strong,
    All by one impulse swayed.
One impulse – bread: one impulse – work!
    How hope at each heart knocks
As mute and meek, they crush to seek
    A day's work at the docks.

"Stand back! Stand back!" a hoarse voice storms,
    With curses muttered lower,
The straining ring of human forms
    But closes in the more.
Well fed, you foremen scarce can know
    How Want the judgment mocks,
When, mute and meek, men eager seek
    A day's work at the docks.

How many must be turned away,
    The streets to idly roam,

With dull, sad hearts, and minds that prey
    O'er hearts as sad at home!
Oh! boast we of our prosperous land
    While thousands on life's rocks
Stand, mute and meek, poor wrecks, that seek
    A day's work at the docks.

Sudden and stern are Fortune's blows –
    Her ebbs and flows of tide.
How many, 'mid those eager rows,
    Could boast of bygone pride.
And now, all humbled, they but ask,
    As brothers to the ox,
To labour meek, as here they seek
    A day's work at the docks.

Ye kings of commerce, who but see
    Life's bright and sunny side –
Who dream not of the misery
    The walls of class may hide –
If e'er God's key of charity
    Some kindlier heart unlocks,
Think of the meek, mute men that seek
    A day's work at the docks.

And you that hold the reins of power,
    Remember, now and then,
That life is brief and judgment sure,
    That men are fellow-men.
It is not brave to ply the whip
    When men, like helpless blocks,
Stand mute and meek, because they seek
    A day's work at the docks.

1910

The Tearaway Boss

Number Two is a man of note,
   In charge of a hatch, maybe,
Leading hand aboard of the boat,
   Or a foreman down on the quay.
Wherever he is it's the same old plan,
   Roaring and ranting around –
The poorest "puke" in the shape of a man,
   That down at the dock is found.

Poor himself, and born of the poor,
   No shame to him, though, for that –
You would think him lord of the world, for sure,
   With all mankind for a mat.
A bully he, with the brain of a flea,
   Neither a man nor a mouse,
Is a cur in his heart, for, between you and me,
   He hasn't the pluck of a louse.

How do they get these bossing jobs?
   Where does their worth come in?
As a brother-in-law of Tom's or Bob's,
   From the first they came "well-in".
Then, always fawning down to the firm,
   This specimen rare and choice,
Though he hasn't the principle of a worm,
   Has, what a worm hasn't – a voice!

"Come on! Come on, there! Heave away!
   What is the stoppage now?"
Hear him roaring the livelong day,
   And never a pause allow.

Strength cannot please him, do what it will,
　　You may work away till you burst,
It's "hurry up" yet, and "go ahead" still,
　　Harried, and bullied, and cursed.

So Number Two, the Tearaway Boss,
　　Well – he isn't the docker's pride.
To us it wouldn't be any loss
　　If his type, like the dodo, died.
But an evil is he we have to stand,
　　Like the hangman dark and dread.
'Twas maybe down in a loafer's land
　　The Tearaway Boss was bred.

He, and the scow that will not work,
　　The evil and cure *en bloc* –
If we had our way, with never a shirk,
　　We'd dump them both in the dock.
For each is a pest in his own sweet style,
　　And a foe to all fairplay,
To man and to master traitors vile,
　　They are both in a good man's way!

And we that would do the thing that's right –
　　Who willingly do our shares
Year in, year out, by day or by night,
　　For employer millionaires,
We think it hard, Jack, Joe, or Jim,
　　And of justice hold it a loss –
That *men* should be under the likes of him,
　　The terrible Tearaway Boss!

1910

Freedom

Freedom comes slowly, but remember she
    Must beg from door to door, a barefoot maid;
No high-born dame in gilded car she rides.
    Full oft beneath the stars her bed is made,
And men repulse her often. Yet her eyes
    Rain drops of purest pity; as for hate,
It finds no entrance to her noble heart,
    And she will bless the toiler soon or late.

The thorns along the path of centuries
    Have deeply scarred her delicate brown feet;
Her gown is torn by many a thicket wild
    Which she has wandered through; her broad brow
                           sweet
Is crowned by fadeless roses lovers placed
    To cheer her heart as on her way she came;
Her flesh oft faints beside the roadside hard.
    Her spirit cannot die – 'tis made of flame.

1907

Immortality

In a hundred years or more Spring will come with her
                             garland of bloom,
And her new lovers walk in the sun when her old lovers
                                rest in the tomb;

Whilst for us golden rain drips unheard and the warm
                              sunlight burns all unseen,
And the lilac spray waves in the wind, and the wren takes
                              her mate in the green;
And we sleep well and long underground, and have done
                              with the laughter and tears,
Who are building to-day the fair world that shall be in
                              a hundred years.

In a hundred years or more they will sing sweeter songs
                              than we know,
And the rain that is falling on us now will have helped
                              their red roses to grow;
And we never may hark to the gladness that throbs
                              through the chaos of pain,
That we bore unto them through the darkness, the raging
                              of wind and of rain;
But the music shall echo for all time that grew from our
                              striving and tears,
And shall ring down the ages with joy unto men in a
                              hundred years.

The best thoughts we are thinking to-day shall be living
                              and active and strong,
When we sleep at the end of the fight, caring not for the
                              war-hoop or song,
And it matters far more than we know that we keep our
                              hearts steadfast and brave,
For the strength that they held shall walk forth when they
                              mix with the dust of the grave.
And immortal, and lovely, and young shall our dream
                              live unclouded by tears,
When we take the long rest that is sweet after toil in a
                              hundred years.

1911

Earth's Song to Her Children

The earth is weary waiting you, O people!
    She yearns to hold you in her glad, green arms;
Each morning as the sun lights up the valley
    She tries to lure you with her hundred charms.
And sadly sighs, "Why do you stay away, Love,
    Why do you timorous wear those self-forged chains?
Cannot the blackbird's magic music reach you,
    Who calls and calls, and calls in rose-starred lanes?

"The water-lily holds the sunbeam for you,
    And wonders why you never come to look;
The river glides or rushes to the ocean,
    And under drooping willows runs the brook.
All things fulfil their mission, and are joyful,
    Why do you stay so long, O Love of mine?
Waiting for you, I deck myself in beauty
    Of sward and fern, gay flowers and stately pine.

"O break your chains and come, for years are fleeting!
    These flowers I wear are for your absent eyes,
Soon it will be too late, dust will have filled, dear,
    Your sight, and all in vain will shout the skies.
These waves of shade that wander o'er the cornfields,
    These bursts of sun, and cool clouds scattering rain,
Cornflowers, convolvulus with silver trumpets,
    Birds singing mad, will come, O, ne'er again!

"Others like to them may troop forth for others –
    But you may never see them, O come now!
Now, whilst the sun is shining on the meadows,
    And let me send the hard lines from your brow.
A long, long rest would follow; I would give you
    Sweet joy and beauty ere Life's gem be lost.

Your mother calls her truants to her bosom,
    O come and claim her what may be the cost.

"I pour and pour, and pour my glorious treasures
    That you may live and laugh, nor be a slave;
They come and lay you dead before your time, dear,
    And rend my breast to make your early grave.
Up like the sun, my boys, in morning splendour,
    Smiting aside the gloomy cloud's array:
Tell them the dreary hours of night are over,
    You come to claim your mother and the day."

1911

Run Down

In the grim dead end he lies, with passionless filmy eyes,
  English Ned, with a hole in his head,
Staring up at the skies.

The engine driver swore as often he swore before –
  "I whistled him back from the flamin' track,
An' I couldn't do no more."

The gaffer spoke through the 'phone "Platelayer Seventy-
                           one"
  Got killed to-day on the six-foot way,
By a goods on the city run.

    "English Ned was his name
    No one knows whence he came,
He didn't take mind of the road behind
    And none of us is to blame."

    They turned the slag in the bed
    To cover the clotted red,
Washed the joints and the crimsoned points,
    And buried poor English Ned.

    In the drear dead end he lies
    With the earth across his eyes,
      And a stone to say,
      How he passed away
    To a shift beyond the skies.

1912

The Song of the Drainer

(On Toward Mountain, 1907)

He is the Drainer. –
    Out on the moorland bleak and grey, using his
spade in a primitive way, through chilly evening and
searing day. Call him a fool, and well you may –
               He is the Drainer.

The toil of the Drainer. –
    Only the simple work to do, to plod and delve the
quagmire through, for thirty pence, his daily screw. –
The labour is healthy – but not for you,
               Just for the Drainer.

The artless Drainer. –
    It doesn't require a lot of skill to dig with a spade
or hammer a drill, but it's bad enough for a man when
ill with fevery bones or a wintry chill –
               Even a Drainer.

The home of the Drainer. –
    A couple of stakes shoved into the ground, a hole for
a window, a roof tree crowned with rushes and straw,
and all around a waste where lichens and weeds abound.
               Is the home of the Drainer.

The rugged Drainer. –
    The sleepy bog breezes chant their hymn, the rushes
and lilies are soft and slim, the deep dark pools the sun-
beams limn – but what do these beauties matter to him –
               The rugged Drainer?

The poor old Drainer. –

Some day he'll pass away in a cramp, where the
sundews gleam and the bogbines ramp, and go like a
ghost from the drag and the damp – the poor old slave
of the dismal swamp –

> The hapless Drainer.

Such is the Drainer. –

Voiceless slave of the solitude, rude as the draining
shovel is rude – Man by the ages of wrong subdued,
marred, misshapen, misunderstood –

> Such is the Drainer.

Two Poems Dedicated to Karl Marx

I

Rich men, what of the Night?
    The night you have made your day –
    That you laugh and you dance away,
        Whilst we and our children slave,
You, in your halls of delight,
    Feast on our blood and breath
        Till our souls be too famished to save
And our bodies too weary for death.

Workers, what of the Night?
    Tho' the night be not o'er for us yet
    We must rise for the day must be met
        With the flag of our faith flung free.
We must rise by the lantern's light,
    And sharpen the swords of our hate
        And the end of the darkness shall be
The end of the slave ridden State.

II

If God were dead in heaven
    And Reason reigned on Earth
        The shock and the shame and sorrow
        Of slavery's day and morrow
Would cease, and love would leaven
    New days of Wealth and Worth.

If God were dead in heaven
　　And Reason reigned on Earth.

If men were born to Beauty
　　And Laughter's Rule and Right,
　　　　And Mammon's puerile passion
　　　　Were dead and out of fashion –
Then living would be Duty
　　And Duty be delight,
If men were born to Beauty
　　And Truth's own Rule and Right.

1914–15

And It Shall Come

Strong men came from the Eastern way
　　To storm the gates of the West,
In the heat and glare of a hateful day
　　They came at hunger's behest,
　　　　To end the wrong and to end the shame
　　　　They came with eyes and hearts aflame
　　To burn the golden West.

Women sad, with hearts grown grey,
　　And little children, too,
Came with men from the Eastern way
　　To do what they could do.
　　　　To gain the right of Life and Light
　　　　For those who toil in the day and night,
　　And for little children too.

Oh for the end of the carrion class,
　　And the crime of palace and slum;

Oh the fierce joy when the night shall pass,
  And the day of reckoning come –
     When the storm sweeps down from the Eastern
                              way,
     And the poor demand that the rich shall pay,
And the great be stricken dumb.

And as sure as time and the world go on
  And the sun sails the sky so blue,
The Earth will be cleaner and sweeter by far
  When its clear and shut of you.

        So let it be: – and he and we are giving
        All that we have so the dead become
                     the living,
        So we shall fight while the strength
                   and passion last,
        And we shall win.

1915

JAMES CONNOLLY
1868–1916

A Dying Socialist Speaks to His Son

"Thy father is a poor man," mark well what that may
mean;
On the tablets of thy memory that truth write bright and
clean.
Thy father's lot it was to toil from earliest boyhood on,
And know his latent energies for a master's profit drawn . . .

Yes, son of mine, since history's dawn two classes stand
revealed,
The rich and poor, in bitterest war, by deadliest hatred
steeled,
The one, incarnate greed and crime, disdaining honest toil,
Had grasped man's common birthright and treasure-house,
the soil,
And standing 'twixt their fellow men and all the earth
could give,
Had bade them render tribute if they would hope to live.
And building crime on top of crime, had pushed their
conquests on,
Till arbiters of life and death, they stood with weapons
drawn
And blades athirst to drink the blood, on land and over sea,
Of him who dared for human rights to stem this tyranny . . .

"The past?" Aye, boy, the method's past; the deed is still
the same,
And robbery is robbery yet though cloaked in gentler
name,

The means of life are still usurped, the rich man still is
                                                    lord,
And prayers and cries for justice still meet one reply –
                                              the sword! . . .
And we, who live by labour, know that while they rule
                                                we must
Sell freedom, brain and limb to win for us and ours a
                                              crust . . .

Treasure ye in your inmost heart this legacy of hate
For those who on the poor man' back have climbed to
                                            great estate,
The lords of land and capital, the slave lords of our age,
Who of this smiling earth of ours have made for us a cage,
Where golden bars fetter men's souls, and noble thoughts
                                          are aflame
To burn us with their vain desires, and virtue yields to
                                              shame.
Such is your foe, foe of your class, of human rights the foe,
Be it your thought by day and night to work their over-
                                              throw . . .

Be it your task, oh son of mine, the rich man's hate to
                                              brave,
And consecrate your noblest part to rouse each fellow-
                                              slave,
To speed the day the world awaits when Labour long
                                          oppressed,
Shall rise and strike for freedom true, and from the
                                        tyrants wrest
The power they have abused so long. Oh, ever glorious
                                              deed!
The crowning point of history, yet child of bitterest need.

From *The Legacy*

The Rebel

I am come of the seed of the people, the people that
sorrow,
That have no treasure but hope,
No riches laid up but a memory
Of an ancient glory.
My mother bore me in bondage, in bondage my mother
was born,
I am of the blood of serfs;
The children with whom I have played, the men and wo-
men with whom I have eaten,
Have had masters over them, have been under the lash of
masters,
And, though gentle, have served churls;
The hands that have touched mine, the dear hands whose
touch is familiar to me,
Have worn shameful manacles, have been bitten at the
wrist by manacles,
Have grown hard with the manacles and the task-work
of strangers,
I am flesh of the flesh of these lowly, I am bone of their
bone,
I that have never submitted;
I that have a soul greater than the souls of my people's
masters,
I that have vision and prophecy and the gift of fiery
speech,
I that have spoken with God on the top of His holy hill.

And because I am of the people, I understand the people,
I am sorrowful with their sorrow, I am hungry with their
desire:
My heart has been heavy with the grief of mothers,
My eyes have been wet with the tears of children,
I have yearned with old wistful men,
And laughed or cursed with young men;
Their shame is my shame, and I have reddened for it,
Reddened for that they have served, they who should be
free.
Reddened for that they have gone in want, while others
have been full,
Reddened for that they have walked in fear of lawyers
and of their jailors
With their writs of summons and their handcuffs,
Men mean and cruel!
I could have borne stripes on my body rather than this
shame of my people.

And now I speak, being full of vision;
I speak to my people, and I speak in my people's name
to the masters of my people.
I say to my people that they are holy, that they are august,
despite their chains,
That they are greater than those that hold them, and stronger
and purer,
That they have but need of courage, and to call on the
name of their God,
God the unforgetting, the dear God that loves the peoples
For whom he died naked, suffering shame.
And I say to my people's masters: Beware.

Beware of the thing that is coming, beware of the risen
   people,
Who shall take what ye would not give. Did ye think to
   conquer the people,
Or that Law is stronger than life and than men's desire to
   be free?
We will try it out with you, ye that have harried and held,
Ye that have bullied and bribed, tyrants, hypocrites, liars!

Arise Ye Sons of Labour

Arise ye sons of Labour!
  Arise while yet ye may,
Your Rebel brother calls you
  To help him in the fray.
From every land he calleth
  On you to help along
The Day of Revolution
  By word and deed and song.

Chorus

    Then rouse, ye sons of Labour!
      Strike hard while yet ye may,
    Break down these superstitions
      That block the workers' way.
    Raise high the Crimson Banner
      That all the world may see,
    And work for Revolution
      And the Days that are to be.

Arise, ye sons of Labour!
  Stop war of want to-day,
Your Comrades in the battle
  Are bound by destiny.
Your Brothers are in prison
  For words or trifling deeds,
Your women toil as vassals
  To serve your masters' greed.

Arise, ye sons of Labour!
  Fear not the master-class,
Have faith in your own Brothers,
  And fight unto the last.
For all the world awaits you,
  Awaits the Coming Day,
The Day of Retribution,
  The end of slavery.

May Day 1916

REV. P. O' NEILL

The Foggy Dew

As down the glen one Easter morn to a city fair rode I,
There armed lines of marching men in squadrons passed
me by;
No pipe did hum, no battle drum did sound its loud tat-
too,
But the Angelus bell o'er the Liffey's swell
rang out through the Foggy Dew.

Right proudly high in Dublin Town they flung out the
flag of war,
'Twas better to die 'neath an Irish sky than at Suvla or
Sud el Bar;
And from the plains of Royal Meath strong men came
hurrying through,
While Britannia's Huns with their great big guns
sailed in through the Foggy Dew.

O, the night fell black, and the rifles' crack made
'perfidious Albion' reel,
'Mid the leaden rain seven tongues of flame did shine
o'er the lines of steel;
By each shining blade a prayer was said that to Ireland
her sons be true,
And when morning broke still the war flag shook
out its folds in the Foggy Dew.

'Twas England bade our Wild Geese go that Small
                              Nations might be free,
But their lonely graves are by Suvla's waves or the fringe
                              of the great North Sea.
O, had they died by Pearse's side, or had fought with
                              Cathal Brugha,
Their names we'd keep where the Fenians sleep,
      'neath the shroud of the Foggy Dew.

But the bravest fell, and the requiem bell rang mournfully
                              and clear
For those who died that Eastertide in the springtime of
                              the year;
While the world did gaze, with deep amaze, at those fear-
                             less men but few,
Who bore the fight that Freedom's light
      might shine through the Foggy Dew.

Ah! back through the glen I rode again, and my heart
                              with grief was sore,
For I parted then with valiant men whom I never shall
                              see more;
But to and fro in my dreams I go, and I kneel and pray
                              for you,
For slavery fled, O glorious dead!
      when you fell in the Foggy Dew.

1916

LIAM MACGABHANN

"A Man Like That –"

(The son of a Welsh miner, a member of the firing squad that shot James Connolly, afterwards visited Connolly's relatives to implore forgiveness. The poem is an impression of the soldier's story to his comrades.)

The man was all shot through that came to-day
Into the barracks square;
A soldier I – I am not proud to say
We killed him there;
They brought him from the prison hospital:
To see him in that chair
I thought his smile would far more quickly call
A man to prayer.

Maybe we cannot understand this thing
That makes these rebels die;
And yet all things love freedom – and the spring
Clear in the sky:
I think I would not do this deed again
For all that I hold by;
Gaze down my rifle at his breast – but then
A soldier I.

They say that he was kindly – different, too,
Apart from all the rest;

A lover of the poor; and all shot through,
His wounds ill drest,
He came before us, faced us like a man,
He knew a deeper pain
Than blows or bullets – ere the world began;
Died he in vain?

Ready – present: And he just smiling – God!
I felt my rifle shake
His wounds were opened out and round that chair
Was one red lake:
I swear his lips said "Fire!" when all was still
Before my rifle spat
That cursed lead – And I was picked to kill
A man like that!

192–

The Levellers

We walked the world once with a wayward yearning,
Learning the new things the rich men may not know;
Ours is a strange and queer prophetic learning,
Secrets the first men knew – ages long ago.
A baby's cry comes in the grip of hunger,
Pierces the dark veil that rings the years between,
Till in the future the universe grows younger,
Fate of the poor man, to bring the might-have-been.

One wilding song of ours breaks up an empire;
Millions of us marched once and broke the swords of Rome;
Thousands of us shrieking to stake a Bourbon vampire;
We razed the towers of Muscovy to build ourselves a home.

324

Down along the dark years the rich men grew stronger,
Squandered our souls on us, filched away our bread;
Dimly we thought it out, as agony grew longer –
Our fight was terrible, ruthless, and red.

Submarines and bombers, Thompsons and trench-mortars
Blaze along their battle-front where the empires go;
Slums and fever'd alley-ways, these were our headquarters –
Multitudinous armies, dazed, and dumb, and slow.
Gas bombs and shrapnel cloud along the trenches,
Hell fume and shell reek numb the helot's ire;
Dust bins and plague pens were our battle stenches,
Shrieks of our women-folk louder than their fire.

Slow came our vengeance, the planning, the first of it –
Buy our women's bodies, blast our children's souls!
But vengeance, ye devils! ever the thirst of it?
Waiting for vengeance and taking out your doles.
We walk the world now Justice comes behind us,
The great, grim Justice the worst of us demands,
Come we as levellers, break us and blind us –
But, tyrants, turn and face us – with weapons in our hands!

c. 1933

The Parable of the Old Men
and the Young

So Abram rose, and clave the wood, and went,
And took the fire with him, and a knife.
And as they sojourned both of them together,
Isaac the first-born spake and said, My Father,
Behold the preparations, fire and iron,
But where the lamb for this burnt-offering?
Then Abram bound the youth with belts and straps,
And builded parapets and trenches there,
And stretched forth the knife to slay his son.
When lo! an angel called him out of heaven,
Saying, Lay not thy hand upon the lad,
Neither do anything to him. Behold,
A ram, caught in a thicket by its horns;
Offer the Ram of Pride instead of him.
But the old man would not so, but slew his son, –
And half the seed of Europe, one by one.

Dulce et Decorum Est

Bent double, like old beggars under sacks,
Knock-kneed, coughing like hags, we cursed through sludge,
Till on the haunting flares we turned our backs,
And towards our distant rest began to trudge.
But limped on, blood-shod. All went lame, all blind;

Drunk with fatigue; deaf even to the hoots
Of gas-shells dropping softly behind.

Gas! Gas! Quick, boys! – An ecstasy of fumbling,
Fitting the clumsy helmets just in time,
But someone still was yelling out and stumbling
And floundering like a man in fire or lime. –
Dim through the misty panes and thick green light,
As under a green sea, I saw him drowning.

In all my dreams before my helpless sight
He plunges at me, guttering, choking, drowning.

If in some smothering dreams, you too could pace
Behind the wagon that we flung him in,
And watch the white eyes writhing in his face,
His hanging face, like a devil's sick of sin;
If you could hear, at every jolt, the blood
Come gargling from the froth-corrupted lungs,
Bitter as the cud
Of vile, incurable sores on innocent tongues, –
My friend, you would not tell with such high zest
To children ardent for some desperate glory,
The old Lie: *Dulce et decorum est
Pro patria mori.*

The Glory of War

What does it matter if men are torn, and a village razed
to desolation?
'Tis a little thing for men to die, and houses can be built
of brick and stone;
The glory of a just war surely spreads its mantle over all.

This battle is ours: our men rest where yesterday lay the
enemy;
The village is ours (for torn earth and smoking bricks
were once a village).
What is the cost? A thousand men are killed who did not
want to die.
What does it matter? Their country needing them, they
gave their lives.

Happy ones, though ignorant of their happiness, they died
to make the battle ours;
And their bodies lie grotesquely on the torn slopes about
the village.

A lad was shot, just as we started to move forward;
Perhaps you saw him where he lay, with eyes still open,
With eyes still looking out upon the world, dazed and
horror struck.
There lay a hero – who did not want to die.
My sergeant-major's dead, killed as we entered the village;
You will not find his body, tho' you look for it;
A shell burst on him, leaving his legs, strangely enough
untouched.

Happy man, he died for England;
Happy ones are they who die for England.

Did he, did that poor lad, truly die for England's sake?
Did all those thousands who are gone, did they all die
                              for that bright cause?
All England wages war:
The flower of her manhood lies waiting in the cold pale
                              days of Springtime,
Waiting for the harvest that reaps so many souls.
Some are brave and unafraid, some shrink in mortal
                              apprehension;
But all are happy, for they know that by their efforts they
                              are helping
So many of their fellow-countrymen to make their fortunes.

February 1918

The Sleepers

As I walked down the waterside
  This silent morning, wet and dark;
Before the cocks in farmyards crowed,
  Before the dogs began to bark;
Before the hour of five was struck
By old Westminster's mighty clock:

As I walked down the waterside
  This morning, in the cold damp air,
I saw a hundred women and men
  Huddled in rags and sleeping there:
These people have no work, thought I,
And long before their time they die.

That moment on the waterside,
  A lighted car came at a bound;
I looked inside, and saw a score
  Of pale and weary men that frowned;
Each man sat in a huddled heap,
Carried to work while fast asleep.

Ten cars rushed down the waterside
  Like lighted coffins in the dark;
With twenty dead men in each car,
  That must be brought alive by work:
These people work too hard, thought I,
And long before their time they die.

192–

Remember Scarborough

The Appeal

Working men of England! have you forgotten Scarborough
The white drawn faces of the children that were killed?
How can you forget the women slain at Hartlepool?
How can you rest with your vengeance unfulfilled?

The Answer

Vengeance for these must our German brothers take for us;
When the day shall come for vengeance, we have other
                                        work to do!
There are blood-stains still on the paving-stones of Dublin:
And hundred years have passed – but we remember
                                        Peterloo!

There are widows in the streets of Tonypandy:
In Mitchelstown and Featherstone our brothers' blood
                                        was shed.
Take heed, oh, our masters, how you talk to us of
                                        vengeance,
Lest we turn on you – and take it – and avenge our
                                        English dead.

May 1915

May Day, 1917

Spring should be with us – but spring is a laggart.
We are weary of waiting; and winter is long.
Slowly, ah, slowly, the boughs come to burgeoning;
Tardily, tardily, birds wake to song.

Over a year ago, flaming to westward,
Spring came to Eirinn: the dark Rosaleen,
Clad in white cloud, golden gorse and green meadow,
Rose in a glory of gold, white and green.

Now once again the old earth is a-tremble
With the joy and the passion and pulse of the spring:
Far to the eastward the new buds are blossoming:
Fruitful, O God, be the promise they bring.

Spring, that has come to the east – and the westward,
Soon may it come to rouse England again;
Come to her, red as her own English roses,
Red as the blood in the hearts of her men.

1917

A Ballade of Reconstruction

Our masters – seeing us a little tired
        Of war – for even wars begin to pall;
Seeing us growing restless, are inspired –
        Lest we should once again begin to call
        For liberty and justice, and to bawl
For things we've tended to forget of late –
        To promise, lest some graver thing befall,
They'll reconstruct our England while we wait.

They, in our very green and pleasant land,
    Will build Jerusalem; will overhaul
The older England, till an England planned
    To give each Englishman, or great or small,
    That which he wishes – if it's not too tall
An order – comes to being; from a state
    Better than ever graced this earthly ball;
And reconstruct our England while we wait.

Wherefore – some politicians, one or two
    Leaders of Labour (not the kind who brawl),
Some trusty Civil Servants, and a few
    Ambitious youngsters with an Oxford drawl
    Will sit on sub-committees in Whitehall,
And draw up schemes to settle England's fate;
    Will draft reports, and sit and talk and scrawl,
And reconstruct our England while we wait.

Then, when we've waited for a year or so,
    Always expecting that they'll soon instal
The new millennium for high and low,
    Into our minds it will begin to crawl
    That Labour still is hopelessly in thrall.
That Capital's not going to abdicate,
    That Governments do not intend to fall
To reconstructing England while we wait.

Envoi
Princes, the thought may very well appal
    You and your henchmen that some sudden spate
Of revolution may engulf you all,
    And we rebuild our England – and not wait.

1918

Comrades

As I was marching in Flanders
A ghost kept step with me –
Kept step with me and chuckled
And muttered ceaselessly –

Once I too marched in Flanders,
The very spit of you,
And just a hundred years since,
To fall at Waterloo.

They burried me in Flanders
Upon the field of blood,
And long I've lain forgotten
Deep in the Flemish mud.

But now you march in Flanders,
The very spit of me,
To the ending of the day's march
I'll bear you company.

1916

Out of the Pit

You are just out of the pit?
                        I'm out of the pit.
And lucky, my lad, to escape with your life out of it!

Ay, to be sure, in a way – and yet, I don't know
I can't say that I'm out of the pit, while a lad's left below.

1925–27

Fire

Across the Cleveland countryside the train
Panted and jolted through the lurid night
Of monstrous slag-heaps in the leaping light
Of belching furnaces: the driving rain
Lacing the glass with gold in that red glare
That momentarily revealed the cinderous land,
Of blasted fields, that stretched on either hand,
With livid waters gleaming here and there.

By hovels of men who labour till they die
With iron and the fire that never sleeps,
We plunged in pitchy night among huge heaps –
Then once again that red glare lit the sky
And high above the highest hill of slag
I saw Prometheus hanging from his crag.

1930

Unity

When the cooling tyre contracts
Round the felloe of the wheel,
Do not spokes that once were boughs
In close-knitting fibres feel
A glow in being ironbound
In unity secure and round
For conquest of untravelled ground?

The Answer

Give us security! to life we cry.
And would you, then, have death before you die?

Murderers

And so we're hanging Robert Smith to-day.
We're hanging him?

                    Ay, so the papers say.
But I'm no hangman.

                    No, to save your face,
You pay another man to take your place.
Mine? Nonsense! I know nothing of the case:
Murders are not in my line: I'd not heard
A thing about it — hadn't read a word ...
Why, till you spoke just now, I didn't know
There'd even been a trial!

                    Ay, just so.
Murders are not in our line, as you say,
And yet we're taking a man's life to-day.

Karl Marx

With the infinite wealth of his learning,
    In the temple of Genius planned;
And the strength of a limitless yearning,
    He peered in all doctrines and scanned
Every creed of the past and the present,
    Writ in star or in cross or in crescent,
And high in a night which was blackened with shame
    Bore the Promethean brand.

In the noontide, the twilight, and dawning
    He wrought for Futurity's ends!
Every whisper of selfishness scorning,
    Save their love and his love for his friends:
And the touchstone of selfless endeavour
    Illumined the spark that forever
Shall gleam in the peerless forever of Man,
    A forever that nothing transcends.

We have gazed at mankind in the making,
    Down the horrific depths of the past;
We have followed the trail of his breaking,
    And shrank from its horror aghast:
By blood-sodden paths have we striven,
    For the secret his labour hath given;
A secret revealed by a sacrifice made.
    In a struggle titanic and vast.

337

In Humanity's birthday abysmal,
  When man was but more than the brute,
In an Eden afflicted and dismal,
  Was Freedom the name of the Fruit
That we lost at the moment of tasting?
  Or was it the fruit that is wasting
The race, from the tree that has Gold on its boughs,
  And Corruption and Hate at its root?

As the minstrels of eras grown olden
  Solved part of the problem by guess,
And hymned it in narrative golden,
  Bedight in a sanctified dress,
So vouchsafed to him was the solving
  Of the riddle recurrent, revolving,
The social enigma of baffled mankind,
  The problem of Wrong and Redress.

With the lancet of Wisdom he probed
  To the heart of the question awry;
And bared to the vision unrobed –
  Foul Greed with the hate in its eye;
And the message to men undiscerning,
  He gave in the utterance burning –
Greed is the God of the beast-like, and crept
  From the cancerous womb of a lie.

With his back to the past and its errors,
  Where the red blood of martyrdom drips –
A city of ignorant terrors,
  In a land of eternal eclipse –
He hastened for toilers awakening,
  The day of a dawn that is breaking!
With purpose magnificent writ on his brow,
  And the Music of Truth on his lips.

Unto Labour he pointed the Birthright,
  Witheld since Nativity's hour –
To shiver the gyves of the earth might,
  And encompass a world in its power:
Erect and undaunted achieving,
  Its mission of Destiny's weaving –
To idleness weeds that are sapless and sere,
  And to Labour the fruit and the flower.

He was not for one folk or one nation,
  Nor for Gentile alone nor for Jew;
He sought not a crowd's adulation,
  Nor the sycophant praise of a few!
He is timed by no measure diurnal,
  But for all and forever eternal;
For of all things eternal the greatest is Truth,
  And all that he gave us is true.

And the sound of his name shall be token
  Until the Red Banner is furled,
That the chains of mankind shall be broken
  And the Wrong from its eminence hurled!
Till the earth is delivered of madness,
  And Liberty, reigning in gladness,
May fold the tired wings that now flutter in vain
  On the winds of a blood-stricken world.

May 1918

To the Memory of Liebknecht and Luxemburg

From Past's cimmerian night to Present's morrow,
    Through ages stained with wrongless blood and tears,
Sweeps a grand symphony of human sorrow,
    One throbbing masterpiece of hopes and fears:
In cadence soft from trembling swell descended,
    The story pours of that divinity,
Which bade men living, live with courage splendid,
    And dying, die to set their fellows free.

The chords of hate with age grown old and wrinkled,
    The staves once filled with the accursèd lore
Of thrones with sacredotal incense sprinkled,
    Are blotted deep on that eternal score:
No song divine but Discord's idle wailing,
    Did these inspire in mortals weak and vain,
The censer hides the stench of human failing,
    The crown obscures the brand of murd'rous Cain.

The song is there of many a grand Isaiah,
    Whose name has perished in the far-away,
Daring with burning scorn's ironic fire,
    Some puny despot of a little day:
Or Nathan bold whose troubled spirit brooded
    Alone in lair of some wild beast or bird,
And to a lecherous throne his truth intruded,
    To contradict a lustful tyrant's word.

And many a Spartacus of glorious daring,
    And Eunus of the wide Sicilian plain;
And many a Jesus who with gentle bearing,
    Carried the world's gigantic cross of pain.

And all who lived with purpose strong yet tender,
 Treading the path of sacrifice sublime,
Who held aloft the flaming torch of splendour,
 And fell beneath the blows of ruthless crime.

The battle's roar, the plash of warfare's torrent
 Are drowned in harmonies divinely pure;
What man has glorified in crime abhorrent
 With melodies of Love can ne'er endure!
But not one feeble effort is forgotten
 Of those who tried to magnify the race;
The deeds that live are those by Love begotten,
 Far mightier they than Death, or Time, or Space!

Of such the dead whose deathless inspiration
 Evokes the humble tribute of my song:
Who on the stone of selfless immolation,
 Gave up their lives to slay tyrannic wrong;
Who with untiring labour abrogating
 Earth's foulest curse, have sealed it with their blood –
Now with avenging call reverberating,
 From the great sanctuary of Brotherhood.

193–

The Proletarian Pedigree

Working folk in the days of old
By lords and ladies were bought and sold
For so many pieces of silver and gold,
 According to their worth;
And babies born to a vulgar slave
Had neither bodies nor souls to save
But until they sank to a nameless grave
 Were somebody's slaves from birth.

341

At a later day it came to pass
That every lad and every lass
Wore round the neck a girdle of brass
   Engraved with a neat inscription –
Of the lowly name of the thrall abhorr'd,
The lordly name of his noble lord,
   And things of a like description.

The years flew by and they drove away
The humble thrall of inferior clay,
And onto the stage in this brutal play
   Stalked the "villein" of sad disaster;
He wore no longer the brazen gyve,
But had, in order to keep alive,
To wretchedly toil and woefully strive
   In the fields of a lordly master.

And thus he lived with a mind distraught,
Till another ingenious change was wrought
In the distant life of this abject sport
   Of the dark and horrible ages;
When the worker, freed from his master's land,
Heard Capital's word of stern command,
And from being a villein became a "hand"
   To toil for his weekly wages.

Once slave of a man, now slave of a class,
To render docile the two legged ass,
They took from his neck the circlet of brass
   And fastened it round his brain:
He adds with zest to his master's store
By toiling as never a slave before
Was ever compelled in the days of yore,
   And loves each link of his chain.

Superstition and idiot war,
Political cant and lunatic law,
He licks each hideous, festering sore,
   Blind as a bat unseeing:
Drugged by phrases honeyed and bland
To work for the good of a dronish band,
As slave, as thrall, as villein or hand,
   But never as human being.

But 'tis said that even a worm will turn,
And common folk are beginning to learn
The RIGHT TO LIVE they may quickly earn
   If they only but act correctly:
And the plundering gang that are out for loot
Shall discover some "rare and refreshing fruit"*
When REVOLUTION – the ugly brute –
   Has given them Hell directly.

* An historic cant-phrase invented by Mr. Lloyd George.

The Soul of Silas

My name is Silas Dirtydog – I've earned it, so they say;
I travel with the "bookies" and I'm canned up every
   day.
I've been at pocket-picking ever since I was a waif;
I have burgled many a mansion and I've rifled many a
   safe.
I've engineered a fire or two when biz was pretty slack;
I've faked 'em with the loaded dice and sharped 'em
   with the pack.

I might ha' been a pirate, too, I'm made o' proper
      stuff –
For I've scuttled ships afore to-day – when pay was big
      enough.

No doubt yer think a cove like me should ne'er ha' had
      a birth –
A dirty hookem-snivey cuss not fit to live on earth.
You're maybe right, old party, but – a whisper in your
      ear –
There's bigger swine than me about have very little fear.
In spite o' my confession, mate, o' worthless knavery,
I've always drawn the blinkin' line at servile slavery.
And I reckon I'm a cherubim – a seraph if yer like –
Beside the skunk as scabs it when his mates are out on
      strike.

Oak-Leaves

1. Mr. Churchill states that it is contemplated that men mentioned in despatches shall have permission to wear a small oak-leaf on the ribbon of the Victory Medal.

2. William Parry, a discharged soldier, has died in a hospital in Bath after going seventeen days without food in one of the arches of Newton Bridge.

> Eighty thousand oak-leaves
> >Leaves in hordes and batches,
> Oak-leaves for the heroes
> >Mentioned in despatches.

> Eighty thousand oak-leaves
> >As well as stars and crosses,
> To keep our memories evergreen
> >And help us bear our losses.

> Eighty thousand oak-leaves!
> >We learned when we were younger
> How robins covered up with leaves
> >Babes who died of hunger.

> Eighty thousand oak-leaves
> >Won on dangerous marches
> To cover William Parry up,
> >Who starved in Newton Arches.

1920

Nine Men's Morris

It was Nine Merry Morrismen, as May Day requires,
It was Nine Merry Morrismen went dancing like their
sires,
With bells and with handkerchief, with pipe and with
tabor,
And each Merry Morrisman danced better than his neigh-
bour,
On May Day
On May Day
As they went through the shires.

And what are you looking for, you Nine Merry men?
We're seeking Merry England by field and by fen.
But where has she hid herself, so blithe and so pretty?
Oh, is it in the village, or is it in the city?
On May Day
On May Day
That we'll find her again?

We've sought her in the factory, we've sought her in the
mine,
And the dance is a hard one for the strongest of the Nine,
For everywhere the dance goes, not one of our paces
But is watched by lean and hungry eyes, and white,
anxious faces –
Oh, May Day
Sweet May Day,
What's come to thee and thine?

It was Nine Merry Morrismen, as May Day requires
Went seeking for the England called Merry by their sires,
And their bells ceased from ringing as their feet ceased
from leaping,

And they used their coloured handkerchiefs to dry the
children's weeping,

On May Day
On May Day
As they went through the shires.

1921

Promises

"Stand by me!" said the Government
Twelve years since, in 'Fourteen.
"The Country's in a fix, lads,
And needs you on the scene.
Stand by the Country's Standard
And see the trouble through –
And when the war is over
Count on US to stand by you!"

"Stand by us!" says the Government,
In Nineteen-Twenty-Six,
"There's trouble in the air, lads,
And the State is in a fix."
"Stand by us!" says the Government
"And see the trouble through –
And when the Strike is over
Count on us to stand by you!"

Oh hark! the twelve-years' Echo:
"Count on US to stand by You . . ."

May 1926

Meditations of a Trade Unionist on Reading Mr. Baldwin's
Latest Guarantees to Strike-Breakers

So you will "guarantee" that all I'd lose
In Union benefits should be made up,
And you MIGHT keep your promise, though the woes
Of them that gave up everything to fight
And now are starving with their wives and kids
Make one a bit suspicious;
Still, you MIGHT!

Also you've promised you'd protect my skin
And save my bones and make it safe for me
To walk about and work and earn my keep,
I'm not afraid for that. I know my mates;
They're decent, quiet chaps, not hooligans.
They wouldn't try to murder me,
Not they!

But could you make them treat me as a pal,
Or shield me from their cold, contemptuous eyes?
Could you call back my ruined self-respect,
Give me protection from my bitter shame,
From self-contempt that drives out happiness?

Such guarantees are not in mortal power.
I'm sticking to my mates:
That's my reply.

May 1926

To the Memory of John Maclean

Why do the crowds assemble, why do the tear-drops fall?
Why is the solemn music played, the march of death from
Saul?
Old and young are weeping, moved by the sad refrain,
As they march to the grave with a rebel — our comrade
John Maclean.

He smiled in the face of danger, with torture his hair was
grey,
He feared not the bars of the prison, his path was the
thorny way;
He sneered at the traitors and cowards, he battled with
might and main
To free us for ever from bondage, did comrade John
Maclean.

Woe to the tyrants ruling who sneer at his resting clay,
The power they have o'er the people will yet be swept
away.
The workers rise from slumber to break the binding chain,
'Tis then they'll understand the words of comrade John
Maclean.

He looked on a world of plentry and saw the makers
starve,
He then proclaimed this should not be when parasites
could carve.

In war he saw the workers killed, the tyrants to maintain,
"All power to those who make all things!" cried comrade
John Maclean.

He longed to see the dawn of light break thro' the dark-
ened skies.
The men who knelt at Mammon's shrine he always did
despise.
He told the truth and shamed the world, he suffered grief
and pain.
We seldom see a man so brave as comrade John Maclean.

Although the grave his body holds, his soul they cannot kill,
They are but fools who think him dead, his spirit's with
us still;
The firm determination with the courage to attain,
Were left us as a legacy by comrade John Maclean.

Good men are few and far between, they leave their mark
and go.
And John Maclean was one of those who struck a deadly
blow
At all the vile hypocrisy, the murder and the stain
That cloaked itself in pious robes to fight against Maclean.

Then let us o'er his ashes swear and by the tears he shed
"We'll never rest till o'er the earth there flies the flag of
Red!"
This fight for Human Brotherhood can never be in vain,
"The darkest hour's before the dawn!" said comrade John
Maclean.

1923

Hail to the Revolution

Hail to the Revolution,
  It comes o'er the misty hills;
I stretch my hands to meet its light,
  And I feel its mighty thrills;
The workers from mine and factory
  Are running to hail its light;
Gone for ever the rusty chains,
  Gone for ever the night.

Hail to the Revolution!
  Welcome to mine and loom;
Kings and rulers from bloody thrones
  Are driven to their doom;
I hear the laughter of children,
  And joyous songs of the free,
I see the dance of victorious crowds,
  Where tyranny used to be.

Hail to the Revolution!
  The slaves at last are free,
I hear the sound of a million feet,
  Marching to victory.
The nocturnal beasts of poverty,
  Flee in a dismal plight
For the dawn of truth, in rhythmic waves
  Spreads o'er the hills of night.

Hail to the Revolution!
　　The hosts of the mighty have fled;
Millions welcome the red, red dawn,
　　And they hail the banner red;
The crown, the throne and the sceptre
　　At last have lost their charm;
The day of the pick and shovel has dawned,
　　The day of the mighty arm.

Hail to the Revolution!
　　With thundering guns it comes;
It speaks to the great in accents of lead,
　　It speaks in the bursting bombs;
What if the blood of the tyrants
　　Is mingled with the red of the dawn,
The workers are marching to victory,
　　The workers are claiming their own!

1930?

The Image o' God

Crawlin' aboot like a snail in the mud,
  Covered wi' clammie blae,
Me, made after the image o' God –
  Jings! but its laughable, tae.

Howkin' awa' 'neath a mountain o' stane,
  Gaspin for want o' air,
The sweat makin' streams doon my bare back-bane,
  And my knees a' hauckit and sair.

Strainin' and cursin' the hale shift through,
  Half starved, half-blin', half mad,
And the gaffer says, "Less dirt in that coal
  Or ye go up the pit, my lad!"

So gie my life to the Nimmo squad,
  For eicht and fower a day,
Me! made after the image o' God –
  Jings! but its laughable tae.

The Awakening

We have served the rich for a thousand years,
　　Through blood and tears and shame,
As serf and slave our manhood gave,
　　To win them wealth and fame –
They have slain our best in the vile gold-quest,
　By war and toil and death –
If blood be the price of their hoarded gains,
　　Good God! we have bought the earth.

There's never a war been waged
　　But we were the men that bled;
We've left our bones in all their lands
　　(Right well are they mapped out red).
The spoils we share are the medals we wear,
　　While widows and orphans wail;
Who writes the story of Empire,
　　　Good God! writes a shameful tale.

There's never a paper published now
　　But tells how the worker died,
That the tale of wealth might be increased,
　　And Capital justified.
Go! Count our dead at the grim pit-head,
　　Distorted and torn and rent;
If blood be the price of dividends,
　　Good God! they are cent per cent.

Dividends, Rent and Interest,
  Chicanery, Lies and Brag –
These are the Gods of Empire,
  Their symbol – the British flag.
By guile and craft the lands that laughed
  Now weep neath these strange Gods' spell:
Yet – if blood be the price of atonement,
  Lord God! we have ransomed Hell.

We have served the rich for a thousand years
  Sparing neither age or sex;
White slaves in their "hives of industry",
  White rats on their sinking wrecks.
By sea and by track they turn us back
  From all that makes life fair;
The blood of our martyred class cries out –
  "Lord God! there's a debt to square."

1932

The Abandoned City

(Helsinki 1918)

The day dawned grey and cold
The streets in the city were empty
But behind the massive stone walls of the houses
People held their breaths:
Have our efforts been in vain?
Why is the dawn not red?
And the rats in the cellars laughed:
The day of the rats will come!

The day of the rats did come.
When the booming of the guns reached the city
And the last of the valiant soldiers had left
When the people were mourning their heroic dead
Out poured the rats from the cellars and doorways
Grinning with hatred and murder in their eyes.

The day of the rats had come with a vengeance.
The people were dragged from mourning their dead
Many were bitten and mauled to death
Many were thrown into dungeons and cellars
The streets were filled with corpses and blood
With cries of the homeless and starving children.

The day of the rats had come.
The rats are ruling the abandoned city.
Prosperity reigns for the rats in the city.
But behind the massive stone walls of the houses
People hold their breaths:
The day shall yet dawn red.

1935

Love's Hope

What did you say, my darling?
What did you say to me?

'That true love could beat
Life's easy defeat –
And such a love had we.'

What did you say, my sweetheart?
What did you say to me?

'That to live alone
Somewhere on our own,
Were it lowly, we'd be happy.'

Why do we quarrel, my angel?
Why do you quarrel with me?

'It's the torment all day,
Wondering how to pay
The rent, and for bread and tea.'

Why are you haggard, my loved one?
Haggard and careworn like me?

'Because all we now share
Is worry and care,
And days of drudgery.'

But why so downhearted, my dearest?
We'll join others such as we
Who are tearing away
At those chains each day
That shackle love to misery!

193–

Wherefore this Change?

My blood was cold, bitter and cold,
As frozen ice in arctic clime;
But now 'tis hot, aye boiling hot,
Like hunted fox that races time.

> My eyes were blind, completely blind,
> As robot man built from the clay.
> But now they see, aye clearly see,
> Like eagle grim seeking the prey.

My nerve was frail, so very frail,
As tortured bird, ensnared in cage;
But now 'tis firm, aye fiercely firm,
Like oaken tree of matured age.

> My mind was dull, entirely dull,
> As blunted sword of heavy lead;
> But now 'tis clear, aye truly clear,
> Like beaten skin, that's flaming red.

My heart was 'Fear', just frenzied fear,
As feeble mouse in forest fire;
But now 'tis brave, aye bitter brave,
Like sweated slave, with burning ire.

359

My ears were deaf, really stone deaf,
As landlord swine of rotting house;
But now they hear, aye grandly hear,
Like barking dog, calling a spouse.

My body was weak, broken and weak,
As starving mother, feeding child;
But now 'tis strong, aye surely strong,
Like Nature's horse when running wild.

Wherefore this change that alters me
This change loud as a thunderbolt?
'Tis that I heard and answered to
The noble call of Red Revolt!

193–

For Greater Things

Oh, it's nonsense, nonsense, nonsense,
Nonsense at this time of day
That breid-and-butter problems
S'ud be in ony man's way.

They s'ud be like the tails we tint
On leavin' the monkey stage;
A' maist folk fash aboot's alike
Primaeval to oor age.

We're grown-up folk that haena yet
Put bairnly things aside
– A' that's material and moral –
And oor new state descried.

Sport, love, and parentage,
Trade, politics, and law
S'ud be nae mair to us than braith
We hardly ken we draw.

Freein' oor poo'ers for greater things,
And fegs there's plenty o' them,
Tho' wha's still trammelt in alow
Canna be tent o' them –

> From *Second Hymn to Lenin*

1935

The Skeleton of the Future

(At Lenin's Tomb)

Red granite and black diorite, with the blue
Of the labradorite crystals gleaming like precious stones
In the light reflected from the snow; and behind them
The eternal lightening of Lenin's bones.

1934

In Monmouthshire

When greed was born
In Monmouthshire,
The hills were torn for Mammon's fire,
And wheels went round
And skulls were cracked,
And limbs were ground
And nerves were wracked.
No time to dream,
No time to stare,
In that fell scheme
To foul the air,
To grab the coal
And scorn the tree,
And sell the soul
To buy a spree.
And breasts were bruised
In dismal dens,
And streets were used
As breeding pens.
And babes were born
To feed the fire,
When hills were torn
In Monmouthshire.

From *Gwalia Deserta*

1938

Poems of the General Strike

Do you remember 1926? That summer of soup and
                                                 speeches,
The sunlight on the idle wheels and the deserted crossings,
And the laughter and the cursing in the moonlit streets?
Do you remember 1926? The slogans and the penny
                                                 concerts,
The jazz bands and the moorland picnics,
And the slanderous tongues of famous cities?
Do you remember 1926? The great dreams and the swift
                                                 disaster,
The fanatic and the traitor, and more than all,
The bravery of the simple, faithful folk?
'Ay, ay, we remember 1926,' said Dai and Shinkin,
As they stood on the kerb in Charing Cross Road,
'And we shall remember 1926 until our blood is dry.'

From *Gwalia Deserta*

The telephones are ringing,
And treachery's in the air
The sleek one,
The expert at compromise
Is bowing in Whitehall.

And lackey to fox to parrot cries:
'The nation must be saved.'
What is the nation, gentlemen,
Who are the nation, my lords?

The sleek one,
The expert in compromise
Is chattering in Whitehall.

The men who have made this nation,
Who have made her gross in wealth,
The men who have given their flesh and blood
From century to century,
They do not scream and panic,
They do not cringe and whine,
They do not shudder in the hour of crisis.
It is the robber and the gambler and the parasite
Who yell when the hour of reckoning comes.

But the sleek one,
The expert in compromise
Is signing in Whitehall.

The buying and selling is over,
The treachery sealed, and called
A national triumph;
And this Friday goes down to history
Yellow, and edged with black.

1938-53   From *The Angry Summer.*
                           A Poem of 1926

The summer wanes and the wine of words
Departs with the departing birds,
The roses are withering one by one
And the lesser grasses grow sick of the sun,
The mountain tops are torn and bare
And listless grows the secret hare.
Mother to mother begins to sigh
And slander is added to brazen lie
In many a distant seaside town
Where tempers go up when profits go down –

And here and there a traitor crawls
Back to the enemy's coloured walls,
Where food is rich and drink is free
To those who trade in treachery.
But the battle's end is not defeat
To that dream that guided the broken feet
And roused to beauty and to pride
Toiler and toiler, side by side,
Whose faith and courage shall be told
In blaze of scarlet and of gold.

From *The Angry Summer*.
A Poem of 1926

Come Down

Come down, young mountain dreamer, to the crowded
                                public square
Where anger breaks into music and thrills through
                                the common air,
And leave to fade behind you the fantasies you fed
From the sentimental sluices of a culture
                                dying and dead.

Come down from the mindless mountain
                                and let your day dreams die
On the aimless wind that wanders across
                                the friendless sky,
And come with your sense quickened and
                                give the best you can
To speed the day that knows anew the
                                dignity of man.

1943

William Morris

Because the mind is growing cold,
A slave that bends to the God of Gold,
We have no time to learn your lay,
Sweet singer of an idle day.

We have great problems and great pains
And gas mask drills and aeroplanes:
We would not understand your way,
Sweet singer of an idle day.

We have no frenzy in the heart,
We play a mean mechanic part —
You would not understand our way,
Sweet singer of an idle day.

We honour dolts in racing cars
And dirty dogs and talkie stars;
Our fields are brown, our children grey,
O singer of an idle day!

To the Wife of a Non-Interventionist Statesman

(March 1938)

Permit me, Madam, to invade,
briefly, your boudoir's pleasant shade.
Invade? No, that's entirely wrong!
I volunteered, and came along.
So please don't yell, or make a scene,
or ring for James to – intervene.
I'm here entirely for the good
of you and yours, it's understood.
No ballyhoo, what I've to say
may stand you in good stead one day.

   I have to broach a matter that
less downright folk might boggle at,
but none need blush because we try
to analyse the marriage tie.

   The voice that breathed o'er Eden laid
some precepts down to be obeyed:
to seek in marriage mutual trust
much more than sentiment or lust:
to base our passion on esteem
and build a home for love's young dream.
With this in mind, I'll state a case
of interest to the human race.

Suppose your husband yarns in bed
of plans that fill his lofty head,
think what should be a wife's reaction
if he turned out the tool of faction,
who put across the crooked schemes
of statesmen sunk in backward dreams;
whose suave compliance sealed the fate
of thousands left to Franco's hate –
(those very Basques whose fathers drowned
to keep our food-ships safe and sound,
sweeping for mines in furious seas).
Our fleet stood by, but ill at ease:
restive, our sailors watched the shore
whilst hundreds drowned who'd starved before,
victims of Franco's sham blockade –
though in the way of honest trade
Potato Jones and his brave lass
had proved this husband knave or ass.

Suppose he argues: Though I swerved
from honour's course, yet peace is served?

Euzkadi's mines supply the ore
to feed the Nazi dogs of war:
Guernica's thermite rain transpires
in doom on Oxford's dreaming spires:
in Hitler's frantic mental haze
already Hull and Cardiff blaze,
and Paul's grey dome rocks to the blast
of air-torpedoes screaming past.

From small beginnings mighty ends,
from calling rebel generals friends,
from being taught at public schools
to think the common people fools,
Spain bleeds, and England wildly gambles
to bribe the butcher in the shambles.

Traitor and fool's a combination
to lower wifely estimation,
although there's not an Act in force
making it grounds for a divorce;
but canon law forbids at least
co-habitation with a beast.

The grim crescendo rises still
at the Black International's will.
Mad with the loss of Teruel
the bestial Duce looses hell;
on Barcelona slums he rains
German bombs from Fiat planes.
Five hundred dead at ten a second
is the world record so far reckoned;
a hundred children in one street,
their little hands and guts and feet,
like offal round a butcher's stall,
scattered where they'd been playing ball –
because our ruling clique's pretences
rob loyal Spain of her defences,
the chaser planes and ack-ack guns
from which the prudent Fascist runs.

So time reveals what people meant
who framed a Gentlemen's Agreement,
and lest a final crime condones
fresh massacres with British loans,
should not its sponsor be outlawed
from power, position, bed and board?
Would not a thinking wife contemn
the sneaking hand that held the pen
and with a flourish signed the deed
whence all these hearts and bodies bleed?

Would not those fingers freeze the breast
where the young life should feed and rest?
Would not his breath reek of the tomb
and with cold horror seal her womb?
Could a true woman bear his brat?
The millions wouldn't.

                    Thanks, my hat.

1938

Luxury

The long, sleek cars rasp softly on the curb
and twittering women rise from cushioned nests,
flamingo-tall, whose rosy legs disturb
the mirror-surface where creation rests.

Aconite, Opium, Mandragora, Girl!
Essential phials exquisite array!
Poisons whose frail, consumptive fervours whirl
the stony city to a fierce decay.

The churches' sun-dried clay crumbles at last,
the Courts of Justice wither like a stink
and honourable statues melt as fast
as greasy garbage down a kitchen-sink.

Commercial palaces, hôtels de luxe
and Banks in white, immutable ravines,
life's skeleton unfleshed by cynic rooks,
remain to warn the traveller what it means.

The shady universe, once haunt of play,
in leafless winter bares its ways of stone;
the paths we shared, the mounds on which we lay
were ruled by Time and lifted by old bone.

Time has no pity for this world of graves
nor for its dead decked out in feathery shrouds.
The ghoul must perish with the flesh he craves
when stars' hoarse bells of doom toll in the clouds.

Foondry Lane

There's a Juter and a Battener
 Sailing up the Tay,
And a' the wives in Foondry Lane
 Are singing blithe the day.
There'll be pennies for the bairnies
 A pint for Jock and Tam,
Money for the picters,
 The auld fowk get a dram.

We'll gie the secks the go by,
 We canna sew and eat,
And fivepence for twenty-five
 Will no buy muckle meat.
We'll hae steak and ingins frying,
 Lift oor claes a' oot the pawn,
We'll gaither wulks and boil them
 In a corn beef can.

193–

The International Brigade

Not for the medals did these men fight,
Nor for the hope of reward or publicity,
But for the simple yet glorious ideals of the militant
worker.
An ideal that dwelt not in the heavens,
But shone from the earth as a beacon of hope –
The unity of the common peoples.

United they fought, united they drove back
The war machines of barbarism and tyranny.
United in mind and purpose their glorious example will
not die.
Therefore, Proletariat – hear these words,
"These men who gave everything shall behold
The Workers of the World unite."

1939

Thoughts of a Country-Loving Miner

When I rebel against the monotony of the everyday,
I am troubled and my heart is ill at ease –
As I lie by some brook, in some lonely valley
Penning these lines – my mind is not happy
Nor my conscience comfortable.

Rudely, and with impatience, I try
To thrust from my thoughts the diversions oppressing
                                                    them,
And with deceitful selfishness, feast greedily my eyes
Upon the hills, cumulous clouds, and green mosses.

As I gaze my vision becomes disturbed,
And I see my fellow-men toiling in the grime and dust,
Hear them cursing the heat,
See them gulping water from a bottle,
And wipe black lips with a blacker hand –
They think clean sheets and a pillow-sleep,
And their aching limbs move faster,
And the black coal rolls from the biting angry steel –
I see them with the Armies of Freedom – plunging steel
Into the heart of tyranny . . . and I know . . .

I must hurl from softened hands the pen,
Tear into shreds the parchment,
And hurry back into the ranks of my comrades.
I too must sweat and swallow the dust –
Curse the heat with the rest,
And plunge my steel into the black coal,
No solitude must I experience,
I am needed in the struggle,
As are we all,
None is above the other,
We are all one – with one goal,
No favours can anyone be accorded,
We must work and fight –
OURS MUST BE THE VICTORY.

To Karl Marx

We, who have won from the primeval wood
And are self-conscious of our heritage;
Keeping behind our breast, as in a cage,
These brute desires which still must be subdued,
Fear not the consummation of that feud
Prefigured, Marx, upon your passionate page
And rousing to fulfilment, in this age,
From the harsh jungle of our brotherhood.
Yet not the pity, nor the hungry lust
For retribution, nor the wrath made blind
By all the innocent blood sweated to dust,
Shall be the strength that fortifies our mind
For action; but the faith which scorns to mistrust
The magnanimity of humankind.

1939

Advent of Spring of 1939

Nations in hesitancy wait
Assured that change must come;
Yet fearful to unlock the gate
And face the approaching doom.

And like a greyness from the breast
The dark air hides the sun:
The halted buds are unreleased:
The birds but feebly tune.

Blind eyes upon the landscape look:
Blind hands on iron close:
O! men, this hour is a rebuke
While yet your heart can choose.

1939

Direction

We move towards a stormier day
And into deeper glooms,
What sign shall be upon our way
When darkest midnight comes?

What surance shall be at our side
When halted in a waste:
What guidance not to be denied
By blood on hands or breast?

If one cry *brother!* without fear,
Answer him with your faith;
And in the gloom shall be a star,
And in the dust a path.

1941

Soldiers 1939

And every time I see you marching, soldiers,
The same old sergeant and the same old kit ...
I see the windy hills beyond Toledo,
I see us marching, marching from Madrid.

Germans and Englishmen, I see us marching,
Red flags and fire – how the night was lit!
A woman lifts her child. "What are they singing, Mother?"
"They are singing of Madrid, niñito, of Madrid."

And every time I see you marching, soldiers,
The songs you sing are childish, uninspired,
Men with a glorious hope sing not like that,
Your legs are swinging, soldiers, but your eyes are tired.

My father saw your fathers marching, soldiers,
And where your fathers died you die again.
A cross in Flanders, in forgotten deserts ...
Poilu, where do you fight? We fought in Spain.

And every time I see you marching, soldiers,
The same old gun and pack and bayonet,
I see us marching, marching for Madrid.

You do not march like that, soldiers –
Not yet. Not yet.

1939

South Welsh Prophecy

Shall I again from some English gutter
    Sing out my love for the passionate valley,
Shall I again in a lonely city
    Undercut rates of English navvies?

Shall I again tramp over the mountains
    Into the streets of my enemy's pity,
Where no coal is under the pavements
    And no fire in night's jesting?

Shall I again feel flesh grow flabby
    On derelict fists in charity pockets,
Carry a miner's heart in the body
    Of a docile performing Taffy?

      . . .

Breasts of my mother nourished my hungry
    Hatred of masters who crushed my father.
But my father's patience taught me
    Skill of hewing and ca-canny.

Clad in the armour of my suspicion
    I went the road of a black-faced army,
Warm to the warmth of my fervent people,
    Chill to the common sense of owners.

Have I not honoured the hands that fed me?
    Even as death in firedamp crannies.
Have I not treasured their bony wisdom?
    Even as coaldust in my lungs.

      . . .

War has this day at last in my favour
　　Loaded the dice of bargaining power;
I could set silent snares over pitheads
　　Trapping redress in world destruction.

This day of vengeance I must pass over.
　　No, I will not, in hell we have waited.
Traitors and cowards! Steady my anger:
　　Pass this day of vengeance over.

Temper your fetters into new weapons,
　　Steel-breaking steam-coal anthracite volleys,
Learn new strategy from old captains –
　　Coal for your vanguards Tonypandy!

1944

Observation Post: Forward Area

The thorns are bleached and brittle,
The empty folds decay,
The rooftrees creak in the silence
Of inarticulate dismay.

Drought denudes the planting;
In the dry red heat
Dawn spills its ghostly water,
Black heads on the wheat.

Some evil presence quenches
The vagrant drunken theme
Of the swart and skinny goatherd
The black goats of his dream.

A darker beast than poverty
Transfixed the crouching peasants there,
And tore the votive tablets down,
And filled the children with such fear.

The cowdung fires guttered out,
The wizened women cried,
The bridegroom lay trembling,
And rigid the bride.

Love could be had for nothing.
And where is love now?

Gone with the shambling oxen,
Gone with the broken plough,
Death lives here now.

1942–43

Sacco Writes to His Son

I did not want to die. I wanted you,
You and your sister Inez and your mother.
Reject this death, my Dante, seek out Life,
Yet not the death-in-life that most men live.
My body aches ... I think I hear you weep.
You must not weep. Tears are a waste of strength,
Seven years your mother wept, not as your mother,
But as my wife. So make her more your mother.
Take her the ways I know she can escape
From the poor soulness that so wearies her.
Take her into the country every Sunday,
Ask her the name of such and such a plant.
Gather a basket each of herbs and flowers,
Ask her to find the robin where he nests,
She will be happy then. Tears do no damage
That spring from gladness, though they scald the throat.
Go patiently about it. Not too much
Just yet, Dante, good boy. You'll know.

And for yourself, remember in the play
Of happiness you must not act alone.
The joy is in the sharing of the feast.
Also be like a man in how you greet
The suffering that makes your young face thin.

Be not perturbed if you are called to fight.
Only a fool thinks life was made his way,
A fool or the daughter of a wealthy house.
Husband yourself, but never stale your mind
With prudence or with doubting. I could wish
You saw my body slipping from the chair
Tomorrow. You'd remember that, my son,
And would not weigh the cost of our struggle
Against the product as a poor wife does.
But I'll not break your sleep with such a nightmare.
You looked so happy when you lay asleep...

But I have neither strength nor room for all
These thoughts. One single thought's enough
To fill immensity. I drop my pen...

I hope this letter finds you in good health,
My son, my comrade. Will you give my love
To Inez and your mother and my friends.
Bartolo also sends his greetings to you.
I would have written better and more simple
Except my head spins like a dancing top
And my hand trembles... I am Oh, so weak...

Destruction

This is the street I inhabit.
Where my bread is earned my body must stay.
This village sinks drearily deeper
In its sullen hacked-out valley
And my soul flies ever more rarely
To the eyries among the Welsh mountains.

Massive above the dismantled pitshaft
The eight-arched viaduct clamps the sky with stone.
Across the high-flung bridge a goods train rumbles,
Its clanking wagons make my fixed rails rock,
And the smoke from its engine blows higher than my
                                        desire;
Its furnace glowers in my vast grey sky.

Under this viaduct of my soul
The poisoned river makes its dirty bed,
Wherein a girl lies dreaming, diffusing attar of roses.
And I in bitterness wonder
Why love's silk thread should snap,
Though the bands be never so gentle;
And why a destructive impulse should ruin a poem,
Like a schoolboy's sling that slays a swallow flashing
Under the viaduct's arch to the inaccessible eaves.

And now the impersonal drone of death
Trembles the throbbing night, the bombers swoop,
The sky is ripped like sacking with a scream.
The viaduct no longer spans the stream.

But my love knows nothing of that grim destruction,
For the night was about her, blinding her when she
                                        crossed it,
And the train that took her roaring towards the dayspring
Is rocking her through the dawn down empty sidings
Between dark tenements in the neutral city
To the street she must inhabit.

1940–41

Stalingrad

May it for ever live to be
The blood-soaked symbol of the Free
Against whose walls of pride and pain
The might of Evil stormed in vain.

May it, too, stand a beacon light
To help us through the after night
Make a New World in a brave mould
Out of the rubble of the Old!

194–

Back in the Return

Where shall the eye a darkness find
That is a menace to the mind
Save in the coal mine, where one's lamp
Is smothered oft by afterdamp?
Down there is found the deepest gloom,
Where Night is rotting in her tomb:
It is a being, something fraught
With evil, clutching at man's throat.
And O! the stillness underground!
Oppressive silence, ne'er a sound,
Save for the dribble here, and there,
A gas-pop, or a gust of air,
When idle are the wheels, and one
Sits down to listen, all alone;

When one will welcome, with surprise
The unmelodious squeak of mice;
From Baltic beetles gladly take,
And Jaspers, what small sounds they make –
To face it one must needs be brave
This silence of an old world's grave!
But when full work is on the air
Does a more homely garment wear,
When sometimes, floating on the foul,
Comes 'Jesus lover of my Soul',
Between spat Baccy Juice and smut,
From hewers squatting in the 'cut';
Or, coming from more distant stalls,
The rythmic tap of mandril falls
Upon the ear till one would swear
The pulse of *Earth* was beating there.
Back in the foul Return
Where bodies of men burn
Out, out before their time,
Where dead is the sublime,
And murdered is the soul
To keep the brute alive;
Where lust is in control,
Still young the sensitive
Must die, still young –
His songs unsung!

The mine is no romantic place –
It stinks to Hell from sump to 'face';
A honeycomb of headings, stalls,
Airways, drifts, and rubbish walls.
Intake fresh, and foul Return,
Which lighted once becomes an urn
For human ashes!

194–   From *Back in the Return*

George Loveless

Rise up, rise up, George Loveless,
Your spirit lives to-day,
Trade Unions in England
Defend a fair day's pay.

As once you stood up in the dock
Shouting "We shall be free,"
Against the blackest foe of all
We're standing up to-day.

The flame that burns in Stalingrad
In flesh and blood and bone
Belongs to you, George Loveless,
Not Soviet alone.

Man climbed the rungs of history,
And came into his own,
Belongs to you, John Nameless,
They shall not fight alone.

1943   From *The Ballad
                       of John Nameless*

Colour Bar

Lines for a well-appointed Lounge.

O dead men were yellow and dead men were Red,
Dead men were black men who couldn't find bread.
And here stand the living, well-dressed and well-fed.
The living are white men, occasionally tight men –
But always the right men to have and to hold
All the world's factories, all the world's gold.
Unblackened by labour, unreddened by blood,
Their white hands have hastened to nip every bud
That might flower into plenty for poor men, and all men,
For only the white men – and not all the white men,
But only the right men, the happy and few men,
May have and may hold. Yet what if the future,
That uncertain creature, should alter their colour,
Should grieve them, should leave them black and blue men,
Or castless or fleshless, to depend for their whiteness,
On the pie and the vulture, the sun and the sand?

1943

The Miner

He hung around the corners then,
He sometimes sang for bread,
The winding gear was red with rust,
And hope was almost dead.

He looked upon the haunting eyes
Of kids who asked him why
There was no coal upon the grate,
No stack dust in the sky.

Then charging from old Vulcan's forge
Came Mars his sword held high,
"Cwm Rhondda" rolls the drum of war,
And wheels began to fly.

The pit gear whirled away its rust,
The coal came flashing by,
The leaping flame was in the grate
The stack dust in the sky.

The tank and plane, the battleship,
The bullet, bomb and shell,
All came it seemed from that bright dust
That only he could sell.

So once again his pick he swung,
And breathed the dust filled air;
But even while he joked and laughed
The dread was always there.

The dread that Want might yet return
That England would forget
How victory was got of coal,
And coal was got of sweat.

1943

Stepney Green

Where I was born, near Stepney Green,
They toil all day on a sewing machine,
Marry on twopence and live on less,
Bring up a family on watercress.
They're mostly ill-starred,
But they die hard.

Where I was born, near Stepney Green,
They make fighting Cockneys out of margarine.
Some get old, and some T. B.
They're mostly ill-starred,
But they die hard.

Where I was born, near Stepney Green,
Some read Lenin, but none Racine.
Their learning is little, their culture less,
But Oxford's finding is Mile End's guess.
They're mostly ill-starred,
But they die hard.

194–

ANONYMOUS

A British soldier serving in Italy

Greek Tragedy

When down the mountain passes roared
The armour of the Nazi hoard,
The rulers of the invaded states,
Captains and Kings and proud prelates,
Fearing to meet with execution
All found in exile their solution.
The common people had to stay –
They lacked the means to run away.

"We" said the rulers "are the head,
Without our lead the land is dead.
If we were slain, 'tis clear, 'twould be
A national calamity . . .
The common folk, however, can
Bear with adversity, for man
Is born to trouble, as the sparks
Fly upward." With these wise remarks
They "lived to fight another day"
And, let us face it, ran away.

The fighting men laid down their arms.
The land was conquered. In the farms
And factories the people seem
To move as in a hideous dream.
Proud were they once, now they must bow
To fascist rods. They knew not how
To break the spell – until they heard
Spread like a fire the whispered word –

"Resist together! They are few
And we are many. You and you
And you, are needed in the fight.
We'll win at last. Our cause is right!"

But still the exiled bag o' tricks
In London played court politics.

Three years had passed, three years of war.
The people still fought on the more,
Though famine stalked across the land
And death was ever close at hand.
Until at last their allies gave
Assistance. Rescued from the grave
Of fascist might, they cheered amain –
Until they saw our baggage train.

For when they knew the foe undone
The "Government" came back from London.

The Allies came – the flowers of thanks
Had scarcely withered on their tanks –
Before the Old Gang trundled in
And said to ELAS with a grin,
"Now we've secured your liberation
Lay down your arms, you know that we
Are champions of Democracy.
In case you don't see what is meant
We've guns to back our argument."

"Democracy" each Partisan
Retorted, "means that every man
Should share the ruling of the State.
You'd rule alone – you've 'ad it mate.
Besides, in fighting with the Huns,
We too have learnt to handle guns."

The Old Gang said, "You bloody Reds,
We'd all be murdered in our beds
If you secured the power. What's more
You'd best give in to us before
Too late. It's no good getting skittish,
We have the backing of the British."

The rest I blush to tell, for we,
Who came to set the people free,
Upon those people turned the guns
Meant for the Bosche. Must British sons
Take what they came to give, and so
Die "to restore the *status quo*"?

1945

Nostalgie d'Automne

Island of shadow,
Silk of the Kine
Mouse in the meadow
And crab apple wine

Sun on the brambles
Rocking a pram
And driving the yellow
Wasps offa the jam

Sugar-pears hangin
Ripe ready to fall
And a lass stringin mushrooms
In warm Donegal

Starlings at sunset
Linnets at noon
And cat-owl and cricket
Cry out with the moon

Island of shadow
Silk of the Kine
Will Sickle and Hammer
Ever be thine?

Melon and marrow
Stored by the load
Here on a barrow
In Theobald's Road.

1945

Stalingrad

Hushed was the world and O dark agony that suspense
shook upon us
While hate came flooding o'er your wide savannahs
Plunging pestilence against you all that stood to state
That where men meet there meets one human race

Therefore did men from Moscow to the Arctic
Rounding Vladivostock south where Kasbek lifts its peak
Still work and working waited news of Stalingrad

And from cape to wide Sahara men asked
news of Stalingrad
Town and village waited what had come of
Stalingrad
The tom-tom beat across thick forest while
every evening at palaver

Old men told of Stalingrad
The gauchos caught the pampas whisper
Wind swept hope of Stalingrad
And in the far Canadian north
Trappers left their baiting for the latest out of
Stalingrad

In the factories and coalfields each shift
waited
What last had come from Stalingrad
While statesmen searched the dispatch boxes
What they brought of Stalingrad

        And women stopped at housework held their
                        children close to hear
        What was afoot at Stalingrad
        For well man knew that there a thousand years
                        was thrown the fate of the peoples

Stalingrad o star of glory
Star of hope o star of flame
O what a midwife for this glory
Take for the pattern Pavlov and his men
A Soviet soldier and his nine companions
Who full seven weeks sleepless by night and day
Fought nor gave ground
They knew that with them lay
That where men meet should meet one human race

Carpenters who had built houses wanted only to build more
Painters who still painted pictures wanted only to paint
                                            more
Men who sang life strong in laughter wanted only to sing
                                            more
Men who planted wheat and cotton wanted only to plant
                                            more
Men who set the years in freedom sure they would be
                                    slaves no more
They spoke peace to their neighbours at tilling
For in peace they would eat their bread
Uzbeks, Tatars, Letts, Ukrainians, Russians, Muscovites,
                                            Armenians
Who ringed forests wide round Arctic
Brought sands to blossom tundras dressed for spring
These kept faith in Stalin's town
We may not weep for those who silent now rest here
Garland these graves
These lives have garlanded
All our remaining days with hope

Stalingrad o star of glory
Star of hope here spread your flame

Now when news broke
That Stalingrad still lived upon the banks of Volga
That Stalingrad was still a Soviet town
Then the turner flung his lathe light as a bird
And the gaucho spread his riot in the pampas
For this news of Stalingrad
The tom-tom beat wild madness when the elders brought
palaver
These tidings out of Stalingrad
The English housewife stopped her housework held her
child close
And cried aloud now all men will be free
And from Good Hope black miners answered
This will help us to be free
In the prison camps of Belsen sick men routed from their
guards
Now life was certain soon all men would be free
New light broke upon Africa new strength for her peoples
New strength poured upon Asia new hope for her peoples
America dreamed new dreams from the strength of her
peoples
New men arose in Europe new force for her peoples
Once more they stand these men at lathe and spindle
To recreate their hours and each new day
Bid houses rise once more in Soviet country
Men ring forests wide round Arctic
Move rivers into deserts
And with high courage breed new generations
For still the land is theirs
Uzbeks, Tatars, Letts, Armenians
Caucasians, Muscovites, Crimeans
Still they speak peace to their neighbours at tilling

To all the wide world
And men come near to listen
Find by that day of Stalingrad
This voice is theirs.

The then Red star spread your flame upon me
For in your flame is earnest of my freedom
Now may I rendezvous with the world
Now may I joy in man's wide-flung diversity
For Stalingrad is still a Soviet town.

1945

All Men

I hear strong voices calling me brother from the rough
    horsehair tents of Mongolia
In Korea the rivers and mountains leap with the cry of
    their welcome
My heart sings in the lilt of the tear-twisted caress from
    the mountains and far lands of China
I gather like greeting from the red roughened hands of the
    steelmen of Sheffield
My smile is the smile of the miner descending the coalpits
    of Rhondda
I am by the side of the stevedore heaving bales in the
    shipyards of Antwerp
I reach around earth to embrace the Australian docker
For his handclasp assures me victory over subtly plotted
    deception
These are my strength my force their varied conceivings
My calm that in them my living may never decay

And since I am of Africa all that is Africa comes with me
Striding hot storm we come tenting our courage and hope
With the hope and the courage of the men of America
    Europe Australia and all the sea islands
The good men the true men the strong men the working
    men
Whose sweat is their daily bread whose strength is their
    class

Scientists craftsmen teachers painters poets philosophers
    come
We shall work till our power invested together create a
    new world
Till there be no longer famine in India
Till the Yangtse flood no more
Till we plant gardens in Gobi
Till we gather each year the harvest of the Sahara
Till our force bright as the atom blasts the evil oppression
    which cripples all our creations

And so, I rest the little blond German child gently against me
I trace the years with him
I rest the little black African child gently against me
He and the German boy trace the years with me
I rest the litle Kamchatchuan child gently against me
I rest the little Georgian child gently against me
She and the little Japanese boy trace the years with me
Let our love hold them till bright as the atom together
Their power blasts the evil oppression which cripples all
    our creation
Till man cover the earth with his glory as the waters cover
    the sea.

1952   From *My Song is for All Men*

400

Unity on the Clyde

Dedicated to brother members at Strathclyde Foundry

On Clydeside, drab Clydeside where foondries abound,
The pick o' the craftsmen are sure to be found,
And coontless huge castings are proof o' the fact,
Yet that's where some maisters hae least o' a' tact.
For years they've been planning to tighten the screw,
But worker to worker Clydesiders are true,
Wi' cunning the workers they've tried to divide,
But can't smash the unity found on the Clyde.

'Way back in the years when conditions were worst,
When John McLean suffered, but unity nursed,
When big Jock McBain led the workers to fight,
And blazoned the trail wi' his torch well alight,
Wi' things at their blackest such men led us through,
And mony a rhyme frae Tom Bell has come true,
When blacklegs obstructed they brushed them aside,
And nourished the unity found on the Clyde.

Aye, Glesca, yer workers are classed wi' the best,
They've nae time for maister's men, sons o' the west,
Nae creepers or crawlers amang them are seen,
They'd land in the watter that flows through the green.
When victimisation its ugly face shows,
They a' strike thegither and soon brak its nose,
I've travelled ower Scotland and worked far and wide,
But ne'er saw the unity found on the Clyde.

'Twas there I met Charlie the prince o' shop stewards,
Wha' on my behalf wi' the maister crossed swords.
A wee Irish fighter o' sterling and guts,
He said to the maister there's nae ifs or buts,
Such men mak the union oor pride and oor hope,
There's nae situation wi' which they can't cope,
Nae wrong to a workmate is ever let slide,
For such is the unity found on the Clyde.

They're a' brither members and wise maisters pause,
Before interfering wi' yin withoot cause.
They've worked hard for freedom withoot muckle rest,
But first they want freedom right here in the west.
When mealy-mouthed Tories lament o' the loss,
O' man hours through disputes, they ne'er blame the boss,
It's always the workers they try to deride,
Their dread is the unity found on the Clyde.

We might hae been slaves, noses held to the grind,
Had St. Mungo's sons to submit been inclined,
But they faced the maisters in yin solid mass,
And steeled ither workers to fight for their class.
Yet noo federated, proud maisters are strong,
And if we're no' carefu' they'll soon do us wrong.
So, close up yer ranks and wi' strength match their pride,
And follow the unity found on the Clyde.

1945

Song of the Moulder

Wha toils away for profits ne'er divided,
Wha pots and pans and guns has aye provided,
He is the craftsman foremost in the land,
The Moulder wi' his castings in the sand.
His song is in the whistling vent escaping,
While molten stream into the mould is shaping.

Wha crawls into the hottest mould for closing,
While gentlemen their course for golf are choosing?
He is the keystone in the scheme o' things:
We live by moulders though we die for kings.
His song is in the clang o' dresser's hammer,
Wi' yin discord the foreman's ceaseless clamour.

Wha maks the wheels that keep the world in motion?
Wha engines maks for ships to cross the ocean?
He is the Moulder wi' his matchless skill,
What shocks for wealth should he present his bill!
His song is in the mighty gear that's lifting
The fearfu' load beyond his strength for shifting.

Wha maks the stoves and grates for cosy hooses,
The baths and ither things o' coontless uses?
He is the man wha often gaes withoot
The very things he toils to bring aboot.
His song is in the roar o' furnace blasting,
It takes a lot o' hell to mak a casting.

Wha's slavish task is timed to keep him racing
Against the clock, wi' ither workmates pacing?
He is the man wha's back is ever bent,
And by the trade mark on his knees he's kent.
His song is in the scrapin' o' his trooin,
It's to his hand no matter what he's doin'.

Wha pays his dues to keep the union living,
To guard the little bit the boss is giving?
He kens his humble wage wad lower lie
Were he to let the union fade and die.
His song is in the shop steward's voice repeating,
The motions o' the men at ilka meeting.

Wha's day's work done, he hameward gaes to worry,
For moulds are ill to scan when man must hurry.
His is the task that's thankless to the last,
For fate is in the gamble o' the cast.
His song is in the cascade o' the metal –
'Tis life or death to him, the foondry battle.

1948

The Legend of County Louth

Tune: *The Northern Lights of Aberdeen*

In a little town in County Louth
  A strange thing you will see
Though the green, green grass grows all around
  Here none will ever be.
For the Black and Tans here killed a man
  Of the Irish Volunteers,
And where he was laid not a single blade
  Has grown for thirty years.

And in many a colony, I guess,
  Where the British Army goes
And out upon the green, green grass
  A patriot's life-blood flows,
Could children and martyred men
  Leave such a print indeed
The earth would soon lose all her bloom
  Ah! – and crimes no more be hid.

1957

Cypriot Question

Tune: *Boolavogue*

In Famagusta, one February morning
    The market place and the streets were full
When crowds of children marched protesting
    That General Harding had closed their school:
Then the British Army went into action
    With baton charges and tear gas drill
And the children's stones were met with bullets
  For the troops had orders to 'shoot to kill'.

Ah, British Mother, had you a boy there?
    No blame to him for the evil done
Or that a sorrowing Cypriot couple
    Lost that day a beloved son
When at eighteen years, in the cause of freedom
    Petrakis Yiallouris met his eclipse
Shot through the heart, by a conscript soldier,
    'Cyprus, Cyprus!' upon his lips.

When the dockers heard it, they struck in anger
    And our shops were closed and our streets were still
And we drew around us our little children
    Your troops had orders to 'shoot to kill';
But they feared Petrakis more dead than living
    And made us bury him out of sight
Fifty miles from the scene of the murder
  In lashing rain and by lantern light.

Scotland's hero, brave William Wallace
    They slew for the love he bore his land
And they shot James Connolly as he was dying
    And made a mighty crown of the felon's brand;

They make the widow, they make the orphan,
  They shoot the children – it's come to this:
But ah, British Mother, had they a quarrel
  Your conscript laddie and our Petrakis?

In February, 1956, in Famagusta, British troops opened
fire on a demonstration of school children. A shot from a
Sten gun killed Petrakis Yiallouris.

1956

My Country

*I stand here not as the accused, but as the accuser of
Capital, dripping in blood from head to foot.*
John Mac-Lean from the Dock

I

In this land a battle rages
  One side for your happiness
One side, Britain, for your sorrow
  One side for war, and one for peace.

But on which side, beloved country
  Can the naked truth be shown?
Which is Britain, who is Britain?
  Each side claims you for its own.

II

My country dwells in a tenement
    Dark and smoky
My country dwells in a cottage
    Tied to a job
My country toils in a shipyard
    Crawls in a mine
Steals hours from the night in overtime.
    Patriot, my country labours all his life
To keep a roof above his weans and wife.

    He fills this land with beauty and with wealth
And lives and dies in poverty himself.

My country is a mill hand, patriot
Whose darkened eyes watch life slip through her loom
My country is a pale-faced outworker
Stitching and stitching till the crack of doom.

My country is a labourer who toils
In bitter weather, carrying the hod
And when he's old and bent and choked with dust
You leave his widow to the Grace of God.

My country is a soldier, patriot
Who lost his arms and legs in your defense
And reaps the agony of war for life
While you rake in its golden dividends.

A mother who remembers in her heart
How you flung all her family on the dole
And not a child's hungry cry could pierce
Your pocket, or your patriotic soul.

My country is an old-age pensioner
Whose fading eyes stare in an empty grate
Whose trembling hands
For fifty years dug coal out of the earth
And made your children millionaires by birth
Now at the gates of life, my country sits
In a bare room as cold as charity
And he who gave it radiance must depart
From this great shining land in poverty
His precious last days comfortless and dark
That should be crowned with gaiety; his purse
As empty as your patriotic heart.

My country is a young lad doing time
Two years you sentenced him – theft was his crime
While you, great pillar of society
Who steal the golden promises of youth
Murder them in industry and slum
Give them instead of homes, the atom bomb
And march each generation off to war
You, who should be standing in the dock
Live petted and protected by the law.

My country is in a child's eyes
Who sees green fields as they were paradise
My country is a child's happy laughter
But oh, have you not seen my country's future
When that same child in a gully lies
Beside a brother he was sent to butcher?

My country's name in your cruel hand
Is writ in blood and fire by sea and land:
In the ashes of a Malayan village
In the rubble of a Korean town
On the charred lips of a Kikuyu child
Our name in agony is written down.

III

Patriot, on my country
You pour dishonour and shame
With a lash with a row of bullets
'Britain' – you write your name
With overflowing jails, huts put to the flame
With leprosy, with famine
In murder's foul hand
Where'er you chalk up dividends
You vilify our land.

But comes the day my country
Will bring you to disgrace
For the hatreds you engender
Among the human race
For the hatreds you engender
By tyranny and lies
And will stretch the hand of friendship
To the people you despise.

And you, who cast my country
In your own entwisted mould
And strangle love and beauty
With steel and smoking gold
Shall come before my country –
The people you refused
And you who judge the workers
Shall by them be accused.

IV

My country's splendour is the flame of them
Who fight to crush your cruel tyranny
My country's glory in the name of them
Who serve the great cause of humantiy.

My country's hope is in the working class
Who bring the visions of the slave to pass
My country's deep and patriotic love
Is in their heart, who fight your evil plan
And underneath the emblem of the Dove
Will build the grand society of Man.

Then with humanity, my country, march
Against the sway of brutal Capital
That rose to crush, created but to mar
Forged even the plough to feed the mills of war –
And we will build beside the Thames dark water
And we will build beside the rolling Clyde
A new society, that war and sorrow
And hate and avarice shall not divide,
And from land to land across the ocean
Eternal as the stars of heaven shine
Peace shall gather every creed and colour
Beneath her mighty wings –
                              O land divine

Where the ragged-trousered army rose
To fight for bread and freedom long ago
O land where yet the scarlet banner glows
That struck the first, strike now the final blow!
An epoch rests its glory on our shoulders
And deep as heart can think or eye can scan
The age which men have dreamed of is approaching
When joy shall be the natural state of Man.

1957

Socialism

Socialism, comrade
Is the world's most perfect poem
Whose first words were uttered
In the humblest little home;
Long ago 'twas spoken
In the hovels of the serf
In the huts of fisher-folk:
The meanest of the earth.
The wealthy tried to crush it
They tried to strike it dumb
The wealthy tried to twist it
With smooth and pious tongue
The wealthy tried to buy it
But their silver turned to dross
They burned it at the stake
They nailed it to the cross
They flung it into prison
They closed it in the grave:
But they might as well have tried
To stop the breaking wave.

For socialism, comrade
Was bound to come to pass
It was as predetermined
As the motions of the stars
It was in the cradle
When slavery was born
It grew like a green garland
Wherever chains were worn
And blessed men predicted
The time would come to pass
When the rich man's idols
Of silver and of brass

Would be smashed to smithereens
By the working class
            And now the common people
Are bringing it to pass.

. . .

            Socialism, comrade
Is in the hands of men:
            It is with us, it is with us –
Though it fade and fade again.
            The white man shall have it
All the world around
            The black man shall have it
The yellow and the brown;
            The labourer shall have it
With sweat upon his face
            The middle class shall have it –
It is for the human race;
            The millionaire shall have it
Though he hates the very name
            And tries to crush and strangle it –
He shall have it, just the same!

            Socialism, comrade
Is like the red, red rose
            Day by day it opens
And day by day it grows
            Its roots are ever spreading
And its sweetness never goes,
            And soon I think its petals
Will the whole wide world enclose.

1957   From *Socialism*, III, IV

413

Guiana Johnny's Song

Driver, work done weary me.
Sun go down, me eye can't see;
Sun that crawl from day to night,
Burn my blood and dry my throat.

Fields of rice in swamp and wet
Made me grandad's grandad sweat.
Driver's whip did make him groan,
Curse the only life he known.

This old slave man long while dead,
Mud and tree roots hide his head,
Yet he still alive in me –
Him a slave, while I go free.

With my eyes he still look out,
With my voice he talk and shout.
In my bones his strength I find;
All his dreams stir up my mind.

All he want I'll try to bring –
Better change in everything.
Yet though we no slaves but free
Sometimes weighs his chain on me;
Daylight borned these governing men,
Midnight, midnight fathered we.

From *The Sugar Reapers* (Libretto)

WILLIAM DUTSON
1899–1972

The Roberts-Arundel Tuba

To the note of a Tuba,
The lisp of a prayer;
The bastion of dollars
That for almost a year,
Had kept men from working
In organised fashion
Shook, cracked and crumbled,
To earth, it came crashing.
As naught, was the tenacious
Struggle of men
Who believed that attack
Was to break Union.
'Twas only the finding of
A creature so rare
As a man with a Tuba, a
Hope and a prayer.
The boss o'er the ocean
Was by prayer contacted
And 007, the business
Contracted;
Senator X, was the plane
In between,
The boss with the dollars
And Mr. Y, as we've seen
Considered the Tuba and
Prayer, and came clean.

It just goes to show, that
To struggle's no use:
If you think that it is so,
You're just like the goose
Who thought that to peck,
To struggle and cackle,
Was the only sure way to
Escape the kettle.
So just settle down to
Ponder and think
What a prayer and a
Trombone – Pardon! Tuba –
Can bring.
Hard hearts afar, can be
Softened by thought!
So sit still in squalor
As slave, you were taught.

1969

Battle Hymn for the New Socialist Party

The cloth cap and the working class
As images are dated,
For we are Labour's avant-garde
And we were educated.
By tax adjustments we have planned
To institute the Promised Land,
And just to show we are sincere
We sing *The Red Flag* once a year.

Firm principles and policies
Are open to objections
And a streamlined party image is
The way to win elections.
So raise the umbrella high,
The bowler hat and college tie,
We'll stand united, raise a cheer
And sing *The Red Flag* once a year.

It's one step forward, one step back,
Our dance is devilish daring,
A leftward shuffle, a rightward tack,
Then pause to take our bearings.
We'll reform the country bit by bit,
So nobody will notice it,
Then ever after, never fear,
We'll sing *The Red Flag* once a year.

We will not cease from mental fight
Till every wrong is righted,
And all men are equal quite,
And all our leaders knighted;
For we are sure if we persist,
To make the New Year's Honours List,
Then every loyal Labour Peer,
Will sing *The Red Flag* once a year.

So vote for us, and not for them,
We're just as true to NATO.
And we'll be as calm and British when
We steer the ship of state-o.
We'll stand as firm as them
To show we're patriotic gentlemen,
Though man to man shall brothers be,
Deterrence is our policy.

So raise the mushroom clouds on high
Within their shade we'll live – and die,
Though cowards flinch and traitors sneer,
We'll sing *The Red Flag* once a year.

1962

Black or White

"How would you like your sister
    to marry one of them, mister?"
"That I wouldn't! I'd give her a blister . . .
    a risk, I'd hope, enough to desist her;
And gain for our folk a corruption-resister.
Fancy one of our kind cross-screwed by a twister!
There're too many about, a-murking our vista,
And spreading their soil for a seed that's fascister!"

". . . even the blacks fall for their ploys –
    to shake – black or white – *our class* in their poise
And poison completely with buy and sell 'joys'!
Whatever it touches it withers, destroys . . .
But that for my sister! . . . My sleeping tortoise –
    slow hate in mind's shell – awakes with the noise:
God! how I loathe the rotting 'boorjwoys'!"

1964

Decadegeneration

Have we got to do it all over again?
How can you holiday so blindly in Spain?
Who now forget the horror day of Guernica?
Why, the brain-washed of decades in train!

Who know not what they do
Because their ignorance is new;
Remanned decennially by truth-massacre;
Paid for by you to
That potentest few!

1960

.

Praise to Our Class

He has left us:
    bereft us.
Where is the cover
    for his blank-file?
Where now such golden stuff as his?

Eighty-and-one wide-eyed years:
Taken from us in 'affluent' '62:
Courage and fortitude were not enough –
Still he'd to die in capitalist stew.

He was betrayed by his loyalties;
Let us denounce the traitors;
In '45 his world was in grasp;
but flung out by soviet-haters
and no-class conciliators.

                I see him now;
                        I see him shine.
                With artist skill
                        sews he trousers – mine.
                All he did was good.
    I see him as music;
    I see him as tutor;
    I see him as heart.

I see him so much more worth than they
who cheated so brave a soul of seeing that happy day.

A friend has gone;
    the world more empty is.
A guide has gone before.
O! what could he have done,
    for the new and better young,
    who spent his cheer
    in this unrequiting here?

Praise, then, this man!
    who at his death
    was newer than the new;
    whose going fewer makes the few;
    whose leg-less stand
    was still firmer than
    most younger in our land.

    Praise to our class:
    Homage to the dear comrade
                whose courage diadems it!

1962

Cuba

Cuba is not an island
As other islands are
In spirit she resembles
The centre of a star.

A star which radiating
In five enormous points
With every corner touches
One of the continents.

The heart is not an island
But reaches far beyond
So, if you strike the centre
The body must respond.

1964

RUTH MOSS
Aged 10 years

The Price of Coal

The agony of someone's heart,
Is all for the price of coal,
The death of miners, hunger and strikes,
Are all for the price of coal.

But worse still there is another thing,
Just for the price of coal,
The death of one hundred children and more,
Was all for the price of coal.

Is this what we pay for the fire in the grate?
Anger, pain and even hate?
Is this the price of coal?

1966

FELICITY WHITE
Aged 8 years

The Dragon of Wales

The Red Dragon of Wales,
    is what the people say.
But it was a black and slimy one,
    on that foggy day.

Man had dug him up you see,
    in the years gone by.
So he smothered the little children
    with one big smoky sigh.

1966

LYNWEN LLOYD JONES
Aged 10 years

Aberfan

On Friday the sad search began
For the buried children of Aberfan,
Lost, perhaps dead.

Some may still be lying there.
With their parents deep sorrow we share.
Men are working night and day,
With big machines, moving debris away;
Some are scraping with hands all bare,
At thick, black, sludge which has fallen there;
When all the children had been found
They made a cross of grass upon the ground.

1966

Long Live Vietnam

Long live Vietnam! – that land so brave
    Beside the Eastern sea;
It fights, it lives, it shows mankind
    The price of Liberty.
Two thousand years it's stood alone
    Against the foreign foe;
Its children fight for Fatherland
    From Hanoi to Nam Bo.

A thousand years it lay enslaved
    Beneath the Chinese heel;
Although the heroes, Trung and Trieu,
    Oft caused the foe to reel.
At last the day of vict'ry dawned
    Beside the Bach Dang stream –
The shattered hosts of China fled,
    And freedom reigned supreme.

But sad to tell, the freedom won
    Was once again to fade,
When Frenchmen with imperial greed
    Did Viet Nam's land invade.
Their cruel reign, a thousand years
    Of plunder and of pain,
Could not subdue a nation's soul –
    'Twould rise and fight again.

And then arose a leader great
        Who loved his Fatherland –
Nguyen ai Quoc, brave Uncle Ho,
        Lead Vietnam's freedom-band.
With Pham and Giap the people fought
        In Saigon, Hue, Hanoi,
Till vict'ry came at Dien Bien Phu,
        The Viet Minh's day of joy.

Sweet peace at last in this ravaged land;
        Alas! 'tis not for long;
The Yankees soon replace the French
        In the valley of Mekong.
The tyrant Diem rules the land,
        The NLF appears,
And martyrs' names – like young Van Troi –
        Shall echo down the years.

O gallant land; you still resist,
        Your spirit can't be chained.
We salute your worker-peasant League,
        And cheer each victory gained;
O Small Ones of the Earth, uncowed
        By bullets or napalm,
We hail your flag which proudly flies,
        And cry: 'Long live Viet Nam!'

1969

Treasure Island

It's the year sixteen hundred and forty-eight
And Owen Roe O'Neill's on the march.
His legions are laden with Spanish gold –
Doubloons! Pieces of Eight! we're told
By the Castle who called it sedition
With Cromwell supporting its claim
And no one was stupid enough to suggest
That Cromwell alone was to blame.

It's seventeen hundred and ninety-eight
And Wolf Tone has taken command;
Now everyone knows he got plenty of aid
That the Croppies with gold from outside were being paid.
For the Castle preserving tradition
Jostled us out of our trance
With rumours that Wolf Tone's gallant men
Were loaded with bullion from France.

A most lucrative year for sedition
Was the Year Eighteen hundred and three.
Then bold Robert Emmett was calling for help
And Boney, God love him, near bankrupt himself;
From then on the French were in trouble
And the Castle just purred with delight –
If Boney would only stop footing the bill
The Irish would give up the fight.

Held fast in the grip of the doldrums
With no one to sponsor the cause

We reached forty-eight and O'Brien and Meagher
Came out in the open but didn't get far
And the Castle summed up the position
Which only the blind couldn't see;
The Frenchman was broke, he had beggared himself
Paying for our liberty.

We have now reached the twentieth century
It's Easter and Dublin's in flames,
You'd learn if you heeded the paid Castle narks
That the Sinn Feiners' wallets were bulging with marks
And the papers were howling sedition
As the firing-squad searched every street
For the savage pro-German Sinn Feiners
Who taught men to stand on their feet.

It's the year Nineteen hundred and twenty-two
The battle is over and won;
But wait – here's the Russian, he's new to the scene,
His gold put the gold in the gold, white and green
And the Castle cried out it's sedition
In accents unlike those before
But the words haven't changed, they're the very same words
As the words of our neighbours next door.

So now we're back where we started
The mixture's the same as before,
The Russian, we're told, is now pouring in gold
As the Spaniard, the German, the French did of old
And the Castle can go to perdition –
This gold tell me where can it be:
'Stop twisting my arm,' said the Leprechaun,
'It's under the fairy tree!'

1969

The Streets of Derry Town

Air: *The Sally Gardens*

'Twas the fifth day of October
    And the sun was beaming down,
The people had assembled
    To march on Derry Town.

The police were there in hundreds
    And on mercy they did frown,
As they batoned men and women
    On the streets of Derry Town.

They had assembled at the station,
    As all free people might,
And they peacefully marched up Duke Street
    As was their civil right.

The police had formed a barricade
    And they told them turn around,
Then they freely used their batons,
    That day in Derry Town.

Oh come all you Ulster policemen,
    For it's you that are to blame;
Come, all you Ulster policemen,
    You should hang your heads in shame.

The shame that will go with you,
    Though you roam the wide world round,
How you freely used your batons
    On the streets of Derry Town.

Take heart, you Derry people,
    All the world knows of your plight,
And that Government in Stormont
    That denies you Civil Rights.

The day is fast approaching
    When these men they must stand down;
On that day we'll march triumphant
    Through the streets of Derry Town.

1969

The Red Flag

The people's flag is deepest red;
It shrouded oft' our martyred dead,
And ere their limbs grew stiff or cold
Their heart's blood dyed its ev'ry fold.

> *Chorus*
> Then raise the scarlet standard high!
> Within its shade we'll live or die;
> Tho' cowards flinch and traitors sneer,
> We'll keep the red flag flying here.

Look round – the Frenchman loves its blaze;
The sturdy German chants its praise;
In Moscow's halls its hymns are sung;
Chicago swells its surging throng.

It waved above our infant might,
When all ahead seemed dark as night;
It witnessed many a deed and vow; –
We must not change its colour now.

It well recalls the triumphs past;
It gives the hope of peace at last;
The banner bright, the symbol plain
Of human right and human gain.

. . .

With heads uncovered swear we all
To bear it onward till we fall.
Come dungeon dark or gallows grim,
This song shall be our parting hymn.

The Internationale

Arise! ye starvelings from your slumbers,
　Arise ye criminals of want,
For reason in revolt now thunders,
　And at last ends the age of cant.
Now away with all superstitions,
　Servile masses, arise! arise!
We'll change forthwith the old conditions
　And spurn the dust to win the prize.

> *Chorus*
> Then comrades, come rally,
> 　The last fight let us face –
> The International unites the human race
> Then comrades, come rally,
> 　The last fight let us face –
> The International unites the human race.

No saviours from on high deliver,
　No trust have we in prince or peer;
Our own right hand the chains must shiver,
　Chains of hatred, of greed and fear.
Ere the thieves will disgorge their booty,
　And to all give a happier lot,
Each at his forge must do his duty
　And strike the iron when it's hot.

We peasants, artisans and others
    Enroll'd among the sons of toil,
Let's claim the earth henceforth for brothers,
    Drive the indolent from the soil.
On our flesh too long has fed the raven,
    We've too long been the vulture's prey;
But, now farewell the spirit craven,
    The dawn brings in a brighter day.

Acknowledgements

This Anthology contains verses from the following books published since 1900:

Dai Alexander, "The Miner", *Our Times*, 1943.

Anon., "Streets of Derry Town", *Irish Socialist*, 1968–9.

Donald Bishop, "Colour Bar", *Our Times*, 1943.

Peter Blackman, "Stalingrad" and "All Men", extract from *My Song Is for All Men*, Lawrence & Wishart Ltd., 1952.

Nancy Bush, "Guiana Johnny's Song" from Libretto of *Sugar Reapers*.

Ethel Carnie, "Freedom", "Immortality", "Earth's Song to Her Children", *Songs of a Factory Girl*, 1910; *More Songs of a Factory Girl*, 1919, Headly Bros., Manchester.

Maurice Carpenter, "George Loveless", *New Lyrical Ballads*, Editions Poetry, 1945.

John S. Clarke, "To the Memory of Liebknecht and Luxemburg", "The Proletarian Pedigree", "Karl Marx", "The Soul of Silas", *Satires, Lyrics and Poems*, Socialist Labour Press, Glasgow, 1919.

John Clare, "Remembrances", *Poems by John Clare*, Symons, ed. Henry Frowde, 1908; "The Fallen Elm", *John Clare Poems*, Blunden and Porter, ed. Rich. Cobden-Saunderson, 1920 by permission of Eric Robinson.

James Connolly, "A Dying Socialist to His Son", extract from "The Legacy", *Irish Socialist*, 1966.

H. F. Constantine, "The Glory of War", *Paths of Glory*, Bernard Lloyd, 1919.

Leslie Daiken, "Nostalgie d'Automne", *Goodbye Twilight*, Lawrence & Wishart Ltd., 1937.

John Davidson, "Testament of Sir Simon Simplex", *A Selection . . .* MacDiarmid, ed., Hutchinson, 1961.

Idris Davies, "In Monmouthshire", *Gwalia Deserta*, IX, Dent, 1938; "Poems of the General Strike", "Angry Summer", *Gwalia Deserta*, VIII, Faber, 1953; "Come Down", *Our Times*, 1943; "William Morris", *Modern Welsh Poetry*, Keidrych Rhys, ed., Faber, 1944.

W. H. Davies, "The Sleepers", *Collected Poems*, Jonathan Cape.

Salme Dutt, "The Abandoned City", *Lucifer and Other Poems*, Mitre Press, 1937.

W. N. Ewer, "Remember Scarborough", "May Day, 1917", "A Ballade of Reconstruction", *Satire and Sentiment*, Herald, 1918.

Eleanor Farjeon, "Oak-Leaves", "Nine Men's Morris", "Promises", *More Tomfooleries*, Allen & Unwin (no date).

Helen Fullerton, "Legend of County Louth", "Cypriot Question", "My Country" (extract), "Socialism" (extract), *My Country*, Lawrence & Wishart Ltd., 1958.

Wilfred Wilson Gibson, "Comrades", "Out of the Pit", "Fire", "Unity", "The Answer", "Murderers", *Collected Poems*, Macmillan, 1929.

Arthur Hickmott, "Labour Insurgent", "Robert Owen", "Street Propaganda", *Songs of a Shopman*, A. C. Fifield, 1910.

Alun Lewis, "Observation Post", "Sacco Writes to His Son", *Ha' Ha' Among the Trumpets*, 1945; "Destruction", *Raiders Dawn*, 1942, Allen & Unwin.

Julius Lipton, "Love's Hope", "Wherefore This Change?" *Poems of Strife*, Lawrence & Wishart Ltd., 1936.

Hugh MacDiarmid, "For Greater Things", extract from "Second Hymn to Lenin", "Skeleton of the Future", *Selected Poems*, Craig & Manson, ed., Penguin Books, 1970.

Liam MacGabhann, "A Man Like That", "The Levellers", *Rags, Robes & Rebels* (no date).

Patrick MacGill, "Run Down", "The Song of the Drainer", *Songs of the Dead End*, H. F. W. Deane & Sons, Year Book Press Ltd., 1919.

David Martin, "Soldiers 1939", *Battlefields & Girls*, William Maclellan, Glasgow (no date); "South Welsh Prophecy", *Rhyme and Reason*, Fore Publications, 1944.

Huw Menai (H. M. Williams), "Stalingrad", *The Simple Vision*; "Back in the Return", *Back in the Return*.

George Milligan, "A Day's Work at the Docks", "The Tearaway Boss", *Life Through Labour's Eyes*, Sands & Co., 1911.

T. E. Nicholas, "Hail to the Revolution", *Prison Sonnets*, W. Griffiths & Co. (no date).

N. O. M., "Long Live Vietnam", *Irish Socialist*, 1968–9.

Wilfred Owen, "Parable of the Old Men and the Young", "Dulce et Decorum Est", *Poems*, Chatto & Windus.

Patrick Pearse, "The Rebel", *Collected Works*, Mansel & Roberts Talbot Press Ltd., Dublin.

Edgell Rickword, "To the Wife of a Non-Interventionist Statesman", "Luxury", *Collected Poems,* The Bodley Head, 1947.

Leon Rosselson, "Battle Hymn for the New Socialist Party", *Songs for City Squares* & *Sceptical Circles,* Harmony Music, London, 1966.

Alexander Russell, "Unity on the Clyde" and "Song of the Moulder", *Foundry Rhymes* (no date).

William Shakespeare, "A London Riot", *Sir Thomas More,* Complete Works, Alexander, ed., Collins, 1951; Transcript by permission Cambridge University Press.

John Singer, "Stepney Green", *Stars and Monuments,* William Maclellan, Glasgow, 1947.

William Soutar, "To Karl Marx", "Advent of Spring of 1939", "Direction", *Collected Poems,* Andrew Dakers, 1948.

Merryn Williams, "Cuba", *Poetry on the Left,* Ken Geering, ed., 1964.

Larry Wright, "Treasure Island", *Irish Socialist,* 1968–9.

Albert Young, "Two Poems Dedicated to Karl Marx", "And It Shall Come", *The Red Dawn,* Northern Division, Herald League, London (no date).

The Editor and Publishers gratefully acknowledge the kind permission of Mr Peter Blackman, Mr Beverley Robinson, Mrs William Dutson, Mrs Mary Brooksbank, Mrs Nancy Bush, Mrs J. O. Harris, Mrs H. M. Davies, Mr Hugh MacDiarmid, Mr Alex Russell, Mr Edgell Rickword, Mr R. Palme Dutt, Mr Ken Geering and Mr Jack Lindsay; and of Messrs Macmillan, Jonathan Cape, George Allen and Unwin and David Higham Associates – for the reproduction of copyright materials.

Index of Authors

Adams, John Francis, 270–77
Alexander, Dai, 389
Anderson, Robert, 117
Anderson, Tom, 319
Anstey, Christopher, 60
Arnott, John, 191

Barmby, George Godwyn, 228
Binns, George, 165
Bird, Matthew, 349
Bishop, Donald, 388
Blackman, Peter, 396–400
Blake, William, 92–94
Blandford, Edward, 115
Brooksbank, Mary, 373
"Brown, John", 168
Burns, Robert, 89–91
Bush, Nancy, 414
Byrom, Sir John, 59
Byron, Lord, George Gordon,
    103–109

Carnie, Ethel, 304–7
Carpenter, Maurice, 387
Chadwick, R. Sheldon, 221–23
Clare, John, 137–42
Clarke, Charles Allen, 278
Clarke, John S., 337–44
Cole, Charles, 143–48
Connell, James, 432
Connolly, James, 314
Constantine, H. F., 328
Coombe, Ernest T., 292
Cooper, Thomas, 173

Corrie, Joe, 353
Crossland, Vincent Edwin, 374–75

Daiken, Leslie, 395
Davidson, John, 279–91
Davies, Idris, 363–67
Davies, W. H., 330
Davis, Thomas Osborne, 186
De Jean Fraser, John, 188–90
Dutson, William, 415
Dutt, Salme, 356

Eaton, Daniel, 82
Elliott, Ebenezer, 149–52
Evans, Thomas, 101
Ewer, W. N., 331–33

Farjeon, Eleanor, 345–47
Fennel, Alfred, 214
Fullerton, Helen, 405–13

Gay, John, 56
Gibson, Wilfred Wilson, 334–36
G. W. S., 294

Harington, Sir John, 39
Hickmott, Arthur, 296–99
Hobart, W. H., 258
Holcroft, Thomas, 83

Johnson, Robert, 209
Jones, Ebeneezer, 200–208
Jones, Ernest, 193–99
Jones, Lynwen Lloyd, 425

Jones, Samuel Sumner, 177
Jones, William, 216–18

Laycock, Samuel, 255
Leno, John Bedford, 244-53
Leslie, John, 267
Lewis, Alun, 381–84
Lipton, Julius, 358
Lofft, Capel, 155

MacCall, William, 237
MacDiarmid, Hugh, 361–62
MacFarlan, James, 224–27
MacGabhann, Liam, 323
MacGill, Patrick, 308–10
Mangan, James Clarence, 210–13
Martin, David, 378–80
McOwen, J., 185
Menai, Huw, 385–86
Midford, William, 124
Milligan, George, 300–303
Milton, John, 44–46
Morris, Charles, 77
Morris, William, 254
Moss, Ruth, 423

Nicholas, T. E., 351
Nicoll, Robert, 159–62
N. O. M., 426

O'Neill, P., Rev., 321
Owen, Wilfred, 326–27

Paine, Thomas, 86
Pearse, Padraic, 316
Pottier, Eugène, 434
Preston, Ben, 233–36

Rickman, Thomas "Clio", 87-88
Rickword, Edgell, 368–72
Robinson, Beverley, 419–21
Rosselson, Leon, 417
Rushton, Edward, 95–98
Russell, Alexander, 401–404

Shakespeare, William, 40
Shelley, Percy Bysshe, 110–14
Singer, John, 391
Slimmon, James, 262–66
Soutar, William, 376–77
Spence, Thomas, 66–73

Taylor, Robert, 131

White, Felicity, 424
Williams, Hugh, 153
Williams, Merryn, 422
Wingate, David, 242
Winstanley, Gerrard, 48
Wither, George, 47
Wright, David, 176
Wright, Larry, 428

Young, Albert, 311–13